TAKE MY ADVICE, I'M NOT USING IT!

ADVENTURES OF A TRUE AUSSIE LARRIKIN

ROD HALSTED

ALLEN&UNWIN
SYDNEY • MELBOURNE • AUCKLAND • LONDON

Some names and identifying details have been changed to protect the privacy of individuals.

First published in 2025

Allen & Unwin
Cammeraygal Country
83 Alexander Street
Crows Nest NSW 2065
Australia
Phone: (61 2) 8425 0100
Email: info@allenandunwin.com
Web: www.allenandunwin.com

Allen & Unwin acknowledges the Traditional Owners of the Country on which we live and work. We pay our respects to all Aboriginal and Torres Strait Islander Elders, past and present.

EU Authorised Representative: Easy Access System Europe, Mustamäe tee 50, 10621 Tallinn, Estonia, gpsr.requests@easproject.com

A catalogue record for this book is available from the National Library of Australia

ISBN 978 1 76147 218 3

Set in 12.75/16.5 pt Adobe Garamond Pro by Midland Typesetters, Australia
Printed and bound in Australia by the Opus Group

10 9 8 7 6 5 4 3 2 1

The paper in this book is FSC® certified. FSC® promotes environmentally responsible, socially beneficial and economically viable management of the world's forests.

Rod Halsted has lived a knockabout life. He's dealt in drugs, done time, worked in pubs, fossicked for nickel, managed a patisserie franchise and built a pressure washing business from scratch into a million-dollar concern after getting sober 25 years ago. He lives in Albury, New South Wales.

'Rod Halsted was a wild country kid who hit the road to find himself and found crime instead. From a rigged poker game to overseas drug runs, he took crazy risks with deadly crooks and lived to see the funny side of a reckless life. This is his story, scars and all.'

Andrew Rule, journalist, co-author of the *Underbelly* book series

'A wild, brawling and regularly hilarious tale of a country boy's descent into the vicious Australian and international drug-running underworld, into near madness . . . and on to redemption. Frighteningly, it's all true.'

Tony Wright, *The Age* and *The Sydney Morning Herald*

'In his memoir, Rod Halsted, a self-confessed "black belt in bullshit", manages to deliver some searing truths about the amorality of the drugs trade.'

Chris Masters, journalist

'A great story of a "lived in" life. Loved it.'

Rick Grossman, musician, Divinyls and Hoodoo Gurus

'Phew, I feel like I've been physically assaulted reading that book. But in a good way. It's a red-hot read.'

Barrie Cassidy, radio and television host and presenter

Dedicated to the people who had to put up with the most from me.
My family. Thanks for sticking.
I will love you all until my last breath.

CONTENTS

PREFACE

I caught a bus to my first drug deal. At the time, I lived in the inner-city Sydney suburb of Newtown, where you could leave your front door open without fear of being burgled—but only because so many of Sydney's criminals lived in the area. It was the early seventies and I travelled by bus to the upmarket harbourside suburb of Abbotsford because I didn't own a car and didn't have enough money for a cab.

My last deal ended abruptly in 1981 in a country town with a police pistol to my head after I had collected five kilos of the best grass ever grown in Australia. Well, that's what the courts said, anyway.

In between those two events, I made and lost millions of dollars. I had guns pointed directly at me on six occasions. I was part of the inner circle of an extremely successful drug importation ring run by a ruthless man whom I liked a great deal.

I travelled to Pakistan in 1978 in the company of an easygoing bloke, now one of London's crime tsars, to deliver money to members of the powerful Bhutto family. At the time they were in opposition to General Zia, who had just hanged the incumbent president of Pakistan and head of the Bhutto clan, Zulfikar Ali Bhutto.

I picked up from Sydney customs two shipments of drugs so large they required trucks to transport them. I went from pauper to prince and back again and lived to tell the tale.

I married a woman whose father would rather she had taken vows with anyone other than this hard-drinking reprobate. I managed to prove some of his suspicions about me correct. I got myself busted in Wagga Wagga after setting up a cocaine bust for the cops that went so wrong that I, along with two police officers, ended up with a contract on my head—and, in my case, gaol time to serve.

I ended up a hopeless alcoholic with arrest records in four states, including six drunk-driving convictions. I have written off seventeen motor vehicles and three motorbikes, and have had to deal with the fact that I abandoned my two daughters when they were seven and five.

And finally, after I had lost absolutely everything, I found the one thing I'd strayed from years before: my true self.

It's been interesting. Here's my story.

CHAPTER 1

LIFE'S HIGHS AND LOWS

I'm a risk-taker. Always have been. But when I recall one particular event in Sydney in the mid-seventies my blood still runs cold, 50 years later.

I'd been to a boozy lunch with my mates Dr Dave and Corky. We'd arrived back at Dave's place: a unit on the fifth floor of an Elizabeth Bay high-rise. We intended to smoke a joint then move on to a local watering hole. But that was hard to do given our host had locked his keys inside.

While my two addled pals were problem-solving our predicament and alternately scratching their heads then their balls, I instinctively knew the answer.

I walked down the hall and knocked on the neighbour's door, which was quickly answered by a puzzled Chinese gentleman who spoke no English. I said a warm hello as I stepped into his unit and walked past his somewhat stunned wife and two young kiddies, waving to them as I continued over to the curtains. After pulling them aside, I slid the window open and stepped out onto the ledge, which ran along to Dave's unit. This short entryway was only interrupted by a concrete pillar.

Swiftly assessing the situation and not once looking down, I placed my left palm on the pillar and swung my right foot around, placing it on Dave's side of the ledge. Without breaking my movement, or wind for that matter, I pivoted on the ball of my right foot and brought the rest of my body around to where I wanted to be: with my back to the sliding window leading into Dave's bedroom.

It was child's play from there to slide the window open, step inside and, with a few quick strides, reach the front door. I opened the door, beckoned my two reprobate mates into the unit and gave my Chinese host a thumbs up and a loud, 'Cheers, mate.'

He was peering down the hall at me like I was David Copperfield. Which is more than I can say for Corky and Dave. I didn't even get a 'thank you' from them.

But that's not where my story starts or, thank Christ, ends. It all began in the Blue Mountains.

CHAPTER 2

A COWBOY ARRIVES

I was born Roger John Halsted in Katoomba Hospital on a snowy day in late July 1951. I had a sister, Christine, one year older. From six more pregnancies, four live siblings were to follow me into the world.

My parents met in Sydney while they were both serving in the Royal Australian Navy during World War II. After the war they married and were living with my mother's parents in their guesthouse, Yabba Yabba, in Blackheath, up the road from Katoomba.

Not long after my birth my dad, Howard, found a job with stock and station agents Farmers & Graziers in Gunnedah. My mum, Billie, stayed behind at Yabba Yabba with Chris and me. Mum's name was really Helen Gladys, but her father, William (Bill) Brewster, secretly wanted a son, so from conception he nicknamed his younger daughter Billie. His firstborn got to keep her feminine name, Jeanne.

Just before Christmas 1951 Bill, my Pompa, decided he and my grandmother, whom we came to call 'Dinny', were not going to retire just yet, so it was time we joined Dad in New South Wales's Northwest. He informed Mum we would need to leave. On reflection I like his style. Too many parents these days let their kids steer the ship when what they really need is a kick up the arse and directions to the front gate.

So off we went, apparently. My memory of this part of my life is hazy. Remember, I was only five months old. It improved with time.

Mum, Chris and I caught the train from Katoomba to Sydney's Central station, then on to Moree where my other grandparents lived. This was a journey of over a full day, in the height of summer, with no air conditioning in the rattlers they called train carriages in those days. It was just a few years after the war had ended and soldiers, sailors and airmen were still travelling all over the countryside, either returning home or on service business. So, here was this top sort in her mid-twenties being ogled by all these young blokes who were keen for a bit of female company, all the time taking care of a bawling five-month-old kid being cooked by a fierce Australian summer, as well as a curious seventeen-month-old daughter. Mum reckoned it was her and Chris's engaging natures that kept the young lotharios at bay.

We made it to Moree in time for Christmas. My parents immediately called both the local doctor and Catholic priest: the doctor to try to save my life from heatstroke, which he obviously did rather a good job of; and the priest as a backup to administer the last rites in case I turned up my toes and headed upstairs. The latter wouldn't have been so bad: I'd have joined my Uncle Roger—known to all of us as Uncle Rod—the bloke after whom I'd clearly been named.

Rod was my dad's older brother, along with Des and Bill who were older still. Des was already in the Royal Australian Air Force (RAAF), working as a meteorologist for the Pacific region during World War II. Bill joined the Light Horse but, because of his bad feet, was honourably discharged before being able to see active service; this was a tremendous lifelong regret.

Rod, who was helping his father, Hubert, my Poppa, as a stock and station agent, was in his teens when a Moree local dropped a white feather in the family letterbox. The white feather was a universal indication that the recipient was a coward. These feathers were almost always delivered anonymously. It wasn't hard to work out who the coward was in those circumstances.

Against his mother's wishes, Rod immediately packed his bag and headed to Sydney to join the army. After having a beer with his big brother Des, he decided to join him and become a pilot. Des reckoned it was better to be delivering the bombs than on the ground watching the fuckers dropping on your head. So, at the age of eighteen, off Rod went to become Flying Officer Halsted. He found himself at No. 463 Squadron RAAF, Bomber Command, RAF Waddington, England, in command of a Lancaster Bomber, flying bombing raids over Germany and responsible for six lives as well as his own.

I don't know how many raids he flew during his three years of service, but they were numerous. You can imagine the stress of piloting a 30-tonne metal tube loaded with explosives and six of your best mates through flak-filled sky, looking for a target the size of a pinhead so you could unleash those death-delivering missiles on people and places you've never met or been to. Then getting the bloody plane home. All this before you are legally old enough to vote. What incredible fortitude he and his comrades had.

His luck ran out on 22 December 1944 when, after a successful raid over Pölitz, Germany, he flew into fog and couldn't land at his base in Waddington, Lincolnshire. At least five of the 207 Lancasters on the mission crashed that night due to the shocking English weather. Running out of fuel, Rod finally crash-landed just one mile north of RAF Waddington at 2.46 a.m. The tail broke off his aircraft and spun away from the body of the plane, which burst into flames. All bar the rear gunner, usually the first killed in the air, were incinerated. Rod died eight days after his 21st birthday.

So, yeah, I'm proud to carry Roger Hubert Halsted's name forward. What he'd make of my life's story I'm not sure. But I'm bloody pleased I'll get to ask him when I die as an old man rather than as a five-month-old kid. Besides, if the latter had occurred, he would have had trouble deciphering what I was babbling about. Come to think of it, it's a good thing I didn't die while I was on the drink. I made as much sense then as when I was an infant.

CHAPTER 3

ARTHUR AND THE TOFF

The Halsted family moved to Gunnedah, north-central New South Wales. Chris and I were joined by another three siblings in quick succession. That's what happens when your parents are Catholic, have no TV and get on well. It's the perfect storm for procreation.

In his mid-twenties our old man was very quickly promoted to manager of the local branch of Farmers & Graziers (F&G). F&G was a stock and station agency, and a big part of the job was dealing with farmers, visiting their properties and selling their sheep and cattle at the Gunnedah saleyards. He was the best salesman I've ever seen in action, either one-on-one or as an auctioneer. He didn't just have the gift of the gab: he knew how to listen and genuinely engage with people. Later on, I carried those learnt qualities into my drug dealing.

Invaluable.

He was assisted and tutored by an old bloke by the name of Arthur Tapscott who was himself a brilliant salesman. One day I was up on the rail that ran between the pens where the salespeople stood, a few feet higher than the pens of cattle they were selling. Arthur was selling a yard of cattle, the buyers standing in the middle race between the yards. The bidding was moving along at a brisk old pace, with Arthur putting great showmanship into his auctioneering.

'I've got 45 pounds.' Remember, this was when Australian currency was in pounds, shillings and pence and there were 20 shillings to the pound.

'Now I've got 50 quid.' A quid was a pound, the equivalent of two dollars today but, of course, it bought far more in the fifties than it would today—approximately ten times more.

'*Fifty* to the bloke in the natty brown coat, this is cheap boys, bloody cheap, now I've got 52 and a 'alf, *that's more like it*, 52 and a 'alf to the gent wearing the private-school tie.' An audible chuckle at this daring dig at the upper-class toff ran through the hundred or so men attending the sale.

'Come on lads, these are top-line Herefords, let's hear another bid, *there it is, 55 quid*, now we're talking, 55 to the fella in the sporty Akubra hat.' He turned to the toff wearing the tie. 'Come on, ya bald-headed old bastard, don't let 'em slip away.' This time the audible chuckle turned to a collective gasp at Arthur's audacity to insult the upper-class gent in such a public manner; then laughter, getting louder as Arthur, a moment after the apparent insult, removed his pork pie hat from his head revealing a large, gleaming, bald dome. 'There aren't many of us left.'

The severe look on the toff's face evaporated as a broad grin broke out.

'Sixty quid!' he roared.

'Sold!' shot back Arthur, 'to the gentleman in the quality tie.'

The sales ring broke into spontaneous applause coupled with loud laughter. Even the losing bidder joined in, recognising that the theatre of the moment demanded Arthur sell the cattle to the toff.

That wasn't the only time Arthur knocked down a sales item quickly and, as I'm about to tell you, extremely cheaply. F&G was conducting a clearing sale at a property out of town. First, it sold the stock at the Gunnedah saleyards. The following weekend Dad, Arthur, and Dad's offsider, Lionel Daniels, conducted the homestead sale. Lionel was an odd character who, incidentally, treated himself a little unorthodoxly when a snake bit him out in the bush one day. He didn't have a knife, so he shot a 22-calibre bullet across the bite to make it bleed, then drove himself the hour to hospital.

The whole family went to see the old man and his team sell the contents of the sheds, all the machinery and, finally, the contents of the family home. Mum loved an auction. She picked it up from her father, Bill Brewster, our Pompa, who would attend every auction within striking distance of Yabba Yabba. He'd come home with boxes of cutlery, framed paintings and pictures, crockery and anything else he deemed interesting or useful. His wheeling and dealing didn't always give him the result he was looking for, though. On one occasion, in his later years, when Pompa was living with Mum and Dad in Wahroonga, one of Sydney's leafy northern suburbs, he and Mum attended the Sydney railway lost property auction. He wasn't sure what he was after but certainly, when he purchased the lot comprising 30 umbrellas, he didn't expect to find at the bottom of the box 200 pairs of used false teeth. I can understand him preparing for a wet winter but what he did with the teeth I'm not sure. Maybe he sold them to losers at the races so they could put the bite on winning punters. Good luck with that idea. Firstly, winning punters are as rare as honest jockeys, and, in my experience, getting the dosh out of the bookies bag is hard enough. No one is giving anything more than a bus fare to a losing punter.

At the homestead sale, Arthur was in full command, having sold the mahogany dining table and chairs for some outrageous amount. His trousers were held up by a large leather belt circumnavigating his enormous belly, the belt buckle fascinating everyone in the room—the way it would rise and fall, up and down, every time he emphasised a bid. 'I've got *three pound*', up the buckle would rise, 'three pound', down it would drop and so on.

Mum had earlier admired a beautiful timber inlaid sewing table. It was a true, top-level antique that she couldn't possibly afford; an item that would sell in a Sydney antique shop for hundreds of pounds. Arthur had seen Mum admiring the item's intricate workmanship and, without any consultation with the owners, he said, 'Next up we've got this small kitchen table, make me an offer, six shillings from Mrs Halsted, *sold*!' before moving on to the next item. The only thing Mum treasured more than that ornate sewing table was her friendship with Arthur.

The best things in life are free. Friendship is at the top of the list.

CHAPTER 4

A STROLL TO THE SHOPS

Mum managed the tribe. By 1954 she had three kids under school age and was pregnant with Bill. Down to the shops she'd go with a double stroller holding me and my sister, Lindy, Chris toddling along beside her. There was no car. Mum didn't learn to drive until we got to Albury around ten years later. We'd head into McDonagh's Store and Mum would buy the groceries, which the store would deliver later that day at no extra cost. Then off we would wander, heading home. They talk about footballers being heroes, but the real legends are the country women of Australia. It's been said Australia's wealth was built on the back of sheep. Bullshit. It was built on the shoulders of women like my mum and my aunties.

Of course, Mum would get frazzled occasionally. After tea one night she asked, 'Who wants ice-cream?' Of course, all of us, including the old man, answered in lusty voices, '*Me!*' So, to the little freezer she went and, to her puzzlement, found her purse sitting beside the ice tray. It didn't take her long to put it together. She'd left the ice-cream on her nightstand in the bedroom. Where she would normally leave her purse. Looking after three kids was tougher than herding cats. Dealing with a fourth, who was at that moment sitting at the head of the table flicking jelly onto the ceiling, much to the delight of his tribe of billy lids, took the cake. She had to have the patience of a saint to manage us all.

It was a very happy home. No disagreements between parents, not that we ever saw anyway. Mum settled our sibling disputes with patience and wisdom: 'Go down the back and sort it out, or I'll sort it for you. And if I can hear you, you'll all be in trouble!' All of us adored and admired both of our parents. And let me tell you, after hearing some horrendous stories at Alcoholics Anonymous (AA) meetings many decades later, I deeply appreciate my upbringing and the gentle but firm lessons we were taught.

It doesn't take a berating tirade of words to convey a message or teach a lesson. In my case it was a simple, unguarded look of disappointment from the old man. I'd been given a plaited leather cane from an old drover who had spotted me in the yards working with cattle. All the stockmen, including my dad, carried a similar persuader at the sales so they could give the cattle a tap on the rump to move them along. This old bloke had seen me at work and, because he liked and admired my dad, decided I needed a cane, too. He spent endless hours weaving and plaiting it for me and gave it to me at the yards one day. There was no big fuss, but the old man was deeply thankful to him.

One day Dad said, 'Rod, I haven't seen you using your cattle cane for a while. Where is it?'

'I lost it, Dad. In the long grass, I think.'

The fleeting look of disappointment didn't escape me. He didn't go on about it but instinctively I realised the importance of treasuring the things that were gifted to me. Particularly those that were given with extra effort and thought.

CHAPTER 5
HOORAH HOORAH

By the time I was ten I was old enough, the old man decided, to work with him at Gunnedah saleyards in the school holidays. My job, being a dexterous lad, was to go into the triple-decker sheep transporters and open the gates so the dogs could push the sheep out. Then the drovers and yard hands would pen them up. I'd start on the lowest level, getting pissed and shat on from the upper levels, and work my way up. I climbed around, up and down like a monkey on steroids.

I was paid generously and treated well by everyone in the yards. That is, until one day I noticed a bloke poking at some cattle with what looked to be a stick with iron spikes on the end. 'What's that thing?' I innocently asked the rough-looking drover. Whatever it was, it certainly had the cattle moving along at a nice old clip, often running up the arse of the beast in front. 'This thing?' the weathered cow puncher asked. 'This is what's called a cattle prod.' The evil-smelling animal torturer stepped closer to me. 'Here, I'll show you how it works.' He quickly touched the thing to my arse. Well, fuck me, I leapt further than Jesse Owens jumped at the Berlin Olympics. The bloody thing sent an electric shock into whatever hide it touched: man, beast or boy. And it had no trouble travelling through cotton trousers.

'Jesus Christ, Jim, that's Howard Halsted's boy. He'll have your guts for garters,' another drover exclaimed.

'Oh shit, I'm sorry little mate. Fuck, please don't tell your dad what I did. I'll lose my job.' The once-arrogant now-humble shit kicker was begging.

'Mate, you burnt my bum. *No,* stay away!' The silly prick was reaching to give my electrified arse a rub. Even at that age I sensed these drover types spent too much time alone with animals, and whatever the arse-rubbing led to it wouldn't be a good result for me, young Roger. Indeed, as my education expanded over the years, I often reflected that the likely outcome was that young Roger would have been rogered.

One thing I am grateful to Jim the drover for is introducing me to the sweet art of profanity. It wasn't until the second half of high school that I came into my own in the swearing department, but I had some pointers along the way.

The house we lived in, on George Street, didn't have one of the basics that we all now take for granted: an indoor toilet. We had what was commonly known as a 'thunderbox' at the bottom of the backyard. It was a structure not much bigger than a telephone box which had a toilet seat over a can big enough to take regular deposits from our large family. The nightsoil carters would come around in their horse and dray once every two weeks, always in the dead of night, to collect the can. One of them would feel his way down the side path past my bedroom window, carrying a replacement can on his head. He'd pick the can full of bodily waste up, put it on his hat-covered head (hence the term 'flatter than a shit-carters hat'), and trudge back up the path to the dray, where he would sit the shit can on the tray alongside the dunny cans from all the other families in our neighbourhood.

On one memorable occasion, the shit-carter tripped on one of our tricycles on his journey back up the path. I knew something was amiss when I heard, ‘Fark, ah Jesus, Christ Almighty I’ve got shit all over me. Faaaaarken hell!’ And with that, the night went silent. I must say I had trouble getting back to sleep, what with a bad case of the giggles and the foul smell wafting in my window. It wasn’t made easier when I heard the old man chortling away too from the other side of the house.

So, I must credit my introduction to the wonderful world of swearing to a filthy, evil-minded drover and an anonymous shit-carter. A belated thank you, gentlemen.

I reckon my attitude to life and how it should be lived, as well as my unshakeable self-belief (which wasn’t challenged until later in life), were formed during a single event at the saleyards in 1961.

‘Rod, I’m going to hunt a steer down this race to you,’ the old man said. ‘I want you to stand here and hold onto this gate, and when the beast comes towards you, say “Hoorah hoorah” and it will go into that pen the gate’s swinging off. Then close the gate. You reckon you can do that?’

I replied with more confidence than I felt.

‘Yep, Dad, she’ll be right.’

I held onto the gate and waited. Soon I heard Dad urging the steer around a corner and into the alleyway leading to me. But as soon as the brown beast entered my vision, I clamped my arse cheeks together for fear of shitting myself. It was *huge*. To my ten-year-old eyes it looked like a Spanish fighting bull. In truth it was probably a small steer, but not to me. It was certain death on four legs.

‘Hoorah hoorah!’ I cried in my boyish soprano voice. ‘Get in the pen!’ I pleaded, as the beast trotted closer and closer. If I’d known the value of the word ‘fuck’ I’d have used it unsparingly.

I had one foot on the rail next to me, ready to abandon ship and shimmy up the fence. But there was no need. The fighting bull turned left when it was two feet from me and trotted into the yard. I slammed the gate shut and turned to my old man. We stood there for a good few seconds, looking each other in the eye.

'Good job, son,' he said, in his understated way. But he couldn't disguise the pride he had in me.

At an AA meeting decades after the event, I realised that in that single moment I'd learnt four of life's most important lessons:

1) That I could follow instructions.
2) That I had courage.
3) That I could trust my father and he could trust me.
4) That it's always clever to have a Plan B—a foot on the fence.

CHAPTER 6

DON'T CRY OVER SPILT WINE

Dad's brother, Uncle Bill, lived on a property at Coonabarabran, an hour west of Gunnedah, with my Aunty Muriel and their seven kids—a tribe of cousins for us to play with. The shenanigans this lot got up to were legendary. I used to stay with them during the school holidays, living the life of a cowboy. It's where I learnt to ride a horse and shoot a gun. With my two older cousins, Greg and Barry, I would head off in the morning on horseback to act out cowboys and Indians. That said, we weren't playing. We were the real deal: galloping across open country, navigating dry sandy creek beds with two-metre-high walls carved out by the torrential rains that flooded the country every few years. And we always carried guns. Not to shoot birds or animals but to shoot at each other. It was all part of playing cowboys and Indians. If you had a slug gun, which Barry and I did, you were allowed to shoot to hit. If you had a .22, which Greg did, you had to shoot to miss—but only by enough that you could claim to have hit your target if you wanted to.

When I was thirteen our family moved to Albury, on the southern New South Wales border. This move came about because of my sister, Chris. My parents sent her to Gunnedah High School instead of the local Catholic girl's convent. They did this because Chris was top of the class, very bright and inquisitive, and she wanted to study science and maths. The nuns at the convent didn't teach those subjects. They taught cooking and sewing and the other essentials a prospective farmer's wife needed. But no sex education. I suppose they reckoned that the farm boys and girls knew how to work that part out themselves. (And they did, as evidenced by families commonly having five, six or more kids.)

But the local priest, one Monsignor Leahy, gave my folks an ultimatum: either move Chris to the convent or be excommunicated. This was anathema to a Catholic. Dad spoke to the F&G head office in Sydney. Their swift decision was to transfer Dad to Albury. My folks did try to have the Monsignor's decision overturned by the bishop in Armidale, but he was as frightened of the old cassock-wearer as were most of his parishioners. And with good reason.

I was serving at mass one weekday morning with my mate Donny. There were half a dozen die-hard true believers in attendance. God's representative turned towards me and Donny, holding the chalice, ready for the soon-to-be blood of Christ to be poured over his forefingers. But as Donny began to pour, the Monsignor suddenly moved his hands. Wine spilled onto the carpet at our feet.

A look of horror spread across Donny's dial. He innately knew what was coming next.

The red-nosed old fucker calmly put the chalice on the corner of the altar, spun on his heel like a ninja assassin and swiftly and forcefully struck Donny across the face. Then he calmly picked the chalice up and held it out for Donny to again have a shot at pouring the wine over the fingers that had only moments before been used as a weapon. Donny was made of stern stuff, successfully completing his task, albeit with his hand shaking as though he had a 12-volt battery going off in his elbow. He didn't lose a drop outside the cup, with me following with the water and likewise not spilling any. The mass proceeded with not a peep from God's children gathered around the altar rail, tongues extended, ready to receive the body of Christ from the holy man. From that point forward I lost interest in serving God by making myself a target for one of his crazed followers. I went home and told my parents I would no longer be an altar boy. And not long after that, the lunatic Monsignor's actions against my parents caused us to move to Albury.

Before we left Gunnedah, I had been in Year 1 at Gunnedah High with Donny. We were in the Australian Army Cadets and were pretty excited to be heading out on a weekend bivouac along with the other members and the supervising teachers who, when in uniform, carried ranks such as 'major' or 'colonel'. We headed into the bush, each armed with a .303 rifle and some rounds of blank ammunition—bullets packed with gunpowder and wadding but no actual lead bullet. We were told that, when on patrol, we could shoot at the enemy so long as we were a decent distance away, as the brass ends of the bullets would come out with the wadding and could be extremely dangerous if fired at close quarters. Which is precisely what I did when some boofhead leapt up from behind a large fallen log, screaming like a banshee. Instinctively I fired off a round not three feet from his head. I didn't blind him, but it did take some time to pick the bits of brass from his forehead.

We made camp, pitched our tents, laid out our sleeping bags and were settling in for the night when Donny declared he was going for a shit. As he moved off into the bush one of the other lads picked up a long-handled shovel and quietly tracked him, me right on his tail. Donny found a suitable spot, dropped his duds, squatted and prepared to relieve himself of the bully beef we'd had for lunch, now well digested. Very stealthily my companion slid the head of the shovel along the ground from behind and stopped when it was poised under Donny's arse. Out came the processed bully beef onto the shovel, which my mate quickly and quietly withdrew. Donny folded up some dunny paper and did what 99 per cent of people do before wiping their arse: he looked between his legs to examine the result of his efforts. To his consternation there was nothing there. Zilch. He looked further afield until his gaze extended out 10 feet or more. I'm not sure what he thought his arse was capable of, but had he been able to fire a turd that far he was a certainty to be snapped up by Ashton's Circus.

He eventually spotted me and shovel-boy hiding behind a bush, splitting our sides with laughter. I don't know if Don remembers this event but here we are, 60 years on, and I recall it as clear as day. Yet I still can't remember what I had for lunch yesterday.

The memory is a funny thing. Particularly useful at times, but so is forgetting.

CHAPTER 7

SNAKE IN THE GRASS

My regard for God's frock-wearers wasn't high when I began attending Saint Thomas Aquinas College in Albury. Aquinas was a Christian Brothers college staffed by lay teachers as well as a number of brothers with unchristian values. Although I must credit Brother Cusack—Zack, as he was known to the boys—for being a sweetheart of a man. I was quickly accepted by my classmates, forming lifelong friendships with GJ, Bob, Dusty and Phil, plus some boys from Albury High School, and others whom I played Aussie Rules with on the weekends. And, of course, the ones I drank with.

I loved school because of my mates, not because of the environment. I excelled at the subjects that were taught by teachers I liked and respected: Zack for Maths, Olga for English.

I became very good at gambling in the last two years of school, and this gave me a decent, steady income. I ran a Melbourne Cup SP book and oversaw a dice game called Crown and Anchor at the back of our Ancient History class, which was taught by a woman so old she should have been in the textbook. After school my mate Lester and I ran a game of Odd Man Out near the tuckshop, out of the teachers' sight. This game consisted of three players, each with a penny. Each would flick their penny in the air, catch it and place it on the back of their hand, with either a head or a tail showing. Whoever was the odd man out won: two heads lost to one tail, and vice versa. Oddly enough I always had a tail and Lester a head. The third bloke was the guy W.C. Fields was referring to when he said, 'Never give a sucker an even break.'

I also became exceptional at taking the strap, particularly from Brother Powell and Brother Shields. In fact, they were the only two who hit me in my six years at the school. One memorable day Powell wore himself out belting me with his steel-ruler-reinforced leather strap. My mate Bob insists it was 69 times that the flagellating frock-wearer brought his instrument of torture into contact with the palms of my saleyard-hardened hands. All I know is it was difficult to hold a pen as the day wore on. Apparently, that writing is a crucial aspect of the education process was of no concern to Powell. I must admit, in all fairness to the lunatic, that I did prod him along. The first set of six cuts was for failing to do my Latin homework. The second six quickly followed because of some flippant comment I made on my way back to my desk. The third set was because I advised him, 'I think you'll get better purchase if you keep your back foot anchored, Brother.' Who knows what the remaining beltings were for over the course of the day. He only stopped because he ran out of puff, and also because he realised his intended goal of breaking my spirit was never going to eventuate.

Let me assure you, from personal experience, no number of whacks on the hand could come close to the agony of being hit in the arse with a cattle prod.

On one occasion, after we'd been warned by the previous year's class about Powell's psychotic episodes, we trundled into the classroom after play lunch, ready for another bout of English or History or whatever the subject was that period. It was Friday of the first week of the school year. Powell had drawn up a roster for cleaning the blackboard: two boys per week, with the board to be cleaned prior to the start of each period. The two appointed for the first week were Bruce and Squizzy.

As we seated ourselves, Bruce and Squizzy at the front nearest the door, Brother Powell quietly inquired, 'Who is the blackboard team this week?'

'We are!' piped up the appointed duo in unison.

'I see it hasn't been done. You must have been having fun playing handball, I suppose,' the feral educator softly stated. In his leather slippers he advanced on the two choir boys, like a leopard approaching its lunch. The two boys, sensing something wasn't quite right but having no understanding of the danger they were in, innocently replied, 'Yes, sir,' just as the crazed man of God struck. He leapt the last three feet, grabbing a handful of hair on each of his terrified victims' heads, then proceeded to bang their noggins together, all the while spitting out, 'Well, you are funny little fellows, aren't you?' He let go of their hair and began slapping them around the head. Grabbing Bruce by the hair again he dragged him out from behind his desk and made him crawl on his knees to the dais from which he should have been teaching us. '*Put your hands out!*' he screamed at the now terrified boy, white spittle spraying from his slit of a mouth and covering his lizard lips. He then smashed his leather strap down on each hand three times. By this time Squizzy, who could never be called the biggest, strongest or bravest in the class but was a decent lad, had sidled his way to the door. Powell finished with Bruce, bald pate now exposed by his flying combover, spittle spreading out over his gaunt cheeks as his eyes, insanely blazing, sought out his second victim. 'Over here, Taylor, *right now*!' he commanded. Squizzy summed up the situation in a blink, saw the state his best mate Bruce was in and, trembling in terror, turned and bolted like the hounds of hell were on his heels. (Not all that far from the truth, actually.)

Squizzy ran home in record time and told his mum what had happened. She arrived at the college and explained the facts of life to the headmaster, Brother Hall (or Barney as we called him). Squizzy returned to class, never again to be physically touched or verbally abused by Powell or any of the other teachers while attending our college of knowledge.

On one occasion, when Powell had us for sport, he decided we would learn how to tumble by jumping on a springboard, rolling over the pommel horse and finishing with a somersault on the mat on the other side. Everything went smoothly until one boy, Harrow, twisted his ankle and lay prone on the mat. Phibbsy was next in line and pulled up, not wanting to land on Harrow. *'Go!'* screamed our insane instructor. 'Don't worry about him, just *go*!'

So Phibbsy went. He ran, bounced, rolled and landed, trying to avoid Harrow at all costs. Inevitably, he cleanly kicked him square in the mouth, splitting his lip—the same lip he'd had endless operations on to correct a problem he'd had since birth. But there was no problem from our sadistic educator's point of view. Off Harrow went to hospital while we kept jumping the horse. Just another day in the asylum.

Nothing was ever done about Powell. He marched on his merry way, hitting and humiliating boys in his care at will. He was never rebuked, until a young man named Curley Cotter sorted him out. It was our last day of the school year and, as a special treat, Powell had agreed we could ride our bikes out to Mungabareena Reserve on the Murray River for a swim—but only after we had pushed all the desks into a corner of the room, so they would be out of the way for the cleaners.

Curley had ridden his Clydesdale horse to school. (Yep, it was a different time.) Powell said, 'Everyone can go but you, Cotter. I said you could ride your bikes, not your horses.' What a cunt the man was. (As you can see, I'd graduated from 'arse' and 'shit' to 'fuck' and 'cunt' by then.)

Without a word Curley, big man that he already was at sixteen, picked Powell up by his cassock, held him above his head and hurled him across the stacked desks. As the chastened unchristian brother slid to a halt in the corner, curled up in a ball, his black cassock bunched up around his scrawny arse, Curley strode out of the room, never to return. What a man. He was a hero in our eyes, and these days is still a beautiful, kind man capable of settling any dispute with his quiet authority. He went on to run the family stagecoach business, driving drunks on pub crawls around Albury, and did a heap of bouncing in some very tough pubs. When I asked 50 years on, 'Curley, you must have had lots of fights over the years. How many have you lost?' He drolly replied, 'None.'

Brother James Shields, known universally as Jim, was a different type of lunatic: cold, aloof, a master of humiliation. He enjoyed nothing more than picking out one of the boys and remorselessly belittling him, punishing him for the pettiest of crimes. His modus operandi was to creep up behind a boy who was whispering to the kid next to him. Jim would open proceedings with a swift and forceful slap to the side of the head, and then he would take his steel ruler and tap the edge of it onto the boy's knuckles, all the while chanting at him, 'You snake in the grass, you low form of life, *get to the back of the class*, you miserable excuse for a boy!' And as he was destroying the terrified kid's self-esteem with these kind, Christian encouragements, he'd be sucking back the spit that built up in his gob with the same sounds that Hannibal Lecter made when he was talking about his next planned meal of human flesh served with fava beans.

I've often wondered what role celibacy played in the building up of violence in some of the brothers. Perhaps even in the build-up of spittle?

CHAPTER 8

THE PREDATOR

It wasn't just the brothers who were sick, deranged predators. Our school chaplain was one Father Vincent Kiss. If the name is familiar, it's because you've read about this low-life paedophile in the newspapers. He served six years for embezzling around $2 million from charities so he could live the high life in Australia and Asia. Worse, though, he preyed on teenage boys from trusting Catholic homes. I was told his preferred method was to take boys on holidays to Sydney or the Gold Coast, obviously with their parents' permission and trust, fill them up with alcohol and then sexually abuse them. Apparently after the act he would say something like, 'God doesn't see anything wrong with what we've done but, just in case, I'll hear your confession. And because it's a confession it's a mortal sin to speak about it with anyone else.' There is a special place in hell for this grub.

I know of at least two of Kiss's victims who have taken their own lives. This cowardly predator was protected by the church up to and including the time he was in gaol in the late nineties. That's 30-plus years he was operating, that I know of. I've heard from two of his victims that, when they reported his behaviour to their parents, their response was to berate their own child for 'telling terrible lies about Father Kiss'.

Jesus fucking Christ, to be assaulted by Kiss must have been deeply traumatising; but to lose the support of your parents on top of that violent act? I imagine it would be soul-destroying, and I can see why some victims were driven to suicide. And the grub is still alive—no doubt drinking and eating in the lavish way he has always done.

I know who the real snake in the grass is.

Kiss had an offsider working at the parish with him: a stocky young priest in his mid-twenties, named Father Bernard Dwyer. Dwyer summoned me to see him at the presbytery one morning towards the end of my final year at school.

Dwyer showed me to a small room with windows so high you couldn't see out of them. It was very similar to the numerous cells I would become familiar with later in life. He closed the door and disappeared. I sat twiddling my thumbs for a good ten minutes. It turned out he intended to interrogate me and was following police procedure: unsettle the person in question first. What a clown.

I decided I'd had enough and rose to leave when Dwyer re-entered the room.

'What's this about?' I asked, obviously peeved.

The smarmy prick opened with, 'I just wanted to ask you a few questions about your behaviour at the school dance last night at St Patrick's Hall. With the girls from St Joseph's.'

'Righto, fire away,' I replied. 'As long as I have your guarantee this conversation will be treated like the confessional: absolutely private.'

'You have my assurance. Firstly, I wanted to know if you drink and smoke?'

'Sure do,' I replied. 'Why? Do you want a durrie?' I pulled a packet of smokes from my shirt pocket.

'Good God, do you mean to say you bring cigarettes to school?' he asked incredulously.

'Bit hard to have one if you aren't carrying, Bernie.'

'I really think you should address me as Father. Now, tell me, do you also drink alcohol?'

'I've already told you I do, Bern.'

'In hotels?' he asked in disbelief.

'Do you know somewhere else I can buy the stuff?' I was running out of patience with the prick.

'Does your father know about this?'

'Mate, I drink in the pub with him. I turned eighteen in July. Now, I'm running out of time here, mate. What the fuck is this all about?'

He was in so much shock I'm not sure the word 'fuck' registered with him.

'Well, I also want to know if you, ahem, if you, you know, ah, do things with girls?'

'Whaddya mean, do things? You mean talk to them? Play tennis with them? Go to parties with them? What exactly do you mean, Bernie?'

He was squirming around, twisting his cassock into knots, stuttering and stammering.

'Ooh, I get it. You want to know if I fuck 'em. Is that it? Yep, mate, I sure do!' This emphatic statement came smoothly despite me being a virgin.

'Your language is beyond crude. I'll come right to the point. Mrs P said you tried to have sexual relations with her daughters outside the school dance last night.'

At this, I exploded with laughter.

'The P sisters? Mate, I don't know what bullshit you have been fed but I'm done. You and the P family can all get fucked for mine.'

I hightailed it back to school, leaving the naive God-botherer and saviour of the sexually abused with his mouth hanging open.

The next day I was called to Principal Hall's office where he questioned me about my drinking and smoking habits. My reply was succinct.

'Dwyer told me our conversation was sacrosanct. He obviously repeated it to you. That tells me you are both going to be judged very harshly by God. If you've any more questions I suggest you speak to my parents.' And I walked out.

Barney didn't contact my parents on that occasion, but he did a couple of weeks later when he summoned me and other leaving-year students because we hadn't attended sport the day before. It was a week before the final Higher School Certificate exams began. He demanded we leave the school and go directly to our parents and ask them to contact him regarding our absence. We were young men, about to leave school to enter university or the workforce in a month or so's time.

I went to my father's office and explained why I was there. He picked up a pen and wrote a note to Hall, which said, 'Roger will explain verbally why he wasn't at sport yesterday.' When I told Dad that Hall had directed me to bring my prefect's badge when I returned, the old fella pinned the note together with it and put both into an unsealed envelope.

I took a leisurely drive back to school in my 1951 Anglia, arriving at lunchtime—some three hours after the silly prick had sent us on our way. I strolled into the principal's office, flicking the envelope across the desk to him.

On opening the envelope and seeing the badge, he asked why I had included it.

'You said to bring my prefect's badge along. There it is.'

'Well, you realise this badge was given to you in a public ceremony. It will have to be removed in a similar setting. The school concert is coming up; I'll do it there.' He obviously thought the threat of public humiliation would be enough to bring me to my senses.

'Go for your life. And when you have to give an explanation, you can say it was taken from me for not attending sport one afternoon. I'm sure all the parents will understand.' He was going grape purple by this stage. I thought his tiny head was going to explode.

'Well, I'll let it go this one time. Take the badge back.' He slid the small, golden object across the desk towards me. I reached out and slid it back.

'No, thanks,' was my firm reply.

Back it came towards me, glinting in the sun. 'Go on, take it. Please?'

Ah, fuck it, I thought. *I've got the prick.* I reached out and swept the badge up.

'Righto. Thanks. See ya.' I ambled out of his small, small kingdom.

Of course, he had his revenge. Little men can't live without having the last word. He was transferred to a Sydney school the next year and left a letter for the incoming headmaster stating that should Hodda, Percy or Halsted apply for readmittance to the college they were to be denied. Of course, none of us had the slightest desire to re-enter the jackal's lair.

When I later told my mother that Mrs P had gone to Dwyer with an accusation of attempted sexual assault against me, she was swift.

'Right, come on, Rod,' she said. Into the Anglia we hopped, then drove around to the Ps humble abode. We strode up to the front door and Mum knocked.

Opening the door with a shocked expression was the overweight and overbearing matriarch of the house. 'Mrs Halsted, what a surprise, please come in,' she offered in her most ingratiating tone.

'I have no desire to enter your home, Mrs P,' Mum said. 'And if I ever hear of you denigrating my son's name, or indeed mentioning my family name again, it won't *be* your home! It will become my property. My lawyers will see to that.' Turning on her heel she quietly said, 'Come on, Rod.'

Wow. I mean, has anyone ever had a parent stand up for them in that manner? My mother was awesome, and she only got more heroic in my eyes as time went on, right to the day she died.

I look at that experience and compare it with the way my abused mates were treated by their parents. I weep for them and equally thank the Universe for my outstanding luck.

And Dwyer? What of him? Well, apparently, he got a girl from the Young Christian Students pregnant, left the priesthood and married her.

CHAPTER 9

NEVER PLAY LEAPFROG WITH A GREEK

The mates I made outside school were as important to me as my school friends. I made many of them playing Aussie Rules football, which I took to like a duck to water. I was a natural back man, being average height but big and strong for my age—and, having worked in the saleyards, I didn't care much about pain and my reflexes were sharp. I joined my mates GJ and Phil at St Patricks Junior Football Club. It was here I met boys my own age from Albury High School, along with other lads who had departed the hallowed halls of education for more realistic instruction on life and how to live it in the wider world.

We had three different coaches but only one of them left a lasting impression: Des Wynack, an absolute one-off and one of the funniest men I've ever met. We were training one Thursday night at Noreuil Park Oval, next door to the Albury Tigers Football Club. Des had us doing leapfrog exercises around the perimeter of the oval.

'Stop men, pull up,' he said. 'I've something very important to tell you.' We halted immediately, all eyes and ears on him. 'Don't *ever* play leapfrog with a Greek. Righto, on ya go.'

I didn't immediately get it and neither did many of my teammates, but Tony Maloney did. He burst out laughing.

'What the fuck is the joke?' I asked.

'Mate, Greeks are notorious for rooting blokes up the arse,' Maloney said. We all fell about laughing. Des was like that. When things were tense—as they often got in the change rooms, particularly in a finals match at half time—Des would come out with something that either broke the tension or got us even more wound up, so that when we went back on the paddock, we were prepared to run through brick walls for him.

At half time in a grand final when the match was in the balance, Des was giving us a pep talk, spittle flying from the corners of his mouth. With bits of toilet paper stuck to his cheeks and chin where he'd cut himself shaving that morning, he turned to me.

'Big fella, you've got the red hair and the substance. Treat this game like you'd treat ya sheila on a Saturdee night: straight up the middle.' Caught up in his enthusiasm, I replied, 'Fucken oath Des, I'll kill the cunts.' Out we went and literally ran over the top of the opposition. Of course, I'd never been 'straight up the middle' with a girl in my life. The closest I'd come was a knee-trembling kiss with a girl from around the corner that resulted in me coming in my jeans. Fortunately it was late at night and I was close to home, so I managed to get to my bedroom without anyone detecting the enormous wet patch on the front of my strides.

One game we played, I believe against the Albury Tigers, resulted in five players suffering broken bones: collarbones, legs and arms. At that age, late teens, all we wanted to do was win. And pity help the soft individual who showed any fear.

And win we did. In the three years I played with the club, from the ages of sixteen to eighteen, we lost one game and won the three grand finals we competed in.

The payoff for all the hard training and winning flags was the annual trip away to Melbourne. I went on two of them and each had its memorable moments: from one of the boys finding he could see through a small hole into the room of his mate next door, and deciding to make it a little bit bigger, finishing with a cavity big enough to crawl through; to someone dropping a penny bunger into the middle of the Italian wedding reception in the atrium below and us watching as the guests hit the floor, looking to see who was gunning for them; to Maloney standing on a three-storey window ledge pissing on the passing parade in the street below on a Sunday morning. The passersby were holding their hands out, wondering where the rain was coming from out of a clear, blue sky.

We created so much havoc that both hotels we stayed at barred St Patricks Junior Football Club for life. With good reason, considering we turned on the third-floor fire hose at the Federal Hotel and watched as water cascaded down into the atrium. And, at the Southern Cross Hotel, one of our chaperones offered to fix up the hole in the bedroom wall because he was 'a top-notch plasterer', not allowing for being as pissed as a newt at 10 a.m., or that it was a Sunday and he had no access to plaster or tools.

The trip home was always interesting. We would pull up halfway at Seymour so those needing to strain the spuds—which was everyone who had been on the turps the day before—could do so at the service station. Once relieved we would go through the servo shop like a plague of locusts, a couple of us distracting the attendant with minor purchases while the rest filled their pockets with Cherry Ripes, Violet Crumbles and packets of jubes. I reckon for every dollar spent another $50 was stolen.

These were the years my drinking began—along with 90 per cent of others my age, male and female. I had my first drink out of a pub at the Gloucester Hotel, near the Albury Botanic Gardens. I'd purchase ten cans of VB beer for $2. Yep, 20 cents a can. Five of us would retire to the gardens and have a quiet drink on a Friday night. We were fifteen years old, and I was elected to do the buying because I looked the oldest. Not that the publican cared; they would sell to anyone.

I graduated to my first beer over the bar on my sixteenth birthday when GJ and I strolled through the portal of the Albion Hotel, and he bought me a middy. He was fifteen! We settled in at a table, clinked glasses and had a decent pull of the amber fluid. Shortly thereafter, two uniformed police officers walked into the area. I expressed some concern but was assured by my rock-steady mate that 'It'll be right.'

And it was. The coppers walked straight past us and up to three young blokes a couple of tables away, and asked for proof of age. Of course, they were under legal age and were marched straight out onto the street. Their haircuts gave them away. They were AJs, shorthand for 'army jerks'. They were based over the border at the Bandiana army base, the tenants of which were notorious for getting into strife in Albury—not always their own fault. They were sitting ducks for the tough guys who hung around the main street pubs and who loved nothing more than a fight.

From that night on I felt bulletproof in any drinking hole I chose to enter.

CHAPTER 10

THE WILD WEST

At age eighteen, having been blessed with above-average intelligence (or so I think; others may dispute this) and after enduring six years of schooling under the guidance of the Unchristian Brothers, masters of terrorism, all I wanted to do at the end of 1969 was get the hell out of Dodge. Or, more accurately, Albury. Having failed every subject bar English and Mathematics in my Higher School Certificate year I certainly didn't qualify for university. Nor did I want to go. Being enclosed by four walls for a further three or four years was not part of my plan. Indeed, I didn't have a plan, so my old man, well-meaning though he was, pointed me in exactly the wrong direction: towards a job at the National Bank of Australia.

My only memory of that job was of trying to work out how I could steal the suitcase of old bank notes that I carried on the two Tuesday mornings I worked there. I was accompanied by an armed escort. We strolled a hundred metres or so to the local branch of the Commonwealth Bank, where the notes were counted, had holes punched in them and were sent off to Canberra to be destroyed. Even then my criminal mind was at work devising a plan that would make the loot mine.

I lasted a couple of weeks and handed in my resignation. The shock, the horror! 'Your father got you this job, think of the embarrassment!' pleaded my manager. Quickly a compromise was reached, and I was transferred to the bank's North Sydney branch. I moved into the Lansdowne Private Hotel down near the water in Neutral Bay and proceeded to drink as much beer as my pay packet would allow. My drinking pal was my old footy mate John Brady (known as JB), and we had some fun together. I also began to learn the facts of life. One Saturday we went to the races at Randwick where I won $20 on the last race. The bookie overpaid me by $20 so I was up $40—a fortune in those times, when my weekly pay packet would be lucky to top $15. Naturally we thought this reason enough to head into town to celebrate our good fortune. (I have always seen money as 'ours' rather than 'mine', which is probably why I am broke much of the time.)

We headed back to the Lansdowne for a clean-up and to share half a bottle of vodka before walking towards Milsons Point railway station. Our intended destination was Kings Cross, the closest thing to the Wild West that Sydney had to offer. We had to pass the Kirribilli Hotel so, naturally, we called in to wet the whistle. Glancing around at the six or seven desperadoes nursing their ponies and sevens (five ounce and seven ounce beers) I rashly called to the barman, 'Shout the bar!' John, being far more cautious with the folding stuff than I—a fact reflected in our financial circumstances later in life—looked aghast.

'You are a fuckwit!' he said.

I couldn't see the problem, beers being about 20 cents each in 1970. Didn't I get a rude shock when the barman requested $5! Particularly when my weekly wage could be drunk out in a solid weekend of gargling the liquid amber.

'How could it be that much?' I protested. 'They are only drinking small beers!'

'Not anymore, mate. They're all on double scotches and rums with pint beer chasers!'

I paid the money, happy to learn one of life's lessons. Not that I remembered it. I continued to destroy money, literally—there were times I lit cigars and cigarettes with $50 bills, up until I stopped drinking in 1999.

I decided I simply couldn't stay in the bank. Indoors work just wasn't for me. One day I heard from my close school mate, Phil, who told me his father had jobs lined up for both of us in Kalgoorlie with the Great Boulder Gold Mining Company. All we had to do was get ourselves there.

As much as I enjoyed Sydney's attractions, I leapt at the chance to move across the country. How could I not, when my new employer had a name like that? Phil left immediately and I followed after serving my two weeks' notice at the bank and heading home to say bye to the family. I hitched from Albury to Kalgoorlie. The 2400-kilometre journey was memorable, taking sixteen rides and three and a half days. I left home in the middle of winter, early July 1970, with my father's parting words ringing in my ears.

'Son,' he said, 'I've got two things for you. First, a word of advice: the world is full of buyers and sellers; make yourself the agent in the middle. And remember, a good salesman speaks the other man's language.'

'Thanks, Dad. What's the second thing?'

'Thirty bucks,' he'd replied, handing me the cash.

It may not seem much in today's terms, but it was two weeks' wages to me and, as it turned out, just enough to get me to Kal.

My first ride was with Billy Pigram in his semitrailer. He took me from Albury to Melbourne, where his father, Murray, organised a lift in a semi to Adelaide, and introduced me to his brother, Russ, who owned a pub. Russ fed me, gave me a bed and a ride to the highway out of town the next morning, and wouldn't take a cracker.

How easy is this? I thought. *Almost halfway there and I haven't spent a penny.* But then, for much of the next two and a half days I stood on the side of the road with my thumb vainly hanging in the breeze. I got a ride at Iron Knob (still my favourite town name in the whole world), because a pretty girl I stopped to chat with at the petrol station introduced me to a customer as her cousin who was trying to get to Kalgoorlie. The bloke who picked me up was driving a twenty-year-old Holden utility, and he insisted on stopping at every pub and townhouse that sold booze between there and the Nullarbor.

It was my first close-up experience with a dedicated alcoholic. Little did I realise I was looking into my own future.

As we hit the start of that corrugated strip of road that is Australia's main highway connecting east to west, I just wanted to get to my destination as quickly as possible. I was also toey as a Roman sandal about my financial state, as the previous evening I had spent half my savings on a motel after trying unsuccessfully to get some kip on the side of the road. It was just too damned cold.

Fortunately, my benefactor was pissed enough to let me drive. He was happy with his half-dozen stubbies of beer and didn't realise I was pushing the old girl along at a fair clip. As night fell with a thud, as it does out in the wide-open spaces, we spied ahead a flashing light.

'Better pull over,' Boozy instructed. 'Might be someone in trouble.'

All I could think about was the story I had heard of murders being committed along the Nullarbor around this time of night. I could see us being the next victims, then started imagining my travelling companion might be in on it and had arranged for a co-conspirator to assist in my bloody demise. My imagination has always been fertile.

As I pulled the old banger off the road I saw that the flashing light was actually a match held in the right hand of an Aboriginal bloke aged somewhere between 30 and 50. He had been passing his left hand up and down past the lighted match, giving the effect of a flashing torch.

'What can we do for ya, Jackey?' enquired my racist tour director.

'Wanna go up to the camp, Boss,' was the guttural reply.

'Any sheilas up there, Jackey?'

'Sure are, Boss! Lotsa girls.'

'Get in!' was the urgent reply. 'So, Jackey, they young?'

'Some of 'em are young. And me name's Billy.'

'That's good, Jackey. I feel like a fuck.'

'Me name's Billy. Jackey Jackey was another fella!' Billy replied with a little more force.

'How far up the road is the camp, Jackey?'

'Me name's Billy. Along a way little bit, then a few miles in from this road.'

'Mate,' I said, addressing the owner of the old warhorse we were motoring along in. 'Not such a good idea, pulling off the road to go to a camp full of strangers in the middle of the night. No offence Billy.'

'Don't cha wanna fuck? Get sucked off?' the toothless old charmer enquired of me.

'They me sisters, mate, they not sluts,' said Billy.

'They are all sluts, Jackey,' was Boozy's nonchalant reply.

Billy must have had a bit of Dutch courage on board. 'Fuck you, ya drongo. Me name's not Jackey, it be Billy, ya cunt!'

'Well Billy, ya cunt, this is where you get off. Pull the ute over, Rod!'

I obliged. Billy decamped into the dark, more surprised by his outburst than either of us were.

Hastily I stamped on the gas and away we shot, to my relief.

Travelling along the moonlit track laughingly known as Highway 1, Boozy turned to me and said, 'Touchy cunt that Billy, wasn't he?'

There is no explaining some people.

A couple of hours later, I fell asleep at the wheel and ran off the road. Or, more accurately, I ran onto the mound of dirt the regular grading of the goat track had built up. I didn't flip the ute, but I did land us back on the road with a big enough jolt for my now semi-sober fellow traveller to order a halt to driving for the day. He commandeered the cabin and sent me to sleep on the side of the road.

When I awoke the next morning, as the sun started to peek over the horizon, I was frozen solid. Even in a sleeping bag and with six or seven shirts on my back the night had been so cold I was literally frozen. I had to wait for the sun to thaw me enough to be able to move my limbs. It is the coldest I have ever been. Then, a few hours later, the air was so hot I could see mirages all around us. Tough country, the west.

Midafternoon we arrived at Norseman where I was dropped off with a breezy warning: 'The coppers in Norseman give hitch-hikers three hours to get out of town or they lock you up, take whatever cash you have, give you a hiding and keep ya until the circuit magistrate arrives, usually any time in a six-week period, where he then instructs the police to put you on the train with enough money to get ya back to your point of departure. Oh, and good luck, mate.' Boozy then headed in the opposite direction to where I wanted to be.

At least he had dropped me at a servo. I stood by the side of the road, ready to hail the next vehicle going my way. I didn't care if it was a bicycle—I just wanted to be gone. Spotting a vehicle approaching I made ready with my thumb, only to realise it was, of course, a bloody police bull wagon. The two police officers in it gave me a ridiculously hard looking-over as they cruised slowly by. The passenger cop pointedly looked at his wristwatch.

I stood there for more than two hours without a single vehicle pulling into the servo or driving by. Finally a car pulled in, driven by a bloke in his forties, his wife and mother with him. The women entered the cafe while the driver stood by his vehicle as the attendant filled his tank.

Ready to use my absolute best manners, I approached him. 'Excuse me, sir. I'm desperately trying to get to Kalgoorlie. My mother is ill, and I have hitched from Sydney. Could I possibly ask you for a lift if you are going that way?'

'I am going to Kal,' the man said. My heart leapt. 'But I won't be taking you. I've generally found hitchhikers to be a dirty, dishonest bunch and you don't look like any exception.'

I was so frustrated I was close to putting one on his chin when I heard a shout.

'Mate, you looking for a ride to Kal?'

Two blokes, one about my age, pimply faced, and what turned out to be his older brother by about five years, had pulled off the road. Their four-wheel-drive Toyota utility was idling away, just waiting for me to jump aboard. I grabbed my suitcase (no back-packs for me, not back then) and sleeping bag and bolted for the vehicle, a quick 'Get fucked' thrown over my shoulder to the parsimonious prick who had just turned down a loving son, desperate to get to his dying mother's side. (In those days, and many to come, any story that got me a result wasn't a lie—it was a necessity.)

'Sit in the middle' was the instruction from the older of the two as his brother stepped from the vehicle. 'And throw your gear in the back.' He was a big bloke but seemed friendly enough, and I was now so close to my own personal El Dorado that my antenna for trouble had shut down. Besides, I was hardly in a position where I could exercise choice.

As I climbed into the one-tonner the same police van from before cruised slowly by. 'They aren't after you, are they?' Pimples enquired with a certain tone of fear in his voice.

'Nah, they like to lock up hitchhikers. Looks like they just missed me. What's the trouble, anyway?'

'It's all good, mate,' replied the older brother. 'The name's Stan. This is my little brother, Jimmy. He's a little worked up 'cause we pinched the boss's truck. He's gone to Melbourne for a few days, so we thought we'd go to Kal and get on the piss.'

'Rod's the name, Stan, Jimmy. So, by rights the ute's stolen?'

'Only if he gets home before us, Rod my man,' was Stan's calm reply.

We were belting down the road, if you could call the narrow strip of bitumen a road, at about 130 kilometres an hour, massive trucks towing two trailers each going past us in the opposite direction. They were so close all I could see were the tops of the wheels. To say I was shitting myself would be an understatement. Just when I thought it couldn't get any more terrifying, Pimples decided he wanted a drive. He went at his brother like a kid at his mum in the lolly aisle of Woolworths.

'Giz a drive, Stan, carn, giz a drive. It's my turn, giz a drive, ya prick. Sorry Stan, didn't mean ta call ya a prick but carn, giz a fucken drive . . .'

'Fuck me, 'orright,' said Stan while pulling off the narrow strip of tar onto the red dirt that stretched for miles.

No sooner was the whining Pimples behind the wheel than he shot the vehicle forward, forgetting to turn the wheel. We mowed down half a dozen scrawny bushes before big brother's roaring voice got through to him.

'Get on the fucken road, ya blockhead!' was Stan's advice. 'Fuck, not that far over, bring it back, bring it back before that road train kills us!' he screamed, abject terror flowing from every pore of his body (and mine, too). Meanwhile, Pimples was oblivious to the danger. I reckon he thought it was a carnival ride. Thankfully, the whole episode only lasted two or three minutes at most. Sanity prevailed and Stan was back behind the wheel before his younger sibling could have another shot at sending us all into oblivion.

As day toppled into night my two newest mates decided to pull into a motel about ten kilometres short of Kalgoorlie. They offered to let me sleep on the floor but, knowing the younger one's ability to create havoc from the most docile of situations, I declined and went back to the side of the road. I could imagine Pimples burning the motel down simply by lighting a cigarette.

Best to be gone.

CHAPTER 11

STAND YOUR GROUND

I couldn't have scripted the sixteenth and final ride on my odyssey west any better. The first vehicle to come along picked me up, indicative of the nature of Western Australians, who are generous to a fault. It was a truck! Not just any truck but a massive, fully loaded ore-carrying truck towing a trailer. I learnt that the trailer was known as the 'dog' and when there was a second trailer hitched it was known as the 'mother-in-law'. Why? I have no idea. Probably because it was the third part of the combination, and many who have been married will realise the significance of this. Pulling up in a cloud of dust and with a hiss of air brakes the massive unit stopped right beside me. I climbed up the passenger side and poked my head through the window.

'Going to Kal, mate?' I enquired of the smiling, stocky man behind the wheel.

'Sure am, cobber. Jump aboard.'

What a way to arrive at the fabled town of gold: aboard a mighty truck, in the company of a man of boundless energy and good humour. I forgot all about the difficulty and occasional fear of the previous three and a half days. I asked my newest mate for the name of the best digs in town. Without hesitation he recommended the Palace Hotel. It was probably the most expensive, but I was past caring. It was the same pub my mate Phil said he was staying at, so it was no contest.

'Could you drop me nearby please, mate?'

'Do better than that, little mate. Here she is, right beside ya!' And with that he covered the sound of the air brakes hissing with a mighty roaring of his truck's foghorn. *Brraaapppp, brrraaaaapppppppp*. 'Good luck to you, cobber. Just remember this is a tough town. Back down from no man, or woman for that matter . . . except the madams of the brothels, and the publicans' wives. They run this joint.'

I left my life coach behind and entered the crowded public bar. It was fairly humming: lights blazing, beautiful girls behind the bar, and lots of shouting and laughter. It was a sure sign that there was money about. Good, 'cause that's why I was here—to make my fortune. Looking around, a total of $11 in my pocket, I was trying to spot Phil. I must have looked like the total novice I was because, next thing I knew, I felt a tap on the shoulder. A fellow who looked to be in his thirties said, 'He's not here.'

'What do you mean?' I asked.

'The bloke you're looking for isn't here, mate.'

'How do you know who I'm looking for? Do you know Phil?' I stupidly enquired.

'No, mate, I don't know Phil, but I do know you've eyeballed every bloke in this room at least three times and you haven't spotted Phil, so I'd say it's a fair bet he ain't here.'

I must have gotten a bit testy, so he laughingly said, 'Don't get upset, mate, he'll turn up. Meanwhile, you look like you're a bit short of cash. Here, this will help you out.' He offered me a $20 note. Being full of pride I, of course, refused his offer. 'Mate, we all arrived here with empty pockets. The first lesson you learn is to share the wealth. Take it, you'll need it!' He poked it into my shirt pocket.

'Thanks, mate. I'll pay you back first chance.' But he had already turned and was walking back to his mates, his right hand raised in the air in farewell.

I really should have gone to the bar for a beer, but I was bushed. With the backup of $20 I no longer felt guilty about spending $5 on a room. So, my first night in Kalgoorlie was spent in the best pub in town. (This is now a life's habit I have found hard to break, no matter my financial circumstances or where I have put down.)

As Barry Humphries said to me years later: 'Rod, always live just a little beyond your means.'

The next day I began working with Great Boulder Gold Mining Company as a geologist's assistant and general hand. Phil had started with them a couple of days before me and was already out in the bush. I reckoned on catching up with him over the next few weeks, but it wasn't to be. Two weeks was enough for him before he headed home to Albury. I never did ask him why. I suppose homesickness. We were only young, and being his first time away from home, it was understandable.

After checking in with the boss and being allocated to a geologist named Tim, I was handed over to one of the leading hands: a tall, rangy bloke of about 22 or 23 years. The only name I ever knew him by was Hoss. I later found out he was given the name because he was hung like a horse, and was the only one of the young blokes living at the on-site barracks who had a girlfriend. Going on his looks the rumour about his manhood had to be true. He had a head only a mother could love but, like all bar one of the boys, was a likeable larrikin. Others on the crew that I remember were Scotty, who had long, blond hair and was a Brad Pitt lookalike—a 'cool' guy before Aussies started using the word 'cool'. Marty was a bearded, rotund, happy fella with whom

I shared lots of drinks and laughs. Then there was Michael, who came from a family of Sydney doctors. He was expected to follow in the family footsteps but, after failing his uni entry levels three years in a row, he decided, in his words, to 'fuck the family tradition' and become his own person. He was a big bear of a man who we all thought wouldn't say boo to a mouse . . . how wrong we were.

Another man who comes to mind was a dead ringer for Henry Lawson. I don't remember his name, just that he was a bit older than the rest of us; he may even have been a geologist. I do recall joining him on a drive to Perth in his MG. We got halfway there when he remarked that he was a little disappointed in the car's performance. 'If you shift into fourth gear you may get a little more zip out of it,' I suggested. He'd been driving it for years thinking he only had three forward gears!

On that drive he also described the novel he was writing. He told me of a scene in which the driver of a car roughly brushed his calloused hand against the exposed satiny thigh of the desirable young woman he had picked up. He emphasised the point by brushing his hand against my exposed hairy leg. After our pissy weekend in Perth, I rode back to Kalgoorlie in a different car. Not that I thought Henry was after some rough trade, but why take a chance on becoming a character in someone else's novel?

The final member of the approximately dozen or so field hands and geologists' assistants who populated the Boulder barracks was a Sydney boy. He was a strapping lad: blond of hair, blue of eye, muscles in his hair follicles, about 6 foot 2. His name was Steve. Unfortunately, Steve turned out to be a thief, and possibly a psycho. Things had been going missing from the barracks for some months: somebody's transistor radio, cash here and there, my onyx signet ring that Mum had given me and various other stuff. It was just disappearing, obviously pilfered from our rooms and bags.

In my case, I had left the ring on the basin in the shared bathroom after getting tar all over my hands when I climbed an 80-foot gantry over an old mine shaft. The challenge to climb it was issued so I naturally took it up. I climbed it with a glass of rum and Coke clenched between my teeth. When I got to the top, I drained the glass and placed it on the top rail, which happened to be covered in pitch. Down I came, hands coated in tar. Hence the ring left in the bathroom. I also climbed the inside of a round brick chimney which stood higher than the gantry—probably 120 feet high, give or take. It was a dodgy go but, because I had a motorcycle helmet on my head, I knew I had the safety aspect covered. Once I got to the top of the built-in ladder, I threw a leg over and straddled the top of the stack. Heights have always fascinated me: no matter where you are, a beautiful view from an unusual vantage point is always worth the effort. In this case, though, when I looked down I noticed the chimney appeared to be swaying massively. It gave me the distinct impression that my weight may be enough to tip the bloody thing over, so down I came.

Anyway, the loss of the various items cast a pall of suspicion over the entire camp. We were never quite sure who the thief might be. I wanted it to be a guy I had christened TS (short for Toilet Seat), simply because I didn't like him. But no, it wasn't TS, or any of the other more obvious candidates. It was Steve! I don't recall how this was discovered but it was he, without a doubt.

Bloody Steve. As soon as I heard, I realised he would be capable of that sort of treachery. He'd demonstrated his low character a couple of times while I had been in the bush with him.

On one occasion Steve, Scotty and I were travelling in a ute loaded with gear heading back to our bush camp after a weekend at base. It was pissing rain. The dirt track was so slippery that Scotty and I spent six or so hours in the driving rain, cutting brush to put under the ute's wheels. We cut, pushed and ran beside the ute until we hit camp. All this time Steve sat, high and dry, behind the wheel. As we trundled into camp Steve leapt from the ute, a massive smile splitting his handsome face. 'We did it, boys! Well done, we did it!' he crowed.

'Yeah, Steve, we did it,' Scotty replied. 'Rod and me. We did it. Not you, you lazy prick!' This from the Mahatma Gandhi of the gang. I knew then that Steve was unreliable and out for himself.

Another time, the three of us were bush bashing: driving in remote country through the bush, rather than on a road or track. In Western Australia, much of the land is as flat as a tack, but that doesn't mean the country is level. You might run into rock outcrops or holes and eroded ground at any time. Sometimes these obstructions and hazards are obvious because of the sparse vegetation; other times the brush can be quite dense, and you can't see past the nearest bush in front of you. That's the type of country we were in this day.

Steve was behind the wheel, as he always was. He was a leading hand and, as such, had that right. That said, most of the other leading hands liked to give time behind the wheel to the other members of their teams. In rough country, you never know what may happen, and it's useful if everyone can drive to the conditions. Not Steve, though.

As we barrelled through the bush I suggested it may be an idea for him to slow down a bit.

'Why?' he asked with a maniacal grin. Bravado had gone to his head.

'Because,' I replied, 'if you stack the ute this is where we die. No radio, mate, no tucker, not much water and too far from camp. Reasons enough?'

I got through to him and he slowed down to a reasonable speed. But only momentarily. As he swerved around a bush, three wild goats appeared in front of us. With a startled glance our way they bolted—and Steve took off after them. For a short while it was a load of laughs. But only a short while. He drove straight through bushes and smallish saplings, over rocks and through gullies, determined to catch the goats.

As they separated, he zoned in on the biggest: a large billy, hard as nails after living in the wilderness all his life. Without any warning Steve accelerated into the tiring goat and drove over the top of him.

Scotty and I couldn't believe he had done it.

Then, he spun the wheel and aimed the goat up as he struggled to his feet. He slammed the ute's bull bar into him.

'Stop the fucking car!' Scotty and I screamed in unison at the lunatic behind the wheel. 'Fuck you, Steve. You cunt. *Stop the fucking ute!*'

He pulled the ute up with a quizzical look on his face. 'What?'

Scotty and I were out in a flash. The poor old billy, broken legs under him, was bleating. The look of astonishment and pain in his eyes is still clear in my mind to this day.

Without a word Scotty pulled his long-bladed knife from its sheath on his belt. In one swift motion he pulled the goat's head back and slit his throat. He gently lowered the billy's head to the ground—tears in his eyes, and mine, too—and looked up at Steve. Steve had exited the vehicle and was standing a few feet away, a look of orgiastic pleasure on his face. It was as though the goat's death had actually turned him on.

It was as clear as day to me what Scotty wanted to do. He fully intended on stabbing Steve—probably to death, going on the look of hatred in his eyes. I swiftly moved between them.

'No mate, no,' I quietly said to Scotty as I held him by both his upper arms. 'You're worth more than twenty years in the slammer. That's what they will give you if you kill this cunt.' I was much bigger and stronger than him, but it took all my strength to hold him back as he steadily pushed his way towards Steve.

'Fuck off, mate. Move away!' I commanded Steve. 'Just disappear for a while.'

We left the camp early and drove back to headquarters that afternoon. Scotty and I went straight to the general manager and said we wouldn't work with Steve again, under any circumstances. We were asked why but held our tongues. We did, however, tell the boys when they got back to camp a few days later. Shortly after that, Steve was discovered to be the one thieving our belongings. It turned out that he had been posting little parcels containing his hauls back to his mother in Sydney.

The barracks were about 20 metres long with a dirt yard in front. Further over, about 15 metres away, were the gantry and chimney. Hoss called everyone, including Steve, into this area.

'Boys,' he said, 'the thief is Steve. We have proof. We know it's him. What have you got to say for yourself, Steve?'

'Ah, boys, sorry about that. No real harm intended, ah, I, ah . . .' That was as far as Steve got.

Before anyone else could react, Michael, big, soft man that we thought him to be, walked in a few long strides to Steve. He looked him in the eye and hit him in the mouth with one of the best right hooks I've ever seen. He proceeded to punch him up and down the length of the barracks for a good five minutes. Every time Steve fell, and he fell a lot, Michael dragged him to his feet by his mane of golden locks and lathered into him again. Steve made ineffectual efforts at the start of the flogging to throw a few blows but, like every bully I've ever come across, he simply couldn't hit. Who can with their eyes tightly shut? Steve began to blubber, but there was no mercy from Michael.

'You let'—left cross to the head—'everyone here'—right to the guts—'think that'— another right to the kidneys—'anyone but you'—left to the guts—'was the thief'—big right to the jaw—'you low cunt!' Up Steve came from his grovelling position in the dirt, dragged to his feet by his hair. Then Michael delivered another uppercut.

Michael punched Steve from the soles of his feet to the roof of his mouth. He punched his handsome features into red jelly. He broke his nose, jaw and spirit. And we all watched in silent approval. Every one of us was in awe of this mighty warrior.

Someone drove Steve's Morris Mini outside the gates. We carried the prick to his car in a wheelbarrow, no one wanting to handle the creature, and deposited him beside his car. We took all his possessions and burnt them in a pile beside his vehicle. Everything but his money, that is—we used that to buy beer from the infamous Boulder Block Hotel, affectionately known as the Boulder. The next morning the car was gone, and I have never felt a moment's remorse for my part in getting rid of that flea.

It turned out that Michael's time at school hadn't been wasted. He was his zone's heavyweight boxing champion!

Life after Steve, working with the boys, was always interesting. After a three-week stint in the bush, laying grid pegs and taking magnetometer surveys and soil samples for the geologists to analyse, we all arrived back at the same time. Of course, we then did what came naturally to any red-blooded Aussie male: we spent a boozy weekend in town. Friday night, all of Saturday and all of Sunday would be spent in a pub, usually the Tower. Well, all of Sunday besides the hours between noon and 4 p.m. when the hotels, by law, all shut. I don't know if it was observance of the Lord's Day or simply so the publicans could count their cash, but that was the way it was. We would take that window of opportunity to catch up on well-earned sleep, but we'd always head back to the pub for the last session of the week on Sunday night before heading out into the bush.

One Friday night a fight erupted between two blokes in their twenties. Who knows what it was over—probably a look one gave the other. The guy who picked the fight was given a towelling, but not before he got a few good shots away. He was keen, and the other pugilist had to knock him out to beat him. The loser's mates carted him off, presumably home. Saturday morning found us back at the bar in the company of the previous night's victor, when who should walk in but the vanquished.

'I was pissed last night, mate. Now I'm gonna give ya a floggin'!' the loser proclaimed, loud enough for the whole bar to hear.

'Mate, leave it alone,' the champ replied. 'You're not a bad bluer but I'll beat you every time.'

Not to be put off, our challenger was straight into it. Rip and tear, left and right they went until we saw the same result as the night before: the loser again being carted away by his mates. You wouldn't read about it, but back he came that night for a third go. Same result, but not before a lot of blood had been spilt.

Sure enough, the Sunday morning session began and in walked our man, beaten senseless three straight times. Up he strolled to the reigning champion who visibly blanched at the prospect of another rematch.

'Fuck, mate, you have gotta be kiddin'!' the champ proclaimed in a somewhat incredulous voice, lifting his hands up defensively.

'No, mate,' the rugged-featured beaten bastard said, again in a voice loud enough for the bar to hear. 'You're just too good for me!' He extended his right fist so he could shake his conqueror's hand.

'Mate, you are unbelievable.' Then, to everyone in the pub, he proclaimed, 'This bloke is the hardest bastard I've ever fought, bar none. But mate, I'll have to shake hands with my leftie. I broke my right on your concrete skull.' They roared with laughter, the entire bar joining in. By the time the session came to an end at noon you would reckon they were blood brothers. And, in fact, they were. That was the law of the west. No kicking, no bottles. Knock him down. If he stays down, you are the winner, and no one interferes. It's a pity those rules aren't still followed, instead of the law of the gun and knife and coward's punch so prevalent today.

CHAPTER 12

MY FIRST MOVIE

After the weekend we headed out at 6 a.m. on Monday for three weeks of cutting down trees with axes, driving stakes into rock-hard soil and general heavy labour in 100-plus-degree-Fahrenheit heat. To get to where we were headed, we had to drive past the Broad Arrow Tavern, about twenty minutes out of Kal.

The pub was off the road a couple of hundred yards and would generally, at this time of day, be deserted. Not on this occasion. There were cars and trucks (a couple of them semitrailers) parked away from the building. Curiosity got the better of us. I think Hoss was the gang leader and, if memory serves me, Michael was the third member.

'Better have a look,' said Hoss, wheeling our four-wheel drive into a vacant spot.

Walking into the bar we couldn't believe our eyes. Here it was, 6.30 a.m., with the light just starting to peep over the horizon, and the pub was absolutely rocking. There had to be over 100 people, mostly men, in the three bars—all of them with drinks in hand. The barmaids were flat-out serving beer and conversation was buzzing. The larger bar across from us was brightly lit up with two big spotlights.

Turning to the bloke nearest to me I asked, 'What's going on, mate?'

'Mate, they're shooting a film, something called *The Nickel Queen*,' he replied. 'This is the big bar scene, and the best part is the piss is free. They need as many extras as they can get, so to keep us here, they are giving the beer away!'

We stayed, along with every other of the 95 men and five women, for three days, only taking a break to catch some shuteye when we needed it (which wasn't very often). It took them three days to shoot the scenes because, almost every shot, some smart-arse would wander into frame, wave at the camera and say something bright, like 'G'day Mum!'

I don't know if my ugly mug made it to the celluloid screen, but I did meet an American who, his Aussie companion informed us, shot down more enemy planes in the Korean War than any other fighter pilot. He was the most unassuming man: short, with dark hair and intense eyes.

In another memory I have from around this time, three of us were camped out in an isolated section, pegging out ground for the geologists to analyse in detail later. We had been out for two weeks and were urgently waiting for our supply truck. We were completely out of water and food, and the truck was already a day late. During the day the temperature peaked at over 100 degrees Fahrenheit, and it was freezing at night. We came to a unanimous decision that we would have to conserve energy until water arrived. We did this by lying on our bunks in the caravan for three days straight. By the time the supply truck arrived we were all so weak we were unable to rise from our beds. The driver had to tip small amounts of water down our throats until we recovered enough to rise from our bunks and walk on rubbery legs from the caravan.

He had some story about flat tyres, but it was apparent from his embarrassment that he had simply stopped along the way, probably at a pub, and had lost track of time. The upshot is that the experience demonstrated to me how fragile life is and how bloody important it is to be on time. To this day I am rarely late for a meeting or appointment, and I am never wasteful with water or food.

It was 1970, and life in the west was filled with experiences like those I've described here. I don't think I once thought of the future when, like most blokes, I'd presumably be married with children and have the responsibilities that came with that lifestyle. As far as I was concerned, every day held the possibility of a new experience. And, indeed, each day during this time of my life delivered just that. It's probably the reason I never truly lost my sense of being a cowboy, living my own adventure.

CHAPTER 13

THE BOULDER BLOCK

The Boulder Block Hotel lay about two kilometres from the barracks and fifteen kilometres from Kalgoorlie. It had a reputation for being the toughest pub in Western Australia. I'd been told the police only ever attended the pub in the case of a death, which happened occasionally. They didn't come for assaults, robberies, brawls or even rapes.

Naturally, I had to have a beer in the joint. My mates looked at me like I had a death wish. 'Don't go, Rod,' said Hoss. 'Nothing good will come of it.'

'Nah, fuck it, I've gotta have a look.'

I headed off one balmy evening, the hotel's neon sign acting like a beacon. I heard the place way before I got to the blazing slot of light spilling out of the single-width door, beckoning me in. Walking into the den of mayhem, I was stunned. There wasn't a woman in the place. The bar was crowded and there were two fights going on, two blokes in each blue. As near as I could make out they seemed to be swapping opponents every few seconds.

Stepping to an open spot at the bar I waited for the barman to serve me.

'Wadalyaavemate?' a bull of a man behind the beer-covered bar enquired.

'Beer, mate.' Then, seeing the old Aboriginal bloke next to me nursing the dregs of his own beer, I added: 'Make it two. That alright mate? Buy ya a beer?' I asked the old fella.

'Too bloody right, young fella,' the red-eyed old codger replied.

We settled in and by the time we had two more under our belts we were as tight as old mates can be. Turned out he was a stockman washing the dust away.

The fighting continued, with different contestants taking to the floor. In the four hours I was in that bar there wasn't a moment in which there wasn't at least one blue going on. It was amazing, legs and arms going like windmills, blokes getting knocked down, with the knocker waiting patiently for the knockee to get to his feet before the dance continued. Solicitous enquiries such as 'Ya wanna go on with it, mate, or ya had enough?' were the norm. There was no glass used as a weapon, no kicking and no contemptuous abuse.

It became apparent to me that this was a sport, and you participated if you wanted.

Standing with my back to the bar, a lull took place in my conversation with my stockman mate. I was quietly observing the action, occasionally moving position a foot or so either way to accommodate the participants of the dance, as I had come to see them, when I was approached by a young Aboriginal bloke, somewhere around my own age.

Amiably he asked, 'Wanna fight, cobber?'

Before I could consider his offer and give him my reply, which would have been, 'No fucking way, thank you very much,' my imbibing companion stepped in on my behalf.

'Fuck off, ya cunt, he's drinking with me.'

'Sorry Uncle, I didn't know. Sorry about that, mate . . . but if ya change ya mind—'

'Gwarn, fuck off I said,' the wizened older man instructed. He turned to me. 'Sorry about that, Roddy. They all wanna fight.

Me, I much radda drink piss.' Then he paused. 'Shit, I'm sorry Roddy, I shoulda asked ya first. Maybe ya wanted a blue? I can get the young cunt back for ya,' he offered.

'No mate, that's alright. I'm happy drinking,' I replied.

Eventually I stumbled out and rolled down the road to home, pissed as a newt. Walking into the barracks it was like being greeted by Mum and Dad. There were Hoss and Michael waiting up for me, anxiety etched over their faces.

'Thank Christ you're back, Rod. We've been worried sick about you for the past four hours. We'd have come to get ya but, you know, it's the Boulder . . .'

Funny places, pubs. If you show fear, trouble will find you. But if you're there for the grog and you mind your own business, you'll be right. Especially if you shout all night for the boss of the joint. What I didn't realise when I bought my old mate copious glasses of beer was that he was the most senior Aboriginal in the joint and, as such, what he said went. And he quite obviously let it be known, 'Don't knock this bastard down while he's paying.'

Thank Christ for respect!

CHAPTER 14

DON'T JUDGE A BOOK BY ITS COVER

Dennis was a bespectacled, bald-headed company geologist who took it in turns with his twin brother to stand as the conservative candidate for the local electorate whenever state elections came around. Neither of them ever won, as the area was dominated by voters who were rebels, would-be unionists, and ratbags looking to make their fortunes without paying a dividend to the government. The Liberals were never a chance.

One day I was travelling with Dennis when we had truck trouble and found ourselves stuck in Onslow, on the far West Australian coastline, for three days. We were waiting for parts to be flown in, so Dennis gave me my liberty. I think he desired my company as much as I his, although he did open my eyes on one occasion. We were camped out in the back of nowhere, looking over new ground to peg leases on, when he halted at the top of a small hillock we had walked up. It was only about 30 feet high but, in a landscape as flat as the moon, it gave us a great panoramic view of the country. He said, 'Turn in a circle and keep your eye on the horizon.'

'Yeah, Dennis, I've done that. Now what?'

'In every direction you looked, and that's about 15 miles to the horizon, do you realise we are the only human beings for 150 miles or more?'

'Including Aborigines?' smartarse enquired.

'What I mean is, if anything goes wrong there is no help at hand. We would die out here. And furthermore, we are probably the only white men ever to have stood here.'

That night, Dennis forgot to unplug the car fridge, which was connected to the car battery. We had no two-way radio and no spare battery, and the ground we were on was so rocky it was impossible to push-start the car with just the two of us.

'Is this a test, Dennis?' I enquired, silently cursing the boneheaded boffin.

'No, Rod. We are in trouble,' came the less-than-encouraging reply.

Standing there scratching our scrotums through our threadbare shorts and watching the scorching sun climb higher in the sky, I thought our journey was over. But then a motorbike came around the hill with a roar. Pulling to a halt the rider, who turned out to be the owner of the property we were camped on, came to our rescue. After we had cleared enough rocks our saviour and I pushed the car enough for Dennis to jump-start it. While we were doing this, I asked the owner where the homestead was.

'About two miles that way,' the third white man to visit this spot replied, indicating with his thumb.

So much for being the Lewis and Clark of the Australian west. Dennis, for all his knowledge of rocks, also had them in his head.

Back in Onslow I decided the best way to kill time was to have a beer or three in the pub—something that was fast becoming a habit. I no sooner had my first beer in front of me than an old codger dressed in a grubby shirt and dungarees introduced himself.

'Bert's the name, son. Your good self?' He extended his gnarled right hand.

'Rod, Bert. Rod Halsted. Pleased to meet you. Buy you a beer?' I took his hand in mine.

'I should think so, Rod.' And so a beautiful friendship was born—a friendship that lasted three days and remained in my mind for decades.

Bert was the most entertaining man I had ever met. He'd arrived in the mining area of the west fifteen years before. By his account, he walked out the door of his Perth home to procure, on his wife's instructions, a loaf of bread and a bottle of milk. He simply kept on walking, driven as much by his desire for a nomad's life as his lust for treasure, whether that be gold or, as it developed, nickel. He said he went back once with presents for his wife and son, who was eight when he left. When he knocked on the door of the family home, it was answered by a strapping young man.

'Can I help you?' the young fella enquired.

'I was looking for my wife, Jean, and son, Dan, but looks like they must have moved on', Bert replied.

The young man's demeanour turned icy. 'No, you have the right place. I'm Daniel and you must be my father. The bloke who walked out on us ten years ago.'

Bert said he had never felt such shame. Years later, I would understand what he meant.

'Well, ah . . . son, I ah have . . . ah . . . presents for you and your mum,' said Bert, thrusting his hand forward. It held two small packages.

Ripping the paper from the package with his name on it, Daniel flipped open the jeweller's box. As he did so Bert, with horror, realised he still had his son in his mind's eye as an eight-year-old. The box contained a Mickey Mouse watch—all the rage for a tween but hardly appropriate for an eighteen-year-old man.

Thrusting it back into Bert's hand Daniel said, 'It's not me who has trouble with the time, mate. I think you can make better use of this than me.' Turning, he gently closed the door. Bert, horrified as he was, held out hope that his son would pass his gift onto his wife. It was a two-carat diamond ring!

Prospectors—eternally optimistic.

Bert claimed to have had success in his treasure-hunting, at least, camping out in the bush and only coming to town every three or so months for supplies. In my naivety I judged him on his appearance and thought his stories of nickel strikes were fanciful flights of the imagination. I humoured him, though, and hugely enjoyed his company—we two being the last to leave the bar on the nights we drank together.

The truck repairs were then complete, and Dennis informed me we would be leaving the next morning.

Bert's last words to me at the end of our last drinking session were, 'Rod, I'm going to London to sell some leases of ground I've pegged. Why don't you come with me to carry my bags?'

I still hadn't fully grasped that Bert may be telling the truth. I thought he was a Walter Mitty character and, not wanting to offend him, I replied, 'Bert, I'd love to go to London but, when I do, I'll pay my own way.'

We passed through Onslow a couple of weeks later on our way back to base. Of course, when we pulled into the pub the first thing I did was enquire of the publican about Bert.

'Is he still about or has he gone bush?' I asked.

'Oh no, mate. Bert's gone to London. Said something about selling some leases.'

With a knot developing in my gut, I asked the only question that mattered. 'Did he go alone?'

'No, mate. After you left, he got on the piss with a young bloke who was working on a drilling rig. Bert always likes to have a drinking mate with him when he goes on his trips.'

I never made the mistake of judging someone by their appearance again. 'Carpe diem' became my mantra. And I have, from that moment forward, trusted my instincts. I knew in my gut that Bert was for real, but simply couldn't believe someone would make an offer like that to a virtual stranger. I forgot that Bert had been in the bush, living on his wits, far longer than me and he had already learnt those lessons of instinctive trust years ago.

He trusted me; I didn't fully trust him. What a mug.

CHAPTER 15

CLOSE BUT NO CIGAR

After Onslow I had one last foray into the bush—with Mike, the geologist. We went to a place south of Kalgoorlie called Maggie Hays Hill. It was a lease that was owned by another company that Great Boulder was looking at buying into. I was told to look out for any unusually coloured rock. I didn't realise it at the time, but we were, for a brief time anyway, about to hit paydirt.

'Mike, have a look at this. What do ya reckon?' I asked, handing him a piece of bluish-green rock I had dug from the ground after seeing a small section exposed.

I could tell by his eyes that I had found something unusual. Just how unusual I was to find out in the next 24 hours.

After a brief look around, he said, 'We are going back to base.' And we did. Bloody quickly, too, I might add. The next morning, I wandered over to the building used for sample analysis and found Mike.

'So, what's the deal, mate? What are we onto?' I asked.

'Rod, I can't tell you,' he replied. 'I have been sworn to secrecy by the GM.'

'Well, obviously something big is happening. I want in, Mike. I know how to keep my mouth shut.'

'I can't tell you a thing.'

'No problem,' I said as I turned to walk away. 'I'll just slip down to the Boulder Block and make a phone call to the newspapers in Perth. Tell 'em what we've been up to.'

I got two paces before Mike responded.

'Hold on. This is top secret, so not a word to a soul, okay?'

'Yep!'

'The rock you found indicates high levels of nickel in the ground. We don't know how extensive, but it looks bloody promising. There will be a share issued under the company name of Theseus sometime soon. Make sure you buy shares.' He turned back into the analysis shed.

I went to the nearest telephone, which happened to be at the Boulder Block Hotel, and rang my father in Albury. I told him the story and urged him to buy shares for both of us. He assured me he would.

About a week later Theseus was floated on the Brisbane Stock Exchange, which was unusual in itself as it was a Western Australian company. They were 20 cent shares which opened at 30 cents. This was only a year or so after Poseidon shares had gone from 80 cents to over $280, and Poseidon was also a nickel miner. (In fact, I had driven past its operations site a few weeks earlier. It was the oddest thing. There we were in the driest country, not a tree or bush alive, and they had dropped a bore so they could have water to grow grass around the compound.)

Theseus quickly gained momentum and within two weeks had risen to $25. Then Mike informed me that it was a dud.

'If you have shares, sell them now,' he urged me.

I rang my dad and told him to sell immediately. It took about a week for the stock to fall, and fall it did, rapidly and repeatedly. Within a couple of days, the value of the shares had dropped to a few cents. I anxiously called Dad, who informed me he had left a message for his broker to sell the shares a week ago, so all was well. We were looking at a fortune.

Safe in the knowledge that I had a windfall to come home to, I handed in my notice and was on the train from Coolgardie to Melbourne within a week. Not before I had spent half my savings on a gigantic piss-up for the boys, though. I figured my shortage of funds didn't matter, since I was going home to a pot of gold. Set up for life, I thought. Of course I didn't consider the fact I was talented at bleeding money.

Needless to say, when I got home it had all gone pear-shaped. The old man told me his stockbroker, a bloke by the name of Bill S with whom Dad had gone to school, didn't buy the bloody shares in the first place, so there was no profit for Dad and certainly no windfall for me. Bill's reasoning was that he hadn't seen the prospectus, so he thought he was doing the right thing by Dad in not investing his money. What can you do? I have always believed Bill's intentions were noble, so I just took it on the chin and looked for the next opportunity.

CHAPTER 16

HOME AND AWAY

Even after only six months away, when I came back to Albury I knew I had changed so much that I couldn't possibly stay in my old hometown. It was way too small. But I needed to save up some cash, before I could move to the big city. So I took a job as a scaffolder on a new Travelodge but was restless every day.

While working on the Travelodge I became involved in the only strike I've ever participated in. The scaffolders were experiencing a lull, so the site foreman ordered us to assist the steel fixers.

'No fucking way!' was the immediate response from the most senior of us, a grizzled, eyepatch-wearing desperado who moonlighted as a break-and-enter man when he was a bit short of the readies. Without waiting for the boss's response he ordered the scaffolders, all six of us, out. 'Down to the Gloucester!' This was a pub I was very familiar with. We breasted the bar at 7.15 a.m. and gargled our first middies approximately 90 seconds later. After around twenty minutes, old One Eye received a call on the pub phone begging us to come back to work. Apparently the rest of the workforce had gone on strike with us. Solidarity is a powerful tool. One Eye informed the foreman we would be back when we'd finished our shout and that we would receive our full day's pay. Old One Eye sure could negotiate. He wouldn't have been out of place in the BHP boardroom.

I was cut out for scaffolding work, having no fear of heights as well as being a two-bob lair. I took perverse pleasure in hanging by one hand outside the perimeter of the structure, four or five storeys up, acting up for the girls below as they headed to work. Back then a bloke could be a leering, whistling mug lair and still be appreciated for both his acrobatic skills and taste in women, rather than be criticised as a creepy yobbo.

The job had its risks, though. I was warned early days not to upset Leo as he was a touchy individual. Leo wasn't the sharpest tool in the shed, but he was immensely strong.

One day we were on the fifth level of the Travelodge. The area was a maze of acrow props—temporary supports that were holding up the flat boards in preparation for the concrete pour to lay the floor of the sixth level. For a bit of sport, I squirted Leo with a nearby hose. Well, fuck me. Instead of the response I expected, and that any reasonable person would make—a laugh, and maybe a threat to 'get me back'—Leo spun around, fixed me with his beady red eyes, let out a roar that had me reaching for a roll of dunny paper and came at me like the genuine fighting bull I'd imagined back in Gunnedah. All I had in my favour was the forest of props and my agility. Leo was huge and massively strong, but slow as a coat-tugger's tip. I found a hiding place and stopped breathing for five minutes. One Eye found me and said it was safe to come out.

'Like fuck!' was my understated reply.

'No, mate, Leo's got the memory of a gnat. As long as you are out of his sight for a couple of minutes, he'll forget all about you.'

So I tentatively emerged from my hiding spot and sure enough Leo ignored me. I was told later that had he caught me he'd have thrown me from the building. I count that episode as one of my nine lives used up.

I came across Leo again a few years later when I was walking past the Albury Post Office. Leo and his father were painting it, Leo working at ground level with a roller and his father at the top of an extension ladder, working on window frames with a brush. As I was walking past the old man called out, 'Righto, Leo', whereupon Leo put his roller down, moved to the base of the ladder, and—I swear the following is the unembellished truth— leaned it out so it was upright and picked it up, his father still perched on the top rungs. Leo shuffled to the next window and placed the ladder back on the ground, leaning it up against the wall again. 'Thanks, son,' came the call from above as Leo moved back to his roller and the task at hand. A shudder went down my spine as I walked away, my mind back on the fifth level of the Travelodge, a picture of me scuttling between props, desperately trying to avoid being thrown to my death.

Soon enough it was time to go: the big city beckoned. In my short time at the bank years earlier I'd fallen in love with Sydney. These days, having lived all over Australia, I agree with Paul Keating who famously quipped that if you're Australian and live anywhere but Sydney, you're camping out.

I arrived in Sydney in 1971 and bumped into Garth Harrison. Garth was studying at university and making a quid selling fruit juice door to door. He got me a start, but I only lasted a few days. Knocking on doors doing the same sales pitch over and over to frazzled housewives wasn't my idea of a career path. The day I was greeted at the door by an overweight, blowsy blonde in a negligee that hid nothing of her saggy boobs and double belly rolls, not to mention the doormat she had underneath the rolls, put me off the game for good. She invited me in with the words, 'You'll have to be quick, me hubby's due home from the factory any minute!'

'I'd rather poke barbed wire up my cock, darl, if it's all the same to you,' I amiably replied, turning on my heel and walking away from a sure thing. I've continued to be choosy in all things, especially love.

I was with Garth when I smoked my first joint. It was all very serious, the ritual of rolling the thing, licking it down and lighting it up. Garth, Bob Hodda and a couple of other blokes were there. I remember turning to Bob and saying, 'If I don't make it, please tell my mother I was hit by a bus crossing the road, will ya, mate? I wouldn't want her knowing I died of a drug overdose.' How naive, to think I could die from smoking a joint. It didn't stop me from partaking, though. I waited for the 'hit' but it never came. *What bullshit!* I thought. *Well, I've tried it now and I don't have to smoke dope again.*

It wasn't long after that I came to a shuddering realisation: while my friends were all at uni or on career paths, I still had absolutely no clue what I wanted to do with my life.

CHAPTER 17

THE BORDER AND THE BOOZER

One day, out of the blue, an old friend in Albury told me a cadetship had opened up at the local paper, the *Border Morning Mail*.

Given I love the written word, I leapt at the opportunity. I applied and was made third cadet—and that's where I stayed. I started off in the subeditor's room as the gofer-cum-junior subbie. It was great; I worked under the chief sub, John Saxby, who was the most professional and kind man. Sax was totally inclusive and very generous with his knowledge and time. Same for the head sports sub, Bon Phefley, and his offsider, Bernie Leo. Indeed, the whole team of about eight or so subs were welcoming and instructive—all bar one were gentlemen. The exception was Gummy. What a prick.

The first thing Gummy would do upon sitting down was take out his false teeth and put them in open view on his desk.

My memory of him is no doubt coloured by a remark he once made to me. I don't recall the circumstances, but he said, 'Of course, Halsted, you have to remember you are less intelligent than me.' I replied, 'Of course, Gummy, the very essence of your statement gives it the lie,' whereupon the subs' room burst into spontaneous applause.

'He got you, Nigel; no reply necessary,' Sax said, causing Gummy to slam his mouth shut.

I was, of course, back in Albury again, but those were great days—not just because I was working with a wonderful crew at the paper, but also because I was sharing a flat for the first time. Journalist Barrie Cassidy was my flatmate for a time, and we have remained lifelong friends.

While living in a flat on Wyse Street I had an experience that completely changed my opinion of marijuana. Another ex-Albury boy, Marty Pierce, who had made it big in the Melbourne dope-dealing world, arrived in town with some Durban Poison—a strain of grass so high in THC that it was impossible to take one drag of a joint without your reality being totally reorganised.

'G'day, boys,' said Marty as he stepped into our humble abode. 'Got a little surprise for you: a taste of Durban.'

'What the fuck is Durban?' I asked.

'Suck this and see,' was Marty's succinct reply as he handed me a now well-alight reefer. I sucked in a decent lungful, held it for the required amount of time then exhaled what I later realised was the most mind-bending, ball-snapping substance that had ever entered my 20-year-old body. At first, though, I felt nothing. When I said so, 'Just wait' was the advice forthcoming. But being the impatient soul I was, I replied, 'Nah, nothing's going to happen, boys. Grass doesn't work for me. I'm going to my folks' place: Mum's got her Friday roast on.' And with that, I opened the front door and stepped out into thin air.

My feet did not touch the ground.

Somehow I made the fifteen-minute walk home.

'Hello, darling,' Mum said as I walked in the back door. 'Ready for some roast?'

'Sure thing, Mum,' I replied. But in truth I had no idea what I was saying or doing. It was pretty obvious, particularly when I couldn't manage a single bite of the meal Mum put in front of me.

'Are you alright?' she asked. 'Do you feel ill?'

I was tripping.

I mean, I was in another dimension.

I had to get out of there.

Urgently.

Before my old man got home from the club.

'I'm just a bit off-colour. Do you mind driving me downtown please, Mum? I'm meeting the boys at Hoyts. We're going to watch *The Music Lovers*.'

The Music Lovers is not a movie to watch bent. I reckon Ken Russell must have smoked Durban Poison when he directed it. Talk about fucked up. It's a period film about a homosexual music teacher, Tchaikovsky, who tries to deny his sexuality by marrying a woman who turns out to be a nymphomaniac.

At one stage I left the theatre to go to the toilet and, making my way back, I found myself in a different theatre. Of course, I had no idea where I was, so I grabbed the nearest seat and tried to get back into the movie. This theatre happened to be screening *Carry On Henry*, a movie about a randy King Henry VIII. It was also a period piece, so it's not difficult to understand my confusion. Viewing either movie straight would have been challenging enough, but put the two together, with me completely off my trolley, and it was mind-bending.

I emerged from the theatre and bumped into Marty and the others who had joined us, none of us realising the wrong turn I'd taken. The conversation over a few beers afterwards was interesting.

So then I knew I wasn't immune to marijuana. I was very much susceptible to it. And I loved what it did to me.

I worked the evening shift at the paper, and one of my duties was to pick up the night's smoko from the milk bar around the corner. I'd also often grab a box of beer from Waterstreet's Hotel, which is how I met its owner, Bill Waterstreet.

The younger members of the journalistic staff would often adjourn to the pub for a drink after work. Because we'd arrive after closing time, we would park in the pub's car park and enter the bar through the back door. We'd walk by the small pool room, which held an eight-ball pool table and nothing else bar a cue rack. The table was always occupied, often by old Algie: a train driver who, three sheets to the wind, cue wobbling all over the place, would methodically hold the table for hours on end, winning money off all challengers. That was unless another of our colleagues, Jim Barr, decided to have a game. He was unbeatable.

In the main bar we'd see the usual regulars including Ronnie, one of Bill's good mates; and a railway worker known as Lovely Day, so named because that was always his response to a greeting. Even if it was raining cats and dogs, his response to 'G'day mate, how's it going?' was always 'Lovely day, thanks.'

When Bill got tired around 2 a.m. he'd simply leave the keys on the bar and tell us to lock up. He trusted us to honour a system where we would always pay for our grog. No one ever abused Bill's trust.

It was rare for a fight to break out at Waterstreet's, but on the odd occasion one did, Bill, big man that he was, would always contain it without hitting anyone. One night, three young blokes decided to give Algie a tune-up because he'd taken their money on the pool table. Before anyone could move, Bill swiftly gathered the three of them in a bear hug. He carried the three would-be pugilists, now chastened, across the floor and dropped them outside the back door. 'Don't try to come back tonight,' he said. 'You will be welcome tomorrow, but no more of the fisticuffs, okay?' 'Yes, Bill. Sorry,' they replied in unison.

Watching Bill in action—remembering everyone's names, breaking into song at the drop of a hat, using only as much force as necessary—gave me my first lesson in how to run a bar; indeed, how to behave as a host in any business. He was the wisest of men.

Bill offered me a job doing the morning clean followed by the early shift behind the bar—an offer I gratefully accepted. My routine was to rise at 6 a.m., head to Waterstreet's, clean the floor, polish the bar and clean the beer lines before opening the doors at 10 a.m. to begin the day's trading. My first customers would wander through the back door around 7 a.m. after their night shift at the railway had finished, or after they had signed in for the day and were looking for a heart-starter to ready themselves for a hard day's labour (consisting of two hours' intermittent work and six hours' playing cards). Bill would come down around noon when the first lunch orders were coming in, and I'd head off at 1 p.m. to begin my 2 p.m. shift at the newspaper. At the end of the shift at the paper off we would head for a game of pool and a few beers, often winding up at 3 a.m. before heading home to bed. I lived on two to three hours' sleep a night for the length of my cadetship, which lasted a little under a year.

The subs' room was a great place to work, but I wanted my chance to report. I had been at the paper well over six months and still hadn't written a word. Meanwhile the top cadet was honing skills that would serve him well on capital city papers and when working for various politicians, and the second was hearing voices from outer space talking to him from the TV and was submitting stuff that had to be rewritten every time. Still, I couldn't get a start.

Sax took me aside one night and told me not to give up. 'You will get your chance, just hang in there. The fact is our esteemed editor, Rex Mitchell, doesn't like you so it's going to be extra hard.'

'What's he got against me?' I asked, realising if I was offside with the editor I was basically stymied.

'From what I can gather, he had an argument with your father at the Albury Club over some innocuous thing or other, and has decided he doesn't like either of you. Just hang in there, Rod. You will make a fine journo.'

But things never improved with Mitchell and, after taking a sickie one night so my mate and I could go to the drive-in movies to see *The Adventures of Barry McKenzie*, it was reported to Mitchell that I wasn't crook. He called me into his office the next night. Walking in I knew the writing was on the wall, rather than in the typewriter as I would have preferred, so I immediately said, 'I resign.' Mitchell, being half a beat behind me, said 'You're fired!' I responded, 'I beat you to the punch.'

That was the end of that. I must say though that the movie was a cracker. My mate and I drank a slab of 24 cans of VB beer between us and managed to get ourselves locked in at the drive-in. We found an exit that had a low chain rather than a gate closing the gateway. I reckoned we could lift the Volkswagen over the chain and, indeed, we did get the front wheels over, but got stuck from there. Fortunately, the guy who did the locking up saw our swaying headlights pointing at an odd angle and came back to release us.

As for Mitchell, some years later I was amused to witness Barrie Cassidy taking revenge on him in a way I couldn't. Cassidy was emcee for an event when, as part of his opening address, he said:

> Rex Mitchell, are you out there? Stand up, would you, Rex, so we can all see you. Ah, there you are. Yes, ladies and gentlemen, Rex was my editor when I worked at the paper. Do you remember what you told me, Rex? Let me remind you. You said, quote, 'Cassidy, you will never make a journalist, not as long as your arse points to the ground.' Remember that, Rex? Well, I just want to point out that I am currently

the Press Secretary to the Prime Minister of Australia. You can sit down now, Rex.

Brilliant. Life really is all about timing.

During winter I signed up to play AFL footy for Chiltern. I was introduced to the club by Chiltern boy Barrie Cassidy, and Jim, who also had a run. I started out in the seconds, playing matches at Beechworth, where the ground was covered in snow and frozen as hard as concrete, and on other grounds that were mud heaps. My brief footy career was brought to a shuddering halt after one home game, at which I had arrived with Jim after we'd pulled an all-night session on the grog. I lined up at centre half back and played a blinder, only interrupting my attendance on the ground twice when I hurdled the fence so I could have a chunder behind a gum tree. The third time I couldn't make it over the fence, so used it to hold onto as I squatted and dry retched. As I rose up, snot running from my nose and tears from my eyes, I found myself looking directly into the eyes of an old lady who, while knitting, was watching the game sitting on the bench seat on the other side of the boundary fence. She looked me directly in the eye, gave me a wink and said, 'Get back out there, son. You're killing them.' I took her advice, went back out and ended up man of the match. A pretty good result, I thought.

In the pub that night a fight broke out between two blokes, and it was to do with me. One reckoned I should be immediately promoted to the firsts; the other thought my succumbing to the technicolour yawn, not once but three times, brought the club into disrepute and I should be asked not to come back. I made it easy for them: I sacked myself.

CHAPTER 18

SIN CITY

Having been excused from the *Border Morning Mail*, I bid my flatmates farewell and hit the big smoke. In 1972 I got a job as a trainee salesman with the AMP Society in Sydney, with Haydn Heath as my boss. He was a good man, but I simply had no interest in wearing a suit, being part of a company structure or working indoors. It was decided that I should be moved into the collector insurance department, where I'd be on the road and working out of a small office at Circular Quay, across the road from head office.

I spent much of my time in a car driven around by a gung-ho, Dutch-born, hard-sell salesman named Loop. He would drop me and three others off in working-class suburbs such as Stanmore and Newtown. We went door to door collecting premiums for existing policies and trying to sell new ones. Loop also had us approaching people eating their lunch in the park with the idea of selling them life policies. He was a humourless, single-minded man whose whole life was the job.

My last day working for AMP was designed so I could get one back on Loop. I told him I had an appointment in a unit within a block of 50 or so flats. He suggested he come up with me, but I insisted that I would benefit most from doing it alone. 'I will not be leaving the place until I have a signature on the paperwork, no matter how long it takes, Loopy,' I said to my beaming instructor.

'I vill come in viz you,' he forcefully offered.

Equally forcefully I replied, 'Loop, this is one job I must see through on my own, but thanks for the offer.'

'In zat case, Rot, I shall remain here, in ze car, no matter how long it takes you, und I shall drife you home afterwards,' he said. 'You still haffent shown me where you liff.'

'Right. Well, I'm off,' I said as I bolted from the car, the loopy one's voice ringing in my ears: 'Vat unit number, Rot, vat flat are you goink to?'

Too late, I was through the front entry . . . and straight out the rear door, over the back fence, down the lane and, five minutes later, having a beer in the Grose Farm Hotel on Missenden Road.

I like to think that Loop, the man without a sense of humour, sat outside that unit block for at least two or three hours before he went knocking on every unit door.

CHAPTER 19

BLOODY MARY'S

I was living in a semi in Annandale with my old mate JB. It was in that house that I lost my virginity on my 21st birthday. We were having a party to celebrate, and many of the people who were there were complete strangers to me . . . that was the way it was back then. As long as you didn't cause trouble and brought your own grog you were welcome almost anywhere. A lady I'd never set eyes on before heard it was my birthday and decided to give me a present. Before I knew what was going on she backed me into my bedroom and gave me a taste of heaven. The first time we did it I lasted as long as it takes to flip the lid off a bottle of beer. The second time I lasted a few minutes. By the time we hit number four I was a seasoned campaigner. It turned out she was a psych nurse. She was a few years older than me and had a great body, and was very funny and very patient. I never saw her again, but I will be forever grateful to her for making me aware from the get-go that the best sex is when each is giving to the other.

JB and I moved into a flat in Camperdown. It was in a block of nine units with a shop and laundromat on the ground floor. We had a ball. Les, a real knockabout, lived in one of the flats, and Julie and Sally lived in another. It was party central.

I was playing pool at the Grose Farm one day, possibly the day I left Loopy in the lurch, when a casual mention of my old hometown, Albury, helped me befriend fellow Albury boy Dave McLean. Through Dave I met Michael Everingham, one of the world's genuine gentlemen; and Nick Bomford, who became a lifelong friend. At Grose Farm I was also reacquainted with Charlie Waterstreet, whom I had met in his old man Bill's pub in Albury during my newspaper days.

Dave and Michael were both studying medicine at Sydney Uni—hence Dave later acquiring the nickname Dr Dave. Nick was opening a wine bar nearby, Bloody Mary's Wine Bar, for a guy called Toohey Miller, and needed an assistant manager. At the time I was so broke I had been known to walk the streets of Newtown looking for Coke bottles to cash in so I'd have enough to put on the pool table at Grose Farm. With Dave's endorsement, Nick offered me the job.

It quickly became apparent that Toohey saw himself as some sort of crime tsar. He regularly came to Bloody Mary's with his gang of misfits. The primary thug was Fred Harrison, known to all as Freddo the Frog.

With a six-storey nurses' home located 50 metres away, we had our fair share of nurses patronising the bar—and, let me assure you, no women drink like nurses when they are out on the town! Sydney Uni was also just up the road, ensuring we had a full bar of hard-drinking students, along with tradies and professionals. It didn't hurt that we closed two hours later than the nearby pubs. Bloody Mary's was a gold mine.

Unfortunately, Toohey started treating the place as his private club. He carried himself like a gangster, booking up copious amounts of food, wine and cider and never settling. Sure, he owned the joint, but this practice certainly didn't help to keep the books balanced. Nick decided it had to stop, so he barred

Toohey and his boys from the bar. I was somewhat incredulous that anyone would have the nerve to bar an owner from his own establishment but, Nick being Nick, that's what he did.

He told me that if any of them came in I was to politely refuse them service. I didn't have a problem with that. I had recently fronted one of twenty bikies in our back room. The gang would come in once a week on an off night and have their meeting, drinking a keg or two of cider. It was good business, and we kept the fear factor at bay by requiring them to remove their colours. That was the agreement Nick made with their president, and they had complied for the four weeks they'd been coming. One night, I went into their room to collect empty glasses. There was one door in and out, and tall tables with high stools. It was pretty cramped, and every stool was taken. Squeezing between tables and with one hand loaded with glasses I spotted a short-arsed, grubby bloke still wearing his patch.

'Sorry, mate, you'll have to take the colours off,' I said.

'Fuck you,' was his quick reply. 'I don't take 'em off for anyone.'

'You do here, mate. That's the arrangement we made with you blokes.'

'Like fuck. Try and take 'em off me, ya moron.'

Placing the handful of glasses on a table I said, 'Mate, you have put me in an awkward position. You know what awkward means, don't you? See, if I back off now, every one of these blokes is going to reckon I'm a weak cunt. Now, you see, I'm not a weak cunt. I'm a tough cunt. And to prove it to you, if you don't have those colours hanging off the back of your chair in five seconds I'm going to reach across this table and rip your fucking throat out. I know I'll get kicked to death, but you will come with me, you bag of shit. One . . . two . . . thr—'

'Take 'em off, Shorty,' came a voice beside me.

'But—'

'Take 'em off. *Now,* ya cunt!' the big man beside me roared. To me, he said, 'It's all right, mate. Piss off, we'll bring the empties back with us.'

After around fifteen minutes they all traipsed out and never came back. Too embarrassed, I imagine. It turns out the big fella was the club president, and he acted not out of concern for his man Shorty's safety, and certainly not out of concern for me, but because he had given his word. He shook my hand on the way out.

It was only a few days after Nick had refused service to Toohey's mob when Freddo arrived on a slow day. He had a well-dressed woman in her forties with him. Fred was a big man, but he had run to fat. He had a reputation as a brawler and hitman, but that reputation had cobwebs on it. Still, he had a certain presence about him, and he could turn mean in a blink.

'G'day Rod,' exclaimed the affable, melon-headed thug. 'A bottle of your best shampoo, my old son.'

'See you a minute, Fred?' I steered him away from his companion.

'Fred, I don't want to embarrass you in front of your lady friend,' I said, 'but I have instructions not to serve you or any of Toohey's mob any grog, so it would be best if you found another watering hole, mate.'

Suddenly turning, and clearly semi-pissed, the old pug shouted, 'Who the fuck do you think you're talking to, ya young punk? Get that bubbly now. *I said now!*'

'That won't work, Fred. Don't cause yourself more embarrassment, mate, just go now.'

'Come on, love,' the woman said, 'no trouble, there's another bar just up the road.'

'Fuck up the road. You will pour us a couple of champers, *right now,* or I will have you shot, you young smartarse.' He never broke eye contact with me.

'Nope, and don't threaten me, Fred. Just fuck off!' I replied.

'*Fuck you!*' he roared as he pulled his cheque book from his pocket. He scribbled on a cheque, tore it from its butt and handed it to the woman, instructing her to pass it on to someone else with the instructions: 'Tell him what this prick looks like, and tell him I want him shot as soon as possible!'

'Fuck you, Fred. You can explain yourself to the coppers,' I said, and picked up the phone. I dialled Newtown police station, still eye-locked with the crazed boofhead. 'Yeah mate, Rod from Bloody Mary's Wine Bar. I need the detectives right now and, before you go, can you send a car here ASAP? I've got a bloke threatening to kill me. Thanks, mate. See ya in a couple of minutes.'

'Have a seat, Fred. The coppers will be here in a few minutes. You can complain to them that you couldn't get a drink. Hey, Fred, where ya going?' The flabby fool scampered out the door, his girlfriend well ahead of him.

I related this event to Nick who, unbeknown to me, then told his friend, notorious underworld figure John Regan. I also told my dad.

The next day I was getting the bar ready for opening when I heard a tap on the open front door. There stood Fred on the bottom step.

'What the fuck do you want?' I asked, thinking that I was going to have to start dodging bullets at any moment.

'Rod, mate, no trouble. Honest. I just want to apologise for yesterday. I'd had a few and I spoke out of turn.'

Not understanding why the grub would be taking this tack, but also not being slow, I seized the moment. 'Who the fuck do you think you are, threatening to kill me? Fuck you, cunt. Let's go. Out on the street, you and me, no pulling up till one of us is pulped, you fucken bag of wind.'

The look of mortification on his face was priceless.

'No, no, mate, none of that. I'm here to say sorry, and now I'm going. You will never see me again.'

As I turned to go back inside, I saw Nick standing in the shadows of the bar, a little grin on his face.

'What happened there?' I said. 'One day he's going ballistic, threatening to kill me; the next, he's shitting himself. I don't get it.'

'I do,' said Nick. 'I told John Regan what happened. I also told the 21 Squad.' (The 21 Squad was the forerunner of today's tactical response police squads.) 'I believe the Newtown detectives also had a word. I suspect, though, Rod, that John's message would have been sufficient.'

By the time Regan died, just a few years later in 1974, it was thought he may have killed north of a dozen people and buried them beneath the floorboards of the numerous houses he owned. Indeed, his nickname was 'The Magician' because of his ability to make people disappear.

Then the phone rang. It was my father. 'Are you okay?' he asked. 'Any more trouble from that bloke you had the run-in with yesterday?'

'As a matter of fact, he just popped in to say sorry. Actually, more like beg me to forgive him,' I replied, laughing.

'I thought he might,' Dad said.

'Why? What did you do?'

'Not much. Although I did mention it to an Assistant Commissioner of Police with whom I play golf. He might have done something.'

When I told Nick, we rolled around on the floor, laughing.

'Poor old Fred,' I said. 'He wouldn't have seen that coming. Four visits in one day, three from the cops and one from Sydney's most notorious gangster. He's probably gone to Gowings to buy a new pair of undies.' Both of us roared with laughter.

CHAPTER 20
SHARING DIGS

I began to smoke dope, and found I liked it as much as anyone else. It was expensive, though, so my opportunities were limited. I was spending more time with Dr Dave, who always seemed to have both dope and money. My friendship with him and Michael was growing stronger, bolstered by eight-ball at the pub and unlimited cider and wine at Mary's. I was spending less time at the flat JB and I shared, and his life was changing, too. He also didn't share my burgeoning habit of dope-smoking, so we decided to give up the flat and go our separate ways.

We figured we would have a party to farewell the place, which I had not long beforehand almost burnt down. I had left a cigarette burning and it had set fire to the curtains. Fortunately our neighbour Les smelt smoke and called the fire brigade. He then got all the residents out and made his way up the short road to Bloody Mary's, where I was holding court.

'Rod, mate, I need a word,' he said, interrupting a particularly funny story I was impressing on one of our visitors from the nurses' home.

'Yeah, Les, hold on, mate, I'm talking,' I imperiously replied.

'I need to tell you something now, mate. It's important.'

'Les, what is more important than me talking with this beautiful woman?' I turned my megawatt charm on the object of my desire. The fact that I was half pissed may have added to my flowery language.

'I'll tell you what's more important, Rod, mate. Your fucken flat's burning down, along with mine and the rest of the block. Is that important enough for ya, mate?'

'Mmm, I'd say so, Les,' I coolly retorted. 'We will take this up a little later, my beautiful lady!' I said, turning to the alluring young thing and kissing the back of her hand.

I was full of both cider and myself.

I removed myself from the bar as swiftly as my dignity would allow and, once outside, broke into a full gallop. It only took me 90 seconds to get to our abode, Les loping along beside me. By the time we got there the fire brigade had extinguished the blaze, which they had contained to the front room of our flat. The only real loss, apart from some water damage, was the record player my parents had given me for my 21st birthday.

It was excitement all round with the fire brigade there, local residents milling about and me trying to explain my carelessness to JB. Meanwhile, Les was being interviewed by a roving reporter from one of the radio stations. There were no live crosses in those days, so the interview was taped to be broadcast later.

Later that morning Julie and Sally, who lived in one of the flats, Les, JB and myself sat around the radio waiting for the fire coverage. We heard other newsworthy stories about a bashing at Kings Cross, a cat that had been rescued from a tree by the local fire brigade and a man who had to be hospitalised after inserting a bicycle pump up his arse. (He thought that was the best way to extract the olive he had lodged up there . . . no wonder they call it a rectum.)

Then it was Les's big moment on Sydney radio:

Interviewer (I): 'I'm here with Les, who detected smoke in a block of flats in Camperdown last night. Good morning, Les. It must have been quite traumatic for you?'

Les (L): 'What the [bleep] does traumatic mean, mate?'

I: 'Frightening, Les. By the way, we are going to air with this, so you realise we have to bleep out any swear words.'

L: 'No [bleep] worries, mate. Yeah, it was [bleep] worrying, mate. Mainly cause the [bleep] units were all [bleep] occupied. All but JB and Rod's, where the fire was. I was [bleep] worried someone would [bleep] die in there, mate.'

I: 'Right. So what did you do once you smelt the smoke, Les? Remember, we are on air.'

L: 'What the [bleep] do ya think I did, ya [bleep] dunce? I ran through the joint screaming out "*fire*" and banging on [bleep] doors, ya silly [bleep]. I certainly got some [bleep] action I can tell you. Those [bleep] came screaming outta the [bleep] units like [bleep] outta a dunny pipe, they—'

I: 'Right, thank you, Les. Listeners, that was Les, a witness to what could have been a tragic fire resulting in multiple lives being taken. Back to you, Barry, in the studio.'

Bloody Mary's was patronised by larger-than-life people, and it rapidly became the place to both drink and pick up. The nurses came looking for a good time with future doctors and lawyers; the male uni students, tradies and other local guys came looking for nurses and female uni students.

When Nick and I first opened the place we employed a couple of guys named Alan and Keith as security. They were students of karate master Fred Vella, a Maltese immigrant who had made his name around town. In a publicity stunt to raise money for a kidney dialysis machine to send back to his birthplace, Fred once demolished a three-bedroom brick home using only his hands, feet and elbows. It was a phenomenal feat by anyone's standards, but more so considering Fred was barely 5 foot 6.

Fred was deadly, as a carload of pissed detectives found out the hard way one night. They pulled Fred over for a faulty tail-light, but their continual references to him as a 'wog' and 'dago' seemed to indicate their bigotry was driving them more than their sense of civic duty.

As Fred pulled his car to the roadside, Alan and Keith made ready to exit the vehicle with him.

'No, boys, youa staya here!' Fred instructed in his thick accent.

Alan and Keith knew better than to argue with the Little Master; and besides, they anticipated a bit of a show was about to unfold. They were not disappointed.

'Whatta you pulla me up for, officer?' Fred politely enquired.

'Shut ya cake hole, ya dago cunt!' was the succinct reply from Detective 1.

'Yeah, shut ya mouth, wog. We do the talking here,' added Detective 2, removing all doubt that they were rational men.

Pissed, bigoted cops with low intellect are both the hardest and easiest people to deal with. The easy way is to go with the flow, be prepared to kowtow and, more often than not, sling some cash around—then you can generally walk away with nothing more than a light wallet and a bruised ego. On the other hand, if, like Fred Vella, you are completely intolerant of these character traits, if you have built your whole life on discipline, tolerance and acceptance of pain, and have an abiding disgust of bullies, then it's generally the hard road for you. On this occasion, the four members of the police force Fred opposed did not fare well.

Detective 3 was walking around the car. He paused at the left rear and bellowed out, 'The wog cunt's got a busted tail-light.'

'No, officer, my car isa fully roadworthy,' said Fred, maintaining eye contact with the biggest of the four, Detective 4, who was standing back, smirking. Then Detective 3 swung his heavy police-issue torch into the offending tail-light, smashing it. 'It's busted now, ya little prick,' said Detective 3, revelling in the snorting laughs of his comrades-in-arms.

'I reckon thatta tail-light, she costa about $20 to fix, officer, so you justa give me the money and we forget alla this bullshit ever happen,' said Fred.

'You say *what*?' Detective 4 screamed at Fred, his face going an apoplectic purple as he swung all his considerable weight behind a haymaker aimed squarely at Fred's head.

It took about 30 seconds, according to Alan when he told me the story, for Fred to put all four of Her Majesty's finest on the bitumen. He knocked three out cold; the fourth—the boss, and biggest bastard of the lot—he kept conscious long enough for one last message.

Taking a business card from his wallet and placing it into the detective's shirt pocket, Fred said, 'Thisa is who I ama, boofhead. When you wanna to learn how to fighta properly, come and see me. Bring youra cunta mates with you.' Then it was lights out for Boofhead.

It was Alan and Keith, along with a third man, the bouncer—an extremely well-built Englishman called Dennis—who visited retribution on Freddo the Frog, Toohey Miller and his sycophantic band of merry men. Dennis was the Chris Hemsworth of his time: the same long blond hair and movie-star looks, and could he pull the women! I walked into the darkest part of the bar late one evening to see Dennis sitting on one of the stools. He had a very pretty student nurse sitting astride him. I was about to ask him if he could collect some empty glasses for me, if it wasn't too much trouble. The words were off my tongue but hadn't rolled off my lips when I spotted his jeans down around his knees. I slammed my mouth shut and got back behind the bar, leaving Dennis to finish his tete-a-tete.

One evening, just as the sun was going to bed, Dennis came skipping off the footpath and onto the road, heading for the bar's front door. He didn't notice Toohey exiting his Mercedes with his band of would-be cut-throats. One of the men was Toohey's nephew, a perpetually pissed youth about my age. His name escapes me now, but he was an arsehole after two sherbets.

'Skippety skippety skip!' was the nephew's unfortunate choice of words. Doubly unfortunately, he said them directly to Dennis, who had a shorter fuse than the electrical system on a doll's house. Without preamble or consideration of who his target actually was, Dennis hit clever lips so hard in the mouth I am pretty sure he was on custard and jelly for a month. Alan and Keith had been watching from the step and bounded over as Freddo the Frog closed in on Dennis's back. Bad move. Alan, knowing Fred's history with me and that he was barred from the bar, absolutely went to town on him. He rarely used his hands in a fight, preferring his feet. He had this way of crossing his arms in front and basically dancing around his victim, like Riverdance on steroids. He kicked the shit out of Fred, mouthing off about his parentage, his lack of fighting ability and the size of his appendage.

Keith, meanwhile, gave the rest of them, excepting Toohey, a few slaps around the head. Nick came out and settled things down, reminding Toohey that he and his boys were banned from the bar, and it should stay that way if he wanted the bar to remain a paying proposition. Oddly, Toohey agreed. Nick did have a persuasive way about him.

Not long later, the bar burnt down. It was an insurance job, no doubt.

Before it went, though, we had many a memorable party in the place. By this time Alan and Keith had moved on. Dennis was still with us, and the other boys had been replaced by Mike, George the mad Hungarian and Sammy the Thursday Islander.

Mike was the most unlikely looking bouncer: short, roly-poly with the look of a choirboy. His face was in a perpetual half-smile, and he had the fastest hands I have ever seen. He once stood a wine glass, the type with a bowl sitting on a stem supported by a solid glass base, on the bar. He stood a lit candle beside it. With a snap of his wrist he flicked his fingertips at the candle flame. It went out. He didn't touch it, simply sucked the oxygen from the flame's base, and it died. Remarkable, I thought. And then, in one movement, he hit the rim of the glass with the edge of his hand, snapping the stem. Even more remarkably, he caught the bowl before it hit the bar. In a fight he was greased lightning, and he had the other three backing him up.

It may seem odd that such a small bar catering to the type of crowd we looked after would need such firepower, but because of the number of gorgeous women in our bar at any one time, it became well known all over Sydney. That gave us two problems. The first was we could only have so many people in the joint at any one time, and we always had a line-up that went around the block. Often there were several hard cases who decided they were coming inside come hell or high water. The second problem was keeping the peace inside; when you have numbskulls with more muscles than brains alongside university-educated intellectuals with scathing tongues, you are bound to have clashes. The boys' job was to ensure that only the numbskulls got smacked.

Unfortunately the boys were a little *too* good at this on one particular night. Out of the corner of my eye I saw Rick, a patron who was a loose cannon at the best of times, lift a bottle of Blackberry Nip from behind the bar and place it between his feet. I walked to where he was sitting with his girlfriend, leant over and quietly said, 'Put it back, Rick.'

'Put what back?'

'The bottle you just lifted. Put it back and leave the bar, mate. You can come back when you apologise for stealing from me.'

'Fuck you, Rod. I dunno what you're on about!' I could see the dreaded glaze settling in his eyes. I'd seen it before. When he was pissed he could be uncontrollable, and he could go a bit. The prick had muscles in his toenails. Swiftly I dipped down and extracted the bottle from between his feet. By this time the well-tuned security team had taken notice. I knew I was in no danger, but I wanted him out. It's all about keeping both control and face in the bar game.

'You're out, Rick. Like I said, you can come back when you apologise.'

Mike stepped in and took him by the arm.

'Don't hurt him, Mike,' I said. 'Just get him out as quietly as you can, mate.'

Mike got him to the door without any fuss. But then Rick turned and screamed an oath at me, at the same time swinging a punch at Mike's head. Bad move.

Mike dropped to a squat and drove a short right hand into Rick's crotch. Rick dropped like a stone, his balls no doubt expanding to the size of grapefruits. The boys hoicked him out the door, and I went on with the job of extracting dollars from the punters.

I finished up at the end of the night, sometime around midnight, grabbed a couple of bottles of red to drink at home with the boys and headed off at a trot, not a worry in the world.

I walked in the door of a terrace on Longdown Street, Newtown, where I had moved with my friends Michael and Dr Dave after JB and I let the lease go on our flat in Camperdown. As I headed down the narrow hall to the living room, I called a greeting and got back . . . total silence. If I had stopped for a moment, I would have realised something was not quite right, but my momentum carried me forward. As I entered the living room I took in a frightening scene. Michael, Dave, and Rick's girlfriend were seated while Rick, who must have been nursing massively bruised balls, was standing at the foot of the staircase, pointing a rifle squarely at my chest.

'I'm going to kill you, you cunt,' he sobbed, snot running from his nose, his eyes freely spilling tears.

Without breaking stride I said, 'Let me make a cup of tea first, Rick,' and stepped out of his sight into the kitchen, where I proceeded to break into a cold sweat.

'Fuck you!' came the scream from the obviously very troubled, gun-wielding Rick.

And then the sobbing intensified. He broke down and Dave simply took the gun from him. It was Dave's, after all. He kept it, a Lee–Enfield .303 large-calibre weapon, in his room. How Rick got hold of it I have no idea. I forgot to ask, and he and Michael are both now dead. I do remember Michael coming to the kitchen door and motioning me to leave through the window, which I gladly did. I scooted down the back lane and took up a position that gave me a view of the front door from outside. Shortly thereafter, Rick exited with his girlfriend, Dave waving them goodbye like it was the end of a pleasant stay.

I don't know what Dave said to Rick to disarm him, but it wasn't the only time he kept a cool head in a crisis.

As Rick disappeared around the corner I came back inside and the three of us looked at each other.

'Well, that was too fucking close for comfort,' Dave dryly observed.

'Yeah,' I replied. 'He had me shitting, that's for sure.'

And Michael, ever-practical, said, 'I think you should store the bolt for the rifle in a separate place to the rifle itself from now on, mate. We will all sleep better.'

That was the second time I'd had a gun aimed in my direction. The first time I was standing beside my old schoolmate, Phil, when we were on a rabbit-hunting expedition around age sixteen. Phil decided to fossick through a camp we'd come upon, when the owners of the gear appeared. One of them pointed his .22 rifle at us. I didn't think he would shoot but he threatened to, and accidents do happen.

With Rick, it was never going to be an accident. Thank Christ Dave and Michael both kept their heads, or I may well have lost mine.

CHAPTER 21

BY THIS TIME, I WAS GETTING USED TO IT

The third time I had a gun pointed at me was only a couple of weeks later. Michael, his future wife, Chris, and I were in Chris's VW Kombi when she took a wrong turn. We ended up in a dead-end alley. As we slowed to do a U-turn, I noticed several guys who could only be detectives standing at the open boot of a late-model sedan—the type cops drove in those days. I only got a glimpse, but I thought I saw firearms in the boot. As Chris pointed the Kombi in the right direction, suddenly we had half a dozen cops at the windows roaring at us:

'Hands where I can see 'em!'

'Stop the vehicle!'

'Don't move or I'll blow ya fucken head off!'

Understandably, we froze. Little did we know, a woman in a Kombi had helped two dangerous criminals escape from a prison van a couple of hours before. The cops didn't hold us more than a minute or two, but I did have a pocket full of dope, so I don't mind confessing I was a wee bit concerned. All good practice for my life ahead.

It wasn't long before there was a fourth gun-pointed-at-me incident—this time involving the blokes from Bloody Mary's. A team of Navy guys loved coming to the bar when they were in dock. One was named Bill, and he and the bouncers got on like best mates. Among other things he was a naval karate instructor, so he fitted right into the culture that had grown around the bar's security staff.

One day, Mike and his insane mate John from the bush decided we should go pig shooting up around Blayney, a few hours inland from Sydney. It was the middle of winter and there were six of us going—every one of us big lads. Why we thought the best form of transport would be John's utility I don't know, but that's what we drove.

Along with our two trusty lunatic guides we had our sailor mate Bill, Dennis, George the mad Hungarian, and me. Most of the time George had a merry smile on his face, but when he went off there was nothing calm or methodical about him. George lost his temper almost every time someone didn't obey his directions—immediately. One little word back and George would be raving at the object of his disdain. It was bad for business, and I knew Nick planned on sacking him, but he was there for the hunting trip—and it very nearly cost me my life.

Although it was cold, it was a clear sunny day so Mike, Bill and I rode with our backs to the rear screen. The rest of the ute was loaded with high-powered rifles, beer and very little else.

We arrived at a little tin shed out the back of nowhere and the boys immediately started shooting at anything that moved—mostly birds and rabbits. But after a short but consistent barrage of weapons-blasting, any game that may have been in the vicinity was gone. That left target shooting. George challenged me to a shoot-off, pushing a bottle top into the bark of a tree. He paced off 30 metres, carefully looked through the scope of his bazooka and fired. He missed the bottle top and just managed to hit the tree.

'Okay, my go,' I said as I raised the open breech .22 calibre rifle I had been loaned for the day. Compared with the other weapons it was a popgun, but it was the type of gun I had been taught to shoot with by my Uncle Bill. One shot and . . . bingo! Away flew the bottle top, a hole straight through it.

'That's how you do it, Georgie,' I taunted the big Hungarian bouncer. The savage look of humiliation in his eyes should have warned me, but I guess I was pleased with myself and I missed the message.

A little later George let a round go from behind me, just over my head. The *boom* scared the shit out of me, and I dropped to a crouch. George roared with laughter.

'Fuck, you frighten like a girl,' he said.

By then, we were all drinking freely and having a fine old time. I waited until George was shooting at rocks, borrowed Mike's rifle, crept up behind George and let a round go. Problem was, I had the end of the barrel about 30 centimetres away from his right ear and the percussion dropped him like a stone. He literally fell to the ground as if shot. I thought he was playacting, mocking the way I had dropped, and thought no more of it. I walked back into the shed, handing Mike his rifle.

Perhaps 30 seconds later there was a bellow from outside. George came roaring into the shed, rifle gripped in his hands, screaming that he was going to kill me. One look into his blazing eyes and I realised he most certainly was going to follow through on his threat. Only moments earlier it was bye-bye birdie; now it was going to be bye-bye Roddy.

'George, I just hope you aren't a backshooter,' was the best I could manage, not realising he'd lost 80 per cent of his hearing in his right ear. He couldn't hear anything but a ringing louder than the bells of St Clement's. No wonder he was pissed off. I turned my back to him and sat on one of the cots, hoping like hell he wouldn't backshoot me. There was a brief moment of silence and then a deafening roar. George pulled the trigger but Mike, having placed himself beside the door, knocked the rifle into the air. The bullet intended for me went through the roof. Mike's super-quick hands saved my life, no doubt at all.

The ride home was somewhat subdued. It was icy cold by then, and here were these three tough guys spooning each other to save from freezing to death. At least I was able to blame my constant shaking on the cold.

The only good thing that came out of it was George could no longer work the door, being half-deaf and all. I saved Nick the problem of sacking him.

CHAPTER 22

STAND UP AND BE COUNTED

By now I knew that no matter the circumstances or odds, I had to stand up for myself—and any others who didn't have the wherewithal to defend themselves. I'd seen enough shit go down to know that men who travel in packs, such as the bikies in the back room of Bloody Mary's, were essentially weak. There were always one or two who could fight, but most were in the gang for their own protection.

My protective side felt instinctive, and I felt it rise up one night at the White Horse Hotel. I was walking to the bar from the pool room out the back when I glanced into the lounge. It was deserted bar one table in the middle at which a dozen or so leather-jacketed punks were sitting. I noticed a pile of broken glass under the table. They had been downing their drinks and crushing the glasses under their boots.

At that moment a young uni student with an attractive girl on his arm walked into the room. They realised their mistake but, before they could wheel around and exit, three of the bullies jumped up and grabbed them by the arms. They marched the petrified couple into the middle of their group, all on their feet now, with one of the cowards stating, 'We're gonna fuck ya girlfriend, mate, and if you're a good boy you can watch.'

The young bloke was ashen, the girl vibrating with fear. I stepped into the middle of the group, forcibly pushing a couple of the arseholes out of the way.

'What's doing, boys? What's happening? Where's the action? How do I get in on this? Who's the meanest cunt here, apart from me, of course? I'm a killer. I rip throats out, carry my coin in my last victim's testicle sack . . .'

I nattered away, all the while easing the couple out of the circle. They back-pedalled out of the room, the girl with tears streaming down her face.

Once they were safely out of the way I abruptly stopped speaking, my eyes wide, almost popping out of my deranged face, staring at each of the thugs in turn with what I hoped was taken as a direct personal challenge.

'Who the fuck are you? It'd look better if it was purple. I'm faster and *way* more deadly than any of you turds. So, what's the deal . . . we gonna dance? One at a time or all in together, girls, this fine weather, ya know Mary had a little lamb, its fleece was black as charcoal, every time it jumped the fence, sparks flew out its arsehole. Any of you cunts know that one?'

The rhyme completely threw them, as I knew it would, as did the reference to purple shortly before. When you deliver dialogue out of context it is completely disarming and confusing. Half of them were nervously chuckling at Mary's little lamb, the other half playing catch-up.

'So speak up, cunts, do you agree it would look better painted purple?' I went on, confusing myself at this stage, let alone the punks surrounding me. I mean, I wasn't dealing with Mensa here.

Then, out of the corner of my eye, I spotted the law about to enter the room.

'So, what I'm saying is you are a pack of low-life cowards and, basically, I'm gonna kick ya nuts up around ya Adam's apples. So who wants to go first?'

The spell was broken. It dawned on my merry band of Neanderthals that they had been challenged and deeply insulted, all in one mind-bending, nonstop monologue.

'You fucken cunt!' said one of the blockheads, drawing back his massive fist. But it was too late: in strode one of my uniformed saviours, who took my would-be assailant by the jacket and marched him backwards, as another of New South Wales' finest grabbed me by the shoulder. I was a bit wound up by now and responded to this interference with my person with, 'Get your fucking hand off me, mate.'

Although somewhat stunned, the cop was made of sterner stuff than the now-subdued gang of thugs. He started to respond in a forceful fashion before the publican and his son stepped forward.

'No, no, officer, he's the one who saved the girl from being gang raped.'

Ah, so the grateful young couple hadn't abandoned me—they were the reason I wasn't lying in a bloody heap on the floor. No matter how cowardly the punks were, there was no way known I could have towelled up a dozen of the fuckers. The coppers marched them away, no doubt to a good old-fashioned flogging in the cells. This was, after all, Newtown: not a beat for faint-hearted coppers. They needed to be fed red meat now and then, and it looked like Marlon Brando and his sidekicks were tonight's main course.

I grabbed the jack who had put his hand on me and apologised for my harsh words.

'I was a bit wound up, cobber,' I said. 'I've got a couple of local copper mates: Vaughn and Tony.' Mention a mate in the job to another copper and it's like you're in on the giggle, too.

'No problem at all, mate,' he said. 'Fuck me, there was no way I was gonna hang onto you, not if you were prepared to take on the whole gang. Jesus Christ, you must be able to blue. What have you got a black belt in?'

'Bullshit, mate. A black belt in bullshit. I was counting on you blokes arriving. What kept ya?'

I smiled at him as the publican stepped in. 'Rod, I owe you a beer.'

'A beer? What, one single beer?' my incredulous saviour said. 'Jimmy, if this bloke hadn't stepped in, you'd have had a rape on premises which would have closed the pub, possibly lost you your licence and would have fucked up that young girl's life forever. You owe him a beer every time he walks into the joint.' The cop shook my hand before handing me his card. 'If ever you need help you've got your mates, and now me, too, Rod.'

CHAPTER 23

TAKE MY ADVICE . . . DON'T DO THIS

My time at Bloody Mary's came to an end when the joint burnt down. But before that, I crossed the line from citizen to criminal, without so much as a moment's remorse . . . well, until I learnt the ramifications of my actions.

It happened because of a card game. I had got into debt with Mike over a game of poker that, unbeknown to me, was rigged. Mike was not only fast with his hands when it came to a blue; he was, as another player who dropped out of the game very quickly pointed out to me some time later, an expert at dealing a marked deck. And he had no problem fleecing anyone dumb enough to trust him—me included.

I was indebted to him for around $500, a huge sum back in 1973, and I had no way to pay it—not on a glorified barman's wage. I wanted to settle it—not out of fear of the consequences, which didn't occur to me, but because of that bloody machismo culture that I had grown up in: a man always pays his gambling debts. That ego-driven view of life stayed with me, to the detriment of my wife and daughters in particular, for many years.

So, how to fulfill my obligation? Naturally, Mike came up with a solution.

'Mate, what we can do is rob the bar!' he suggested over a cider one Friday night after we had closed. 'I'll take half, you take half, and you can pay me back out of your cut. If there's not enough to cover the $500 we'll call it square anyway.'

After giving his proposal full and due consideration I replied approximately two seconds after he finished speaking. 'Okay, when?'

'Why not tonight?' he replied. Mike was nothing if not able to close a deal. Never let the sucker go cold on you, he reckoned. And the till had been ringing all night; there had to be at least a grand in the safe in the storeroom floor, too.

'Mmm, fuck. How do we do this without getting caught?' I said. 'I mean, Toohey won't take it lying down.'

'No worries, mate, it's all insured,' he said. 'Here's the plan: I'll leave you to do the final clean-up while I drive off around the block. I'll park up the road and walk back down Gross Street. I'll come in the back gate and wait by the back door. You do the till count. Leave the float in the till at the front bar, then take the rest to the safe. Bring the bag of rubbish with you. Put the rubbish bag down near the back door, then put the folding in the safe—but don't lock the safe. Remember it has to stay open so you can put the float in afterwards. Then you open the back door and bend over to pick up the rubbish, and I come in with a mask on and belt you in the head. Down you go, unconscious. When you come to, you find the safe robbed, but the float is still in the till at the front. Okay so far?'

'Yeah, go on,' I replied.

'Then you call the Newtown cops, tell 'em you've been bashed and robbed, and stick to your story. Don't go into detail: they'll trip you up if you do. No matter what they say, it's your word. Stand by it. They will imply you set it up. Don't get pissed off at them, just look shocked and dazed. Reckon ya can do it?'

'Fucken oath I can. So, no time like the present, let's do it.' I was quite looking forward to executing the plan.

'Right, so I'm gonna have to belt you, leave some marks on you. Okay?'

'Yep, no worries. You go and give me fifteen minutes to set this up.' And off he trotted, his pear-shaped body deceptively agile on his dancer's feet.

I did as instructed. I dropped the folding money, around $1500, in the safe, unfortunately not noticing an envelope already in there. I left the safe door open and walked to the back door. I opened it and there was Mike, hidden in the shadows. I'd left all the back lighting off, so there was only an arrow of light emerging from the storeroom doorway. Mike slipped in and pushed the door closed behind him.

'Okay, you ready, mate? There's no easy way of doing this,' he said, as he took three 20 cent coins from his pocket. He placed a coin between each finger on his right hand. When he closed his fist, a little of the edge of each coin was showing below his knuckles. 'These will mark you a bit, but that's the idea, isn't it?' he said.

I braced myself and stuck my chin forward. 'Get on with it, mate, we haven't got all night.'

Mike gave me a short, hard right to the left side of my head just beside my eye. 'Need to give you a couple more, mate. There's not enough marks.'

'Mate, for fuck's sake, make it real,' I said. 'Fuck being gentle. Belt me.'

And with that, he did: three cracking blows to the left side of the head. He opened my eyebrow and blackened my eye. Blood started trickling down my face.

'How is it mate? Realistic?' I asked my partner in my first serious crime.

'Mate, beautiful. Very realistic. Now I'm outta here. Lie on the floor and stay there for about five minutes to give me time to bolt. I'll give you your cut in a few days' time.' He moved toward the storeroom and very quickly removed the contents of the safe—including, I would later learn, the envelope.

As he stepped over me to exit the back door he quietly said, with a touch of admiration in his voice, 'Fucking nice work, Roddy, very nice indeed.' Then he was gone.

I waited the agreed five minutes, rose from the carpet and made my groggy way towards the phone at the bar. I dialled the Newtown cop shop's number from memory. I had daily contact with those boys, especially the detectives, most of whom I got on with like a house on fire. I was praying my mates would attend. After a brief conversation with the desk copper, I was told to open the door only when the police arrived and identified themselves, and to avoid touching anything under any circumstances.

Two detectives arrived. One happened to be the only Newtown cop I despised—and the feeling was mutual. But the other was, thankfully, a mate. We'd bonded one night in the bar when, after closing, I let a bunch of cops drink while I cleaned up. I noticed one particular detective was in a bad way, almost unstable. I poured the drinks while I listened to his story. Apparently, the cops had attended a double murder earlier in the day. The perpetrator, whom they had to non-fatally shoot to arrest, had cut the throat of his last remaining child and his ex-wife, killing them both. The child was a teenage boy, and he had died trying to protect his mother. The perp had also killed his other two children in the same manner a few years earlier. He was found not guilty by reason of insanity for the first crime and, after spending six or so years under psychiatric care, had been deemed cured and able to return to society. He had been out for less than 24 hours; his first act as a free man was to murder his remaining family members.

The thing that had brought my good mate to his knees was that he identified with the killer. My mate was a truly decent man but, sometime in the recent past, he'd had an argument with his wife. He flew into a raging blackout and, when he came to, his wife was on her knees in front of him, his hands around her throat. Thankfully, he didn't choke her to death, but the memory of his actions caused him to identify with the killer. So he did what blokes always do when faced with trauma: he got shitfaced. And, as I listened to his story, it affected me, too. There's nothing like a night on the piss, listening to another bloke open his heart, to bond you.

So it was, on the night of the robbery, that I found myself with my traumatised friend along with Senior Constable Arsehole. They asked me what had happened, and I related it exactly as Mike and I had rehearsed. My mate was nodding and taking notes. When I finished there was silence. Then: 'Bullshit!' bellowed Arsehole. 'You fucken set this up, and you'll do time for it. You're way too clever for yourself this time, you smart young cunt.'

'Mate, say what you like, but that's the way it happened,' I replied, glancing at my friend who had a tiny smile on his face. But Arsehole was way too distracted by the subject of his ire to notice.

'Right,' he said, 'so you can't possibly give us a description of the man who hit you, Rod?'

'Sorry, mate, it happened so bloody fast. All I remember is opening the door, bending to pick up the rubbish bag, and then the lights went out.' The contents of the rubbish bag were still strewn on the back hall floor.

'So you have no knowledge of who it was, or what he looked like?'

'No,' I said in a subdued voice. 'Apart from that he was wearing black shoes. That's all I saw. Mate, I've gotta tell you, I've got a headache you could photograph. Any chance I can go home and put my head down?'

'No problem, Rod,' my mate said. 'Get some kip and I'll call you tomorrow if I need to. Let's go,' he said to Arsehole, turning to leave.

'Sarge, you're kidding, right?' Arsehole said.

'No mate, I'm not. We're outta here.' He turned to me. 'You right to get home, Rod? What am I saying, you've copped a flogging. Lock up and we'll run you home.' He had a twinkle in his eye.

The next day I had to front Nick and lie to him bald-faced. He asked me directly if I'd had anything to do with it. I looked him in the eye and said, 'Absolutely not!'

'Well,' he replied, 'Phillip was in last night, and he asked me to mind an envelope for him. He's on the run from the police and Interpol, and that envelope contained his last $1000. You're positive that money can't be retrieved?' He was almost pleading.

I had my chance to do right, and to this day I regret not taking it. Nick wouldn't have cared about the takings being stolen. They belonged to Toohey, and he was a dud in our eyes. Nick's concern was for Phillip Shine. He had been a friend of Nick's for many years, and he was wanted by the NSW Police, Federal Police and Interpol for being the brains behind what became known as the grannies hash importation bust in late 1977.

'Nick, I can't do a thing. I had nothing to do with it. I swear to you.' As I looked Nick squarely in the eye I saw a small light of trust go out.

Later, I met up with Mike and we split the proceeds of our blatant but successful robbery.

'Well, mate, there was a total of close to $2500 in the safe. That's $1250 each. With the $500 you owe me your piece is $750. But I like your style, so let's call it a grand, okay?'

'Good enough, mate,' I replied. Yes, I could have given Phillip his dosh back, but I chose not to. I had a plan, and it required a stake. Back in the early seventies, $1000 was a shitload of money.

Nick and I remained lifelong friends and when I got sober I told him I'd done the robbery and was sorry I'd lied to him. He drolly replied, 'Oh, I've always known that.'

CHAPTER 24

DOPE IS NO MUG'S GAME

The magic was over. I had worked at Bloody Mary's for less than a year, but what a year it had been. In some ways I had changed from a boy to a man in that time; yet it would take me a further 25 years to realise I remained, in an emotional sense, fourteen years of age.

My life at this time was all about knocking around with wild people. I took my first trip of acid, and discovered that casual fornication wasn't a song title but a way of life. My chief instructor, one of the best pick-up merchants in the business, just happened to live in the room above me. I refer of course to my medical student mate, Dr Dave—or Doc Holiday, as he came to be known, because of his frequent trips to the Philippines. By then we were living together in Woollahra, where I had moved after Longdown Street.

Life was exciting and I didn't want that to end, so I saw to it that it didn't. I loved being stoned on grass and hash. The LSD experiment was, however, very different. Acid scared the shit out of me. My first time should have been my last.

Dave, Michael and I were at home one Monday night when Dave said, 'We are going to drop some acid and go to Chris's place to watch Frank Zappa being interviewed by Bob Moore.

Open your mouth.' With that, he popped a small piece of blotting paper under my tongue. 'Just let it sit there,' my personal physician advised. 'It will kick in in about half an hour.'

No worries, I thought. *Just another high.* Yeah, right.

About twenty minutes later my partners in crime were heading off, calling for me to come with them.

'Yeah, I'll follow you. Just gotta take a piss first.' I headed to the brick outdoor dunny. As I stepped through the doorway, the acid kicked in like a mule. Feeling completely disembodied I unzipped, searching for my average-sized dick which had somehow miraculously been altered to the size of a peanut. I finally extracted it but, as I pointed it at the porcelain, I saw a hundred small objects running laps around the top of the bowl.

'What the fuck?'

They were maggots. As I identified them the bricks of the outhouse started to crumble in on me. I came out of the shitter at a startled trot. As I increased speed, heading for the inside of the house and ultimately the front door, the entire house started to collapse around me. By the time I reached the still-open front door I was moving faster than Superman with a case of the runs.

I launched myself through the door and hurdled the gate, bypassed the footpath, landed on Longdown Street, threw myself into a western roll, regathered my feet and made the 80 metres to Chris's door in the time it takes a lit fart to burn itself out. If you don't know how fast that is, try doing it. (And by the way, take my advice and always wear a pair of cotton jocks when you do this, never nylon, otherwise you'll end up setting fire to your pubes.)

I entered Chris's lounge room with the look of a drug-addled lunatic etched into my features. My peepers were crazed, and latched on to Dave's. 'Mate, I'm dying. You've gotta give me something,' I begged.

In his usual calm fashion, he replied, 'Mate, you're fine. Take a seat and enjoy the interview; and zip your fly up.'

Bob Moore was on the TV: 'Welcome to Monday Conference. I'm Bob Moore and my guest tonight is world-renowned rock'n'roll impresario, Mr Frank Zappa . . .'

And with that, Bob and Frank stepped out of the TV set and into Chris's living room, while Michael, Chris and Dave hopped into the box and onto the ABC set.

I spent the next hour enjoying a chat with Frank and Bob while my pals amused themselves at ABC TV's Ripponlea studio. Unfortunately I have no recall of what Frank, Bob and I talked about. All I could say as the program ended and my astral traveller friends rejoined me was, 'How the fuck did you do that?'

CHAPTER 25

FROM LITTLE THINGS BIG THINGS GROW

I knew my old Albury drinking mate Paul 'Macca' McDonald was dealing dope. I'd met up with him in a pub in Hunters Hill, and he told me he had tapped into a river of cash and he wanted to spend some of it. He offered me a deal. While he was having a holiday in Mexico, I was to keep his operation ticking over. He gave me the introductions, phone numbers and information I would need to keep the business running.

Before Macca left, he told me to go to a certain address in Abbotsford on a certain day at a certain time and take delivery of some Aussie cannabis heads. I was to do my best with it and go from there. It later became apparent that this was obviously a test to see if I had what it took to work in the business.

I didn't own a car in the early seventies, nor did I have enough money for a taxi, so I did what any aspiring drug dealer would do: I caught the bus there.

I remember very little of the meeting other than the guy was polite, quietly spoken and very quick getting the business done. On Macca's say-so he handed me a suitcase containing 10 kilos of what turned out to be excellent quality Australian heads: a damned fine smoke. No money changed hands; I had none! But I committed to return within the week with as much money as I had mustered. I was back in two days with all the cash. My slice of the pie amounted to $200 per kilo: $2000. I was king of the heap.

I saw new-found respect in the eyes of those close to me who knew what was going on. Dave no longer treated me like a kid brother, but as an equal. 'You've got the balls for the business!' he said.

The first thing I did was buy an old Valiant station wagon. No way was I ever carrying dope on public transport again. It was way too dodgy, even without the sniffer dogs I'd face today.

I continued to deal with my man at Abbotsford. I instinctively knew that to gain the biggest profits with the smallest risk I'd need to buy big and sell to as few customers as possible. Macca's contacts helped, but I also developed a few myself.

Within a couple of months, I had accumulated over $20,000. Back then it was a massive sum. It would buy a house in Newtown and leave enough for a round trip to Europe. Naturally, though, I didn't do that. I worked the business, I punted and I partied.

Macca was briefly back in Sydney. He'd been having a good time in Mexico and planned to head straight back there after closing up his house and getting some things in order. His parting gifts to me, over 30 beers and numerous games of eight-ball, were two introductions. The first was to my future supplier, a guy I'll call Gator, in the interests of me staying alive. I'd heard of him but had never laid eyes on the man. The second was to my buyer, Rex, from Melbourne. The whole business was handed to me on a plate.

'Mate, be on the bend outside Rose Bay police station on New South Head Road tomorrow at noon, sharp. Gator will send a car for you.' As Macca spoke, he sunk the black. That boy could play eight-ball like a pro.

'What happens then?' I asked.

'Then, mate, you start running shitloads of smoko down to Melbourne. Your contact down there is Rex. This is his phone number,' he said, handing me a piece of paper. 'He's expecting your call. In fact, I imagine he's sitting by the phone. It's a nice operation, mate. Don't fuck it up. Don't get greedy. That's what'll bring you undone.'

'I'm with you, Macca. It's all good, mate. Your cut will be waiting for you when you get back, whenever that is,' I said, shaking his hand.

I turned to go, and Macca said, 'Roddy, you're in for the ride of your life.'

I parked the Valiant around the corner from New South Head Road and walked to the designated bend, arriving just as a white Merc pulled up. A fit-looking, sharply dressed bloke about five years older than me leant over and opened the door. 'Get in,' he said, so I did.

'Scott.' He leaned across and offered his right hand as he drove off at the correct speed.

I took his hand, quickly deciding how much information I was going to give. I was surprised the man himself, not one of his lackeys, had picked me up. Fuck it: in for a penny, in for a pound. 'Rod Halsted,' I replied.

'You heard of me?' he asked.

'Yeah, but I've also heard you're called Gator. What do I call you?'

The look he shot me gave the impression we had made quick progress to a moment of decision. 'Whaddya think?' he asked in that distinctive, side-of-mouth, nasal way he had of speaking.

'Well, mate, I'd reckon only your mates would call you Gator, so I reckon that'll do me, too.'

After a momentary silence he said, 'Let's have a drink.' He spun the car around and got us back to the Golden Sheaf Hotel in Double Bay in double-quick time.

We drank until neither of us could stand up straight. We talked about everything besides what I understood I was there for. When we'd finished, he said, 'Come around in three days to my place in Bondi, and I'll have 10,000 Thai sticks for you. You reckon you can handle that much first go, Roddy?'

Roddy! We had become buddies on our first date.

'Gator, mate, I'll do my very best.'

'Couldn't ask more than that, my man.' And then he gave me his address. There was no greater sign of instant trust. I wasn't sure that I could resist kissing him if this banter kept up, so I hit the frog and toad.

'See you in three days, mate!' I was goneski.

I wasn't so pissed that I left planning for the deal till the next day. I knew already that time is vital in dope dealing. You must give the buyer as much notice as possible so he can raise the cash. The credit line of business stopped with me.

I had farmed out a few kilos here and there on credit and, although I had got all the cash owing, at times it took way longer than agreed. No way was I giving out another man's gear on credit. I knew of Gator's reputation. I'd heard he and another guy I never got to meet, Bag-'o'-Shells, were the two most dangerous dealers in the city. And there was a third, Jimmy Lollies, with whom I did do business down the track.

During our first meeting, when Gator asked if I knew who he was, and I replied in the affirmative, I added that I'd also heard of both Lollies and Bag-'o'-Shells. That I knew they were supposedly the hardest people in the game; you crossed them at your peril.

Gator had turned to me with that enigmatic little smile he used at times, and softly said, 'Bag-'o'-Shells? Yeah, he's hard, but I put him on his back, mate.'

'Yeah, you look fit, mate. Just so you know, though: I'm just a country boy, but I've been working with cattle and cranky rams since I was a kid. No cunt stands over me.'

He gave me a quick look.

'Just so we are clear. Mate!'

Again, he flashed that little smile and gave a quiet chuckle. Then suddenly he broke into song. By God, he had a gangster way of speaking, but could the bastard sing? He had a voice best described as a male Nina Simone. And I told him so.

'Fuck this dope business, mate. You do the singing, I'll do the managing. We'll make a motza.'

He dropped his guard and laughed out loud with a mix of embarrassment and delight. It may have been the best compliment he had ever been paid.

So, with a bellyful of grog and a head full of plans, I rang Rex.

'Mate, it's your mate from Sydney's pool partner. We've got a comp on in six days and want to know if you can come up for it?'

'I'll check with the missus and get back to you, mate,' Rex replied.

It was a simple code: double all figures and reverse destinations. So, six days meant three and 'come up', presumably to Sydney, meant me 'going down' to Melbourne. Operating on the basis that all home phones are tapped, Rex had signalled to me that he would find a public phone and call me at my local pub, which Macca had let him know was the Lord Dudley in Woollahra. It was a quick sprint from home to the pub where I was, by then, well known. By the time I had a beer in front of me, the barmaid was calling me to the phone.

'Mate, what's the go?' asked the fat little antique dealer. (His build and legitimate trade I came to learn later.)

'Ten after twelve, mate!'

'Shit, that's going to take some organising,' Rex replied.

'In that case, mate, what are you doing talking to me?'

As we hung up we were both chuckling: me thinking about the $2 per stick I was going to make; Rex working out where he was going to get $120,000, over the next three days, to pay for 10,000 Buddha sticks. Beautiful things they were, all sticky buds from the best dope grown in Thailand. They were made by binding the dope to a wooden skewer with cotton. Often the stick was extracted so all the weight was in the finest smoko available to dope fiends worldwide. They were then packed in bundles of 100, then into blocks of 1000. When I got hold of them I would either on-sell them in their original packaged state or I would separate each stick so they could be counted. The buyer was always happy to take them packaged, even if the numbers were sometimes short. In separating them, though, I would end up with a pile of kief which was ideal for personal smoking without losing any product.

Rex got back to me within the hour with good news: he had on-sold the lot and had the cash organised. He needed the gear that night, though. Fuck. The drive to Melbourne was eleven hours sticking within the speed limit, which I always did when transporting dope. There was no chance of getting it there in the timeframe required but, because I was building a reputation—I had decided my policy would be to meet the client's needs whenever possible, and only ever deal in top-quality gear—I decided to fly it to Melbourne. In those days, it wasn't as risky as it may sound: airport security wasn't what it is today. There were no metal detectors or sniffer dogs, and certainly no bag searches unless you looked dodgy—which I did not, dressed in my three-piece suit and tie, and holding my briefcase. I was the model young executive.

CHAPTER 26

ALWAYS KEEP YOUR EYES ON THE PRIZE

I purchased a combination lock suitcase, the biggest I could find. It was on wheels and when upright the handle was at my hip. It was massive, but only just big enough to hold the 10,000 sticks of product I was flying. There was no room left for clothes to at least give a covering over the sticks. I packed the gear in a double layer of plastic, wiping each layer with methylated spirits to remove any trace of smell.

After checking my locked bag through, I boarded my flight and assumed the role that I was playing. I removed papers from my briefcase and fiddle-arsed around with them. I even opened a copy of the *Financial Review*, a paper only read by finance nerds (and presumably not by drug dealers—there was no point, since it didn't include a racing form). You never know who's watching and I knew any slip-up that gave the game away could result in plenty of prison time. I was the business exec, and would remain so until I had the cash safely back in Sydney. Until my supplier was paid, I was in the gun.

After landing in Melbourne, I figured I had ten minutes before my suitcase would appear on the baggage carousel, so I found a pay phone and called Rex. After a bit of a natter I let him know which hotel I was booked into (so he could meet me at the back entrance). I hung up the phone up and ambled back to claim my case.

Fuck!

There was my suitcase, along with one other bag, going round and round on the carousel. There was no other passenger in sight and 24 uniformed Commonwealth police standing in twos and threes around the perimeter of the baggage-collection area. What to do? Bolt and try to explain to Gator how I had lost $100,000 of his money? Or collect the bag and hand myself up for a massive bust?

It was a no-brainer: I'd rather spend years in prison than eternity in a hole in the ground.

I spotted one cop standing on his own. I put on a bad limp and hobbled over to him.

'G'day, mate,' I said. 'I wonder if you'd do me a favour? That bigger bag of the two is mine. The bloody thing weighs a tonne, and I've hurt my leg. Would it be too much trouble for you to lift it off the carousel and wheel it over to me, please?'

'Sure, mate, no problem.' And he did! There was enough dope to get me ten years in the slammer and my personal porter, a federal copper, was none the wiser.

As I wheeled the case away, still limping, I continually scanned the posse of coppers in the reflection of the floor-to-ceiling glass windows. I was ready to leave the case and bolt at the slightest suggestion they were coming after me. All my instincts said they weren't—I mean, twenty-plus uniformed police for a one-man bust? And making themselves so obvious? But caution, constant alertness and peripheral vision are what had kept me bust-free up to now, so there was no reason to abandon a winning formula just as I was heading into the big league. But the cops didn't move.

After catching a cab into the city, I instructed my driver to drop me at the Windsor Hotel where I strode into reception, wheeling the booty along beside me. I paid in advance for three nights' stay and picked up my key to a room on the tenth floor. Once inside the lift I pressed the button for the second floor, where I removed myself and my super-sized, ganga-stuffed suitcase and potential ten years in the company of arse bandits, rock spiders and run-of-the-mill lunatics—possible romantic partners one and all.

As the lift ascended to my booked floor, I caught another lift to the basement where Rex was waiting for me in his Volvo. We drove straight to his antique-filled mansion in Toorak. It was obvious the 'business' had been kind to my new colleague.

I spent the next three days ensconced in Rex's back bedroom. I didn't once remove my shoes or clothes. I didn't bathe. I did clean my teeth, and ate the food provided. Rex got as little sleep as I did, as he constantly came to me for varying amounts of sticks. It seemed he sold the entire lot in about six or seven transactions. I was breaking my own rule, and taking a punt each time, but I let him have anything from 1000 to 2500 sticks on consignment.

It all went like clockwork, and I was back in Sydney three days after I'd flown out. I was $20,000 richer and well and truly in Gator's good books. He had his $100,000 and a new man he could trust. I'd proven I had both the nerves and ability to think on my feet and get the job done. Gator, like all successful businesspeople I have known or read about, had the invaluable ability to select the right personnel to work with and for him.

It was also the start of a very successful business relationship with Rex. I went up and down from Sydney to Melbourne perhaps a dozen times in the next two years, sometimes by air but usually in a rented car. On each occasion I made no less than $20,000. I suppose all up I made over $300,000, at a time in which you could buy a terrace house in Paddington for $25,000. It should have frayed my nerves, but it didn't.

Rex and his three offsiders took 90 per cent of the risk. The only danger to me was if the jacks followed him home, which was unlikely. He was nothing if not professional. As I watched him in action during those first three nerve-wracking days, I developed a confidence in him that he never gave me cause to question.

The only time I got nervous was when I went with him to one of his contacts to sell 5000 sticks: $60,000 was just too much to take a risk on, so I insisted on holding the dope until the money was on show. After driving a circuitous route, designed by Rex to confuse me so I could never identify his man's location, we finished up at around 11 p.m. in the car park of a large building. We were met at the back door by a guy in his sixties who looked like a maître d'.

I had the gear in a suitcase, and was ready to do a runner at the slightest hint of a set-up. But there was no need for concern. He walked us through the dark to a table in what was clearly a room in a reception centre. It was huge and dimly lit. On the table was a briefcase filled with cash. The exchange was done quickly: we were in and out in no more than three minutes.

When we arrived back at Rex's house, backslapping all around, I said, 'Mate, if we need to do that again, with me coming along for the ride, do you reckon we could dispense with the James Bond tactics and go straight there and back? It will save us an hour!'

'Yeah, I understand that, Rod, but security is everything, mate, so probably not.'

'Well, you'd better organise yourself a bit better, mate, and place a little more trust in me.' I flashed him a pamphlet for the White Dove Reception Centre. 'It wouldn't be too hard to make a direct approach to your man, but that's not my go. I'd have thought you'd have me worked out by now.'

The expression on his face was priceless.

'I picked this up from the hall table,' I said, laughing as I dropped the pamphlet for the Doped-Up Dove in his lap.

'I'm embarrassed, mate,' Rex said. He had a nice shiny rose on each cheek.

'It's okay, mate. I'm getting some sleep, but not here. Drop me up at the taxi rank and I'll book into a pub for a few hours' kip before I fly back in the morning.'

Once he'd dropped me off, I did the opposite of what I'd said. I had arranged for a rental car to be waiting for me, so I caught a cab into the city which would drop me off a couple of blocks from my pick-up point. I had no luggage, just a large coat with an inordinate number of pockets, all of them stuffed with $20 and $50 bills. Why take a chance on someone deciding to relieve me of my hard-earned by carrying it around in a suitcase?

The deals went like that. It was as simple as digging a hole and filling it in, just a bit better paid: like a year's wages for a day or two's work. Rex was very easy to deal with. The only hiccup we had was when $12,000 went missing from his car. We arrived back at his house after a handover and went inside, me carelessly leaving my ill-gotten gains on his unlocked Volvo's passenger-side floor. We were only inside for a few minutes when I remembered. I shot back out to the car, which was parked well up the long driveway. I opened the door and . . . no fucking cash. What the fuck? The car had a deep footwell so there was no chance I had kicked it out.

I went straight back inside. 'Rex, what the fuck, mate. Did you pick up my cash for me? You should have told me. Where is it?'

'What are you talking about, mate?' He looked mystified.

'I left the twelve grand on the floor of the Volvo. It's not there now.' My gaze was drawn to his wife, who was doing everything she could to ignore this very unusual turn of events. She was a hard bitch with a foul mouth. I never liked her, and now I was certain she was a thief.

Rex saw the look I gave his missus. He exploded.

'What the fuck are you implying, Rod? Don't call anyone here a thief. The cash was your responsibility. You lost it, so you find it!'

I had to hold myself in check or I was going to do some damage, the worst of it to my business connection. I bit my tongue.

'No accusations being made, mate, but I know the cash was in the car when I got out of it. If it turns up, why don't you give me a call? Meanwhile I'll get my gear together and head home.'

His tone changed immediately. 'Mate, we still have a couple of thousand sticks to get rid of. You can't leave now.' He was almost pleading. Making a buck was more important than anything.

'Nah, mate. All good. I need to get home. I'll grab my stuff and catch a cab out the front.'

I immediately went to the room where my gear was stored. The dope was locked in a suitcase. As I came back through the kitchen, heading for the back door, Rex came after me. The $12,000 was clutched in his sweaty hand.

'Mate, it was there all the time, under the car beside your door,' he said in a rush. 'You must have bumped it out and then kicked it under the car. Anyway, all good mate, stick around for a couple of hours and I'll get rid of the last of the smoko.'

There was no sign of Rex's wife. I absolutely knew I hadn't knocked the cash from the car—it was physically impossible, $12,000 being the size of half a brick. I assumed Rex, being the clever, quick-thinking lad that he was, had realised our business arrangement was in danger of coming to an end. I don't know what he did to his wife to get the cash back, nor do I care, but she didn't reappear prior to me leaving. And I didn't wait two hours for him to run around and collect the required $24,000 for the last of the sticks.

'Well, mate, what a mug I am. Fancy treating $12,000 in such a cavalier fashion. Well found. Now, why don't you dig into your pile and stump up for the last of the product. I need to get out of here posthaste.'

He obliged. I was on the footpath hailing a cab ten minutes later.

'Sorry about that fuck-up, mate,' he whined. 'Everything's cool with us, right?'

'Yeah, mate, no problem at all. We all fuck up.'

I'm not sure he got my allusion that his choice of bride was the major fuck-up on this occasion.

'By the way, mate, it's time for you to do some travelling,' I said, as the cab approached. 'Why don't you pick up from me for a change? And bring the dosh with you, mate. You've made plenty, so no more credit.' It was a statement rather than a request, clearly showing that the trust had gone.

'Sure, mate, no problem,' he said as I opened the cab door. 'See ya in Sin City.'

CHAPTER 27

GOOD MATES STICK

And that's how it went. Rex didn't trust airports, so he drove up and back on each occasion, hiring cars and hotel rooms every visit. He had to get the entire payment together and the deal was always done in two drops, so if one went off at least we had half the gear to sell for legal costs. All in all, Rex's thieving wife did me a big favour: no more travel, no more sleeping in dirty clothes, no more eating with people I normally wouldn't speak to. Most of all, no more handing my safety over to others . . .

Around this time, I took a load of 30,000 sticks to another dealer I was doing business with in Melbourne. I ran out of puff after getting rid of 26,000, so I put the remaining 4000 sticks plus the bulk of the $312,000 I had picked up into a large tan bag—rather like a doctor's Gladstone bag, only much bigger. I covered the lot with a few clothes, but it was hardly hidden. I was getting lazy; putting cash and gear together was the number-one no-no.

I locked the bag and checked it through baggage at the airport on the last flight out that night. I was exhausted after four days of law-breaking, and dozed on the flight home. It wasn't easy:

there was a football team on board on an end-of-season trip. The noisy pricks did their best to drink the plane dry.

When I entered the terminal, there waiting for me as arranged was my housemate, GP to the lonely wives of Sydney's outer-western suburbs, Doc Holiday.

'G'day, mate. How'd it go?' he enquired.

'Yeah, all good, mate. Had to bring a bit of product home but got over three hundred grand to divvy up.'

Three hundred grand! It seemed like only yesterday I was walking the streets of Newtown looking for Coke bottles to cash in to finance some time on the eight-ball table. Now here I was, carrying around enough brass to buy the best property on Sydney's beautiful foreshore. It's amazing how you get used to things: the good and the bad.

'I just want to put my head down, mate. Ah, there's my bag.' I grabbed it off the carousel before the rabble of rat-faced footballers descended on their luggage.

Dave and I got home, and he asked if he could see what $300,000 cash looked like.

'Sure, mate,' I said, inserting my key in the bag's lock. No result; it wouldn't turn. 'What the fuck gives?' Dave reached around me and gave the catch a flick. It sprung open.

Dread spread through me like poison. I opened the bag, and there before us was a pair of platform shoes, the likes of which I hadn't seen outside an Adam Ant video. Under the shoes was a pair of bell-bottom pants. *Fuck! Fuck! Fuck!*

'I picked up the wrong bag. Oh, *fuck*!' I immediately rang the airport. They informed me that one of the footballers had a similar bag to mine, and recognised that the bag left on the carousel wasn't his. 'Could you tell me where he is staying so I can deliver his bag back to him?' I quickly asked. I was given the name of a hotel in the city.

'Mate, I've gotta go and get that bag,' I said to Dave.

'I'll drive you,' he replied.

'No, mate. If I get rolled, they'll pick you up, too. They will take your licence to practice off you and that's eight years down the gurgler.'

'Fuck it. I'll drive and wait in the car in case you have to bolt,' he insisted.

Talk about staunch. Friends like that are rare.

Dave parked outside the hotel. I went in, bag in hand. I found the floor where the team was staying and knocked on the nearest door.

'Yeah?' was all the occupant had to say. He was obviously the worse for the drink consumed.

'Mate, I'm looking for the bloke who got the wrong bag. I've got his, and I want to swap.'

'Ah, mate, that's Barry. He knew straight away it wasn't his when he couldn't open it at the airport. He left it with them. You want to give me his bag and I'll get it to him?'

'Sure, mate.' I handed the bag over. 'Do you know where they sent my bag?' I wasn't really thinking I'd get anything useful from him, but was desperate at this point.

'Yeah, mate, they said they'd have it at the TAA office in Phillip Street,' he replied. 'They said if you made contact to let you know they open at 7 a.m. tomorrow. Oh, that would be today now,' my helpful bag handler said.

'Onya mate, thanks heaps.'

Dave and I didn't get any sleep. By the time I exited the hotel it was after 2 a.m., so we sat at home, had a smoke and drink, and he drove me to Phillip Street at 6.30 a.m. I had him park the car around the corner from the TAA office, which was at the dead end of Phillip Street. I figured if they had the bag under observation, I was half a chance of getting back to the car and away before the jacks could get on my tail.

It was all unnecessary. I bowled in like I owned the joint, asked for a bag that had been left at the airport and had it immediately handed to me—still locked.

You can be lucky, as long as you don't panic. Still, I must admit I needed a change of undies after that little episode.

CHAPTER 28

HAWTHORNDEN

Hawthornden was a once-magnificent mansion set on a Woollahra cliff, overlooking Double Bay and across Sydney Harbour to Kirribilli House, the prime minister's residence. In its glory days, Hawthornden was owned by P&O, the premier cruise operator of the time. It had changed hands over the years and lost its gloss. By the time I walked through its double wrought-iron gates and past the five-bedroom gatehouse, it was in similar shape to a hooker who had started in the penthouse and worked her way through to the basement, then out onto the street.

Now it was home to a diverse group of twenty-plus interesting individuals. It had twelve bedrooms, a ballroom which doubled as a ping-pong and dope-smoking room, and stables, which had been converted into a residence in which two doctors, Tim and Marion, resided.

The other occupants of this magical place ranged from a dapper Englishman named Ken who drove a Lamborghini and did something in the city, to Peter the boat builder, to the daughter of a British peer who was twentieth in line to the English throne, to an eccentric named Michael from the Bushes, so called because he had set up home, with his red setter dog, in a very large, heavy-duty cardboard box set among the extensive gardens.

It was one resident, Corky, who intrigued me most. A robust, rough diamond of a man, he wasn't everyone's cup of tea but to me he was unique. He was up for anything, brave and a bully at times—mostly I think because he had a short temper and didn't expect anyone to stand up to him. When another resident, Vicky, did on one occasion, he wheeled on her and unleashed a tirade of abuse so threatening that I stepped in and pulled him away.

I first met Corky outside the house in Spicer Street that Dave and I had moved to a few weeks before. He was wandering along with a skinny little guy: another resident of Hawthornden, English John. They stopped to say hello, so I invited them both in for a joint. It was some heavy-duty shit. As they were leaving, Corky invited Dave and me to Hawthornden for a game of tennis. We drove to the house, only a short distance away, around an hour later—but there was no Corky, and no John. We backtracked and eventually found them at the end of our street. They had walked a total of 100 metres in an hour. The reason they'd travelled so short a distance became immediately apparent: they were so stoned they were counting the number of bricks in the front walls of each house they passed—losing count, of course, before breaking into uncontrolled laughter and starting again.

It didn't take long for Corky to become my close mate, with the pair of us drinking and smoking dope at all hours. We played tennis on the estate's grass court and table tennis in the ballroom, where we belted the little white pill around. No one complained about the noise; or maybe they did, and we simply ignored them.

I was playing table tennis with Al, another man who became a lifelong friend, around 3 a.m. one morning. English John and a couple of others were sharing a joint while lying about on beanbags, when Vicky burst in with two Scotsmen in tow. 'Boys,' she said, 'I'm taking this guy upstairs for a fuck—he's the manager of the Average White Band. This other guy is the lead singer; entertain him, will you?' And off she went with the manager, leaving an extremely pissed warbler behind.

'John, roll this guy a joint, will ya?' I said.

'Keep the fuck away from the table,' was Al's instruction to the singer. 'This is a serious game.' It wasn't exactly the way rock'n'roll royalty was used to being treated, and certainly not the way to speak to a drunken Scotsman by the name of Al Gorrie. The Scots are well known for their fighting ability.

John rolled a lovely large spliff of the very best quality Afghani hash, got it fired up and gave it to our honoured guest. After a few tokes he disappeared. We finished our game an hour or so later and I headed off to the usual bed I crashed in. Bugger me! There he was, our Scottish frontman, arms and legs akimbo, stretched out on my bed, dead to the world. No matter how much I prodded, he simply wouldn't wake up.

Al, John and I couldn't pass up this opportunity. We headed off and came back five minutes later with a few odds and ends, which we put to good use. We placed a tennis racquet in his right hand, a feather duster in his left, a motorcycle helmet on his head and a very large, black cock-and-balls candle between his legs. We covered his moustache in toothpaste, then squirted chocolate syrup along his legs and arms and down his fly. The final touch was a light covering of sprinkled sugar over his chest hair, and some whipped cream inside his pants. I wrote a note which I placed in his shirt pocket, enough poking out so that he would find it: 'You are now known as the Tasty Morsel.'

With our night's work done, we retired—the boys to their respective beds, me to the first empty nest I could find: a beanbag on the upstairs verandah. It was the safest place to be, as it turned out.

It was only a couple of hours later that I awoke to the sounds of violence: doors slamming, raised voices and one terrified scream. I rolled over and went back to sleep in the safe little nook I had found.

When I finally went down to the kitchen a couple of hours later, Shirley, the 'house mother' and John's girlfriend, had Al, Corky, John, Steve the Chemist and a couple of other likely suspects sitting at the large kitchen table. She was going off her head.

'How dare you treat one of our guests in that manner? You realise that when he woke up he went berserk. The door to Rod's room is off its hinges, and Michael has a suspected broken jaw.' She was howling. 'That man is the lead singer of the Average White Band!' she loudly sobbed. 'And look at the way he has been treated. It is an absolute disgrace.'

'What happened to him?' I innocently enquired, studiously avoiding the other boys' eyes.

'His person was *desecrated*!' she yelled. 'It wasn't enough that he had items displayed around his body, but one or more of you put foodstuffs *on* his person. The sugar caused him to scratch himself stupid.'

'Ah, Shirl, I met him last night. He was already stupid,' Al said.

'Enough!' the crazed human rights activist screamed. 'I want everyone here to write "I am now known as the Tasty Morsel" on these pieces of paper I have supplied. I am determined to find the perpetrator of this abominable act.'

'You don't think you're taking this a little to heart, Shirl?' I said quietly.

'You're the main suspect, Rod Halsted!' she thundered at me.

So, we went ahead and supplied the samples required by our Miss Marple—all of us writing with our wrong hand, sloping and slanting the letters.

'There ya go, Shirl. Let us know when y'all are laying charges,' Corky said in his best western drawl. 'Tennis, anyone?'

I've occasionally wondered if our brand of humour inspired the band to write a song about their encounter with the Hawthornden Heathens, which, on reflection, is probably a better name for a group than the Average White Band.

CHAPTER 29

THE AMERICAN CONNECTION

Out of the blue, four Californian visitors arrived at Hawthornden. They had brought a van full of hash into Australia through Darwin and had managed to get it to the Blue Mountains, and hidden it away on an isolated, rundown farm in the lower foothills.

The main man was a businesslike little guy named Jay, who was married to a stunner named Cathy. Jay had two partners, Bob and Randy. I immediately liked Randy but didn't trust Bob, and Jay was just too up himself.

Jay's main claim to fame was that, at a concert in California, Grateful Dead lead singer Gerry Garcia had called out to the audience, 'Jay, are you out there man? We need your goodies.' Apparently he was referring to cocaine, and to Jay—which our new friend didn't mind letting us know. Corky had found him, and we set out to move the 1000 kilos of hash he and his crew had smuggled into the country.

Unbeknown to us, the US Drug Enforcement Administration (DEA) had been onto them from the get-go, when they packed the van in India. Somehow, the DEA guys lost track of their quarry and ended up a couple of days behind them once they hit Darwin. And that's where they stayed: two days behind.

We began dealing the hash: only ten kilos at a time at first, then upping it to twenty. I had set up to sell to Jimmy Lollies. I knew through Gator he had a shocking reputation as a grass for the coppers, and that he had supposedly murdered people when he thought it necessary. He was also a rip-off merchant, so my method of dealing with him was to sell for a cash exchange, always offering double the amount in a later deal. Greed is a great motivator.

I did the first deal in a railway station car park in the lower Blue Mountains, selling him ten kilograms for $25,000. After doing three more ten-kilo deals I promised twenty next time. It all went smoothly, including the promised twenty-kilo transaction. There were no problems with guns, and the money was spot-on each time.

Meanwhile, I was getting Rex in on the deal, and was preparing to move the rest through him. I knew it was only a matter of time before Lollies decided to rip me off. I predicted that the 40 kilos I had offered him would be too much of a temptation for him. I walked away after completing the 20-kilo deal, knowing I would not be back.

Unfortunately, I was spot-on. It was the last deal I did from that stash. The DEA, with the help of the NSW Police airwing, had spotted the van and came in force to bust the Yanks. They only got the three men, though: Cathy had decided to spend some time in town at Hawthornden. Jay was cool with that, until he realised I was playing hide the sausage with his highly attractive and hugely sexual wife.

It happened quite by accident. It started with the two of us locking eyes in the front driveway of the big house. It was a look that lasted a moment too long. One of us, if we hadn't been drawn together by sexual magnetism, should have looked away. But we didn't, and over the next three days we went at it like teenagers. Fair dinkum, if I'd come one more time I reckon my forehead would have caved in. When she went off it was like being in the middle of a bronc-riding contest at the Tumbarumba Rodeo. Fortunately, we were alone in my rented Vaucluse unit, so only had the neighbours to worry about—and who ever gave a rat's about the neighbours?

'Fuck me, drive it into me you horny fucker. Motherfucker!' she screamed as she came for the 92nd time that afternoon. If orgasms were rabbits, she could have opened her own hat factory. Meanwhile her husband, and Bob and Randy, were being held in Goulburn Gaol.

Getting laid was always near the top of my list, but never ahead of the business. We had to get the boys out of the can, and fast. How else were we going to get hold of the rest of the hash, which was hidden in the bush? There were hundreds of thousands of dollars waiting to be made.

The three men had been pinched on a Friday and transported to Goulburn overnight, due to be brought back to Sydney the next week. It was Christmas and everything had shut down. But then, Charlie Waterstreet saved the day. He organised for a Sydney QC to go to the gaol on the Saturday, for a very handsome fee of course, and whatever he said to the screws there, they released the lads on nominal bail of a few thousand dollars.

Meanwhile, I'd been busy. I'd spoken to one of my criminal contacts who, for a very reasonable $1000 each, had come up with passports good enough to get the boys and Cathy out of the country and home. The four left so quickly we had no chance of finding out where the stash of hash was buried.

It was a bit of a bastard that the whole thing had come undone. It cost Corky and me somewhere around $300,000 in commission. We did drive up to the area we believed the van had been hidden in, hoping to find the remainder of the gear that Randy told us they had buried: some 500 kilograms. I went through the bush, which was nearly as dense as me, looking for the stash.

What the fuck was I doing, wandering around in scrub so thick you could barely see five metres ahead, hoping to find a hole that someone else had dug and disguised? All I did was get myself lost for a couple of hours. I only managed to make my way back to the car right on dusk because I found a dirt track, which I followed back to the car and Corky. It was sheer luck. By rights, my bones should be lying out there undiscovered, along with the buried hash.

As Ned Kelly said, 'Such is life.' Fortunately, unlike Ned, we lived to tell the tale.

CHAPTER 30

HITTING THE TOE

Hawthornden was a brilliant place to live, but I had to leave abruptly when two things happened in succession. First, I arrived home to be told that four detectives had descended on the house looking for a red-headed bloke, mid-twenties, suspected of dealing in drugs. Not the sharpest knives in the drawer, those boys. Thanks for the warning.

While I was quickly packing a few clothes in an overnight bag, the phone rang. It was Gator. Someone called me to the phone, and I took it, knowing I'd need to be cautious in what I said in case it was tapped.

'Yeah, mate?' I said.

'Ah, yeah, mate, can you meet me in an hour at that place where we play squash?'

Something in Gator's voice told me that his intentions for me were not in my best interests. Knowing him as I did, I knew how easily he could jump to a conclusion. I also knew I had picked up a crate at the airport only three days prior, and that same crate had been stored in a vacant house on the Central Coast. I knew I had been paid for the pick-up with 5000 Thai sticks worth at least $60,000 to me, and that they were the only sticks removed from the crate before it was stored. I knew that the crate had been discovered earlier that day by a real estate agent who was showing the property and that he had called in the cops. I quickly surmised that Gator had drawn a long bow and decided that I had given the stash up.

There wasn't an iota of truth in this or any reason to come to that conclusion, but I simply didn't feel like explaining to Gator that I wasn't the guilty party—particularly in some lonely part of the national park, a shovel in my hand as I dug a shallow grave. I had plans for the next few years that didn't involve being worm food.

I mean, what was he thinking? I was the one who had risked ten years in the can when I did the pick-up from customs.

The way we planned the collection from customs was simple but ingenious. I had parked my utility outside a pub near the airport and chatted up the barmaid over half a dozen beers. The idea was that she would remember me if she were questioned by the police.

Then, in through the door Gator walked. 'Anyone here got a ute or truck and want to make a quick $100?' he asked to the bar.

Quick as a shot I shouted, 'Over here, mate!' As he joined me at the bar, within hearing of the now-nosey barmaid, I said, 'What's the go?'

'Mate, Trevor's my name. I've got a box I need picked up at customs, but my ute has shit itself.'

'It's your lucky day, Trev. Rod's my name, and I've got my ute parked out the front. And believe me, I can use the dosh. What's the drill, mate?'

'Come with me, mate, and I shall reveal all.' With that, he turned on his expensive loafers and strode towards the door.

I turned to the barmaid and said, 'How about I come back later, and you and I can have a bit of fun with my new-found wealth when you knock off, darlin'?' I gave her a wink to get the juices flowing.

'See ya soon, big boy!'

Not fucken likely, I thought.

So off to customs I motored, and met Gator's contact. He was someone high up in customs, and he walked me through the pick-up and exit in double-quick time. I left with a box big enough to make the springs on my utility groan. We transferred the box, crammed with Thai sticks and nothing else, to Gator's garage and I left with my payment of 5000 mind-benders.

Apparently, Gator had arranged to leave the box in a Central Coast house that had been vacant for months. He really should have signed the lease, because within a few days the real estate agent handling the property walked some prospective tenants through the joint. Bingo. One box filled with a million bucks' worth of imported ganga. In came the cops, out went the box, onto the radio news it was broadcast—where I heard it. A-hunting Gator went, looking for the grass. Not the green kind, that was gone for good. No, the grass who gave the game up.

That's when the phone call came.

I had learnt from Popeye, Gator's minder, that 'Gator' was short for 'Alligator'. I'm sure I don't need to explain why that nickname was appropriate for the man.

'Sorry, mate,' I said. 'Things are really hot here. I'm heading to Tasmania for a while. And this phone's no good. Gotta go!' I hung up and got a lift to the airport as quickly as the cab I hailed on Edgecliff Road could take me. I told no one where I was going. I scarpered to Adelaide, where I had visited my sister only a few weeks before.

I gave him a call a couple of months later, by which time he realised I'd had nothing to do with the loss of the shipment. Our bromance was back on.

During my time at Hawthornden, through Corky I'd met a couple of top birds, Margaret and Jill, who lived on Brown Street,

Paddington—not too far away. One day I dropped in to see them with a couple of kilos of Thai sticks in a suitcase. The sticks were hidden between a heap of newspapers, but the suitcase had hash oil residue in the lining. It was brown, obvious, and pungent when sniffed up close. Why I'd kept such an incriminating piece of evidence Christ only knows.

I asked Margaret to hide the sticks for me and to leave the suitcase handy so I could pick them up later. She agreed to help, and I headed off to do some other dodgy business, borrowing Margaret's car. She said she was off-colour and planned to spend the day in bed.

When I returned later that afternoon, I bounded up the entry path and in through the wide-open front door, of course not bothering to check out the lie of the land. As I leapt into the middle of the living room, I realised I was in the presence of three rather large, besuited gentlemen which, rightly as it transpired, I took to be the law.

'So, who might you be, young sir?' Detective 1 asked.

'Ah, my name is Rod. Who the fuck are you?' (Only the guilty are polite.)

'Listen, cunt—watch your mouth,' said Detective 2. 'Answer the question.' (Now I knew who was bad cop I decided that cooperation was probably the way forward.)

'Sorry, mate, you wrong-footed me. I've just realised you must be police. I didn't mean to be rude. My name is Rod Halsted.' (Well, they were going to work that out when they checked my licence, weren't they?)

'And what are you doing here today, Rod?'

'I've just brought Margaret's car back to her.'

'Wait here.'

Detective 1 headed upstairs, presumably to check with Margaret as to her affiliation with me. Then I saw Detective 3 walking towards the room in which the suitcase was stashed.

I had no idea if Margaret had removed the sticks from the suitcase. If not, things were about to get as sticky as the resin that held the smoko together.

Detective 1 came back from talking with Margaret, who was tucked up in bed.

'Okay, Margaret says you took her car for a service, so you are clear on that. But before you go, turn your pockets out.'

I did as I was told. Along with a dirty handkerchief and a few coins and loose notes, I also had $1000 in folding money held together by a rubber band. My interrogator's eyes lit up.

'This is a shitload of cash to be carrying. Where did it come from?'

'Mate, I work some jobs for cash. This is everything I've earned over the past month in cash. I can't hand it up. I've got a sick mum I'm looking after.'

He looked me over with an eagle eye, waiting for me to blink. Blink? You have to be fucken joking. I was known in the trade as No-Blink Roddy.

'Yeah, alright, you can go,' he said.

I had been waiting for Detective 3 to start yelling, but heard nothing.

I calmly walked out the door, up the path, turned right, got to the corner and ran like a scalded cat.

I went back some four hours later to be informed that they had searched the place from top to bottom and found zilch. They'd searched the suitcase, which was sitting on the floor, wide open, full of old newspapers. When I removed them I found, nestled between the sporting pages and the *Weekender Magazine* my—wait for it—my fucking passport! What head space was I in that caused me to put my passport in a suitcase with two kilos of smoko as well as hash oil residue I really have no idea. I guess it shows that I had sampled the product before letting it loose on the market.

It was then that Margaret told me she had been lying on the dope, hidden under her mattress, the whole time the jacks were rampaging through the house. I wasn't the only one who held their nerve that day.

Another time I was at Brown Street shooting the breeze with Margaret, Jill and Al when the doorbell rang. Jill headed for the door, saw a bloke with a uniform and hat through the opaque glass and quietly hissed, 'Police!' Without a second thought I hurdled the back fence. It was about two metres high, and I assumed the same drop on the other side. Wrong. The fence was built on the edge of another two-metre drop to a bitumen road below. And I was barefoot.

I landed like a cat and started running. Fuck, I could feel someone rapidly catching up. I spun around, ready to go the knuckle, when I saw Al's mad smile closing in on me. I turned and kept running. When we eventually stopped, I asked him why he had jumped the fence, too, since it was only me who was holding smoko.

'Instinct!' was his succinct reply.

It turned out it was the postman at the door.

Al helped me out on another occasion. He gave me a lift on his motorbike to Drummoyne, where Gator had a truck delivering a load of dope. I was to direct the truck to a vacant warehouse, down a side street from the main road it was coming from. Gator was parked down the road with Popeye. Al was sitting on his bike in the side road.

I had a look around the area and noted what appeared to be an electricity linesman up a pole, walkie-talkie in hand. I also noticed three groups of men seemingly doing nothing but chatting.

A warning stirred in me, but before my brain could tell my body to abort, the truck came into view. Throwing caution to the wind I stepped onto the road and attempted to wave the truck into the side road. No luck. The fucker ignored me and kept on driving. I continued to yell to the driver when a sharp whistle from Gator had me turning my head in his direction. Our eyes met and, despite him being about 50 metres away, I could see he made a slashing motion across his throat—the universal sign for 'stop'. Which I did, turning immediately and striding towards Al on his motorbike. As I reached him and jumped on the pillion, the groups of men began running towards us.

Fuck me! Al floored it and we were goneski: in and out of backstreets, across the Iron Cove Bridge and home in double-quick time. That boy could handle a bike.

I did pay him back in a small way another time. We were returning to Hawthornden on his bike, nicely lubricated on neck oil, when the cops pulled us up. They knew we had been on the turps but were decent blokes, and we had them laughing in no time. One of them said, 'Now, we won't book you this time, but you are pissed, so push the bike home. Do not ride it. Okay?'

'No worries,' we both replied. They drove off, around the bend in Edgecliff Road. Unbeknown to us, they turned into the next street, which coincidentally happened to be Roslyndale Avenue: our home street.

'Fuck it,' said Al. 'Jump on'.

'No fucken way, mate. Let's not press our luck.'

We pushed the bike 100 metres up the road, around the corner and into Roslyndale where, surprise surprise, we found our two newest mates parked. As we pushed past them, the driver gave a smile and said, 'Smart move, boys.'

One day I borrowed an old rattler of a car that was parked at Hawthornden. I drove into the city with $30,000 in $10 and $20 notes that I wanted to change into $50 notes. I intended to go to several banks so I didn't produce a large sum to any of the tellers I dealt with.

I finished the task at Martin Place, exchanging the final $5000 at the CBA. I had lazily parked the car in a time-limited area and, by the time I got back to it, the street was a clearway. As I put the key in the lock, a uniformed cop politely asked me to leave the car and step onto the footpath.

First, he pointed out the car was unregistered and then he asked to look inside the satchel I was carrying. I showed him $30,000 in nice, crisp $50 notes. He asked me to come to Phillip Street police station. It was all very civilised.

While he and his partner were driving me the short distance to the cop shop, I heard over the radio the name of a twenty-to-one winner that had arrived at Randwick racecourse that day. I stored that bit of useful information away.

They sat me in a cell without processing me or the cash, and asked me to wait. Shortly two detectives came in and questioned me. How did a young bloke like me happen to be in possession of enough cash to buy a house in Paddington?

'I won it at Randwick today.'

'What's the name of the horse?' One of the detectives asked. I told him the horse's name I'd heard on the radio.

'Who did you have the bet with?'

'Les Tidmarsh.' He was a rails bookmaker who I knew would hold a bet of that size, but naming him was a crucial error on my behalf. It was easily checked.

They left me for all of five minutes and came back.

'Les didn't hold that bet. Let's cut to the chase: 60/40 split.'

'Fuck you; 50/50,' was my rejoinder.

'Done. We will sign you out. My mate will wait for you on the footpath. Don't want you tempted to do a runner.'

He released me, with the cash and without charge.

There was no point in hitting the toe: they knew who I was, if not where I lived. I met the detective on the footpath outside the station and we found a quiet nook in a building up the street.

I extracted one of the two bundles of money in the bag—the cops had counted out their $15,000 and separated it from my cash.

Handing it to the detective I said, 'There you go, your half.'

'You're a silly cunt,' he replied. 'When I said 60/40, I meant 60 per cent for you.'

I had the last laugh though. Some ten years later I saw in the paper that the same detective had been convicted of criminal offences and was sentenced to a stretch in Silverwater Gaol. There is a God.

CHAPTER 31

WHERE'S THE FUCKEN VEGEMITE?

Sometime during the mid-seventies I did another customs pick-up of a large crate filled with a mish-mash of items from Afghanistan. I backed my ute into the bay at the customs warehouse and handed up the paperwork Gator had given me. We worked the same scam as we had previously.

The customs guys weren't at all friendly like the last time. They removed every item from the box, which was about 2 metres long, 1 metre wide and another metre high. As they pulled out pieces of cloth they ran their fingers along the seams, obviously checking for hidden items. But there was nothing. They drilled holes into the wooden items and found nothing seeping out. They were thorough and methodical. Eventually every item was out of the box and on the warehouse floor. The box, constructed with three-ply pine glued to a wooden frame, stood empty.

Clearly disappointed, they told me I could replace the items in the box.

'Like fuck,' I replied. 'I'm only being paid to deliver the bloody thing, and I'm only getting 50 bucks for that. You blokes emptied it; you can refill the bastard!'

And, begrudgingly, they did. They even helped me slide the thing onto my utility. Good thing, too: it was heavy.

I drove back towards Gator's rented Randwick house, him following in his Merc. Unfortunately, I lost him in traffic, so I found a phone box and called him. He picked up on the first ring.

'Hello?'

'Yeah, it's me; is—'

'I'll fucken kill ya, thieving my gear!'

'For fuck's sake, I'm around the corner. I rang to make sure everything's clear.'

There was a brief silence.

'Yeah, mate, all good here.'

'Okay, I'll see you soon.'

I drove the box back to the rendezvous house, where Gator was waiting for me. He was outside, washing the car—or pretending to.

As I got out of the car he gave me a big grin.

'What the fuck?' I said. 'Accusing me of ripping you off? Fuck you. You owe me an apology.'

'I don't apologise to anyone.'

'You do to me.' I was glaring at him now.

After a long silence, our eyeballs locked, he dropped his eyes, gave an embarrassed smile and said, 'Sorry.'

It was quite possibly the only time he's apologised to anyone in his entire life.

We placed the box on the garage floor with the help of Popeye and John R, one of Gator's associates. Then Gator turned to us and offered a grand to whoever could guess where the dope was hiding. I was best placed, and even I had no idea, so the other two were even more baffled.

We unpacked the box, and Gator offered us the pick of the items. I chose a crystal ball about the size of a softball, which was etched with a map of the globe; a cream and brown vase carved from a single piece of alabaster; a small brass bell; and two small brass figurines. The best piece, though, was a Hindu goddess cast in bronze. Remarkably, 50 years on, I've still got every piece.

With the box now empty, Gator carefully prised the three ply from the framework, which was held together with glue and finger joints—not a nail to be found. Swiftly we put the pieces of framework into the boot of his Merc, and all four of us headed to Gator's parents' place in north Wollongong.

When we arrived around 4.30 p.m. Gator's parents were both dressed in their night gear: his mum in hair curlers, nightie and night coat, and his old man in striped pyjamas and a checked dressing gown with a golden tasselled cord holding it closed.

I was the only one who hadn't previously met them. After introductions we moved inside, taking the contents of the boot with us. Gator immediately put the timber in a big, empty freezer sitting on the back veranda. By 5 p.m. we were seated at the formica dining-room table. Well, the men were. Mum brought chops and three veggies to each of us and then ate alone in the kitchen. She wasn't disrespected; this was obviously the way they operated. I suppose the less you hear the less you can reveal if questioned.

It was apparent from the conversation that the old man was a real scallywag who had, in the past, played with the big boys from Griffith. I mostly sat back and listened, laughing along with the rest of them at the funny stories the old fella was relating. While he was talking he picked up a piece of bread and spread it using the butter on the table. He paused momentarily, gave a puzzled look at the items in front of him, then smacked his hand down on the table. The noise rang out like a pistol shot. I levitated out of my chair as the old bloke roared.

'Where's the fucken Vegemite?'

Mum came ambling in from the kitchen. As she placed the jar of spread in front of him, a gentle hand on his shoulder, she soothingly said: 'Here it is, dear. Don't get upset; you'll give yourself a heart attack.'

As she retired to the kitchen, not the least bit upset, the old man went on.

'Well, for fuck's sake, a man reaches for his Vegemite and it's not there. What the fuck's goin' on? Now, as I was saying about that load of grass we transported from Griffith . . .'

Jesus Christ almighty. I glanced at Popeye, who was seated next to me. He gave me a wink, muttering out the side of his mouth, 'You'll get used to it.'

I bloody hope so, I thought, *otherwise I'll need to carry a spare pair of jocks every time I come up here.*

Dinner over, Gator finally did his big reveal. He took one of the pieces of timber from the freezer and used a tomahawk to split it cleanly down the middle. It had been hollowed out, stuffed with hash-oil-filled condoms then glued back together, and sanded so the join couldn't be seen.

Ingenious.

The oil was now solid enough to handle, so we set up a production line with Gator splitting, me taking the condoms and handing them to Popeye, who would remove the rubber and weigh oil into glass canisters. John noted the net weight of each jar as the old man packed them into boxes, which found their way back into the boot of the Merc. We were out of there by 7.30 p.m.

Had to be: Mum and Dad went to bed at 8.

CHAPTER 32

MELODY AND THE GOUGER

Sometime prior to the dope being found by the real estate salesman I had done a deal in Melbourne and was heading back to Sydney when the airline cancelled my flight. I checked the available flights, and found that if I detoured via Adelaide I could be home in Sydney before the next available flight from Melbourne left. It was a no-brainer. I also wanted to see my little sister, Lindy, who had left the carnage of Cyclone Tracy in Darwin and was working for her friend, whose mum owned the Broadway Hotel in Glenelg, bayside Adelaide.

I walked through the pub doors around noon and immediately saw Lindy behind the bar, working alongside a cute little barmaid.

'How ya goin', sis?'

She broke into a big grin, came around the bar and gave me a hug.

'I'm flat-out with lunch so can't talk just now. How about I intro you to someone you can have a beer with?'

She steered me over to a big man with a fighter's face, massive hands and a big gut. He was sitting at the end of the bar drinking what I quickly came to know as a 'butcher': Adelaide-speak for a six-ounce beer.

'Gouge, I'd like you to meet my brother, Rod. Rod, this is Ray Harris. We all call him the Gouger, or Gouge.'

Lindy quickly got back behind the bar.

I later learnt the Gouger's nickname came from his time in the shearing sheds where he worked with Mick Young, a future Minister for Immigration and Ethnic Affairs, to whom the Gouger later introduced me. The nickname derived from his method of settling an unruly sheep by gouging his knuckle in its eye. It's not acceptable behaviour now, nor then, I imagine, but apparently it was highly effective.

'Gouge, pleased to meet you, mate,' I said.

'You too, Rod,' he said with a lopsided grin. 'Shake the hand that shook the world.' He offered me a hand the size of a dinner plate and as hard as Chinese arithmetic.

'Can I buy you a beer?' I asked. I didn't wait for his reply: his answer was as obvious as if I'd asked a man in the desert if he'd like a swig from my water bag. I turned to the sexy girl working with Lindy and said, 'Hi, my name's Rod, and I'd like to buy the Gouger a beer and you dinner!' A cheeky grin was smeared across my gob like butter on toast.

'Wow, for a handsome guy you're pretty clever with words,' she replied. 'My name's Melody. Yeah, I can get you the beer. Dinner might be another matter, though.'

It was the beginning of two beautiful friendships.

It happened to be a Wednesday: midweek racing day. It was no great surprise to either of us that the Gouger and I both liked the ponies. We found, to our delight, that punting and piss-drinking were like breathing to us both.

As Melody fed us butchers of Southwark beer, the Gouger and I proceeded to drag around a grand from local bookies Charlie and Lord John. That was a lot of dosh back then: roughly $8000 in today's terms. We split it 50/50 and, since my punting pal had been near broke when I walked in the door, you might say he was delighted to have made my acquaintance. It was my Sydney racing tips that found us the winners.

I flew home that night with a roll of cash and a burning desire for a roll in the hay with Melody. So, after Gator made me an offer I had to refuse, I arrived back in Adelaide and went straight to the Broadway to check in with Lindy, and to wash the taste of Sin City out of my mouth. Bowling through the door, who should I see but my newest best drinking mate, the Gouger. He welcomed me warmly.

'Well, well. And how's my punting pal going? Melody, do you think we might have a refreshment for my old mate Rod, please?'

'Mmm, I'll need to think about that, Gouge,' said the object of my lust. 'He looks like he's been up to no good to me. Have you been a naughty boy since I saw you last, Roddy?'

I'd gone past desire two seconds after I'd first laid eyes on her.

'I'm not entirely sure, Melody,' I replied, with more of a blinding flash than a twinkle in my eye. 'I think I might need to sit down with you privately to discuss that. I don't know what you would classify as naughty.' I had a bone in my trousers that Lassie would break her teeth on.

I settled into Adelaide, renting a unit in an upmarket area known as the Patawalonga Canal. It was near the pub, and I set about giving my liver a severe talking to on a daily basis, wooing Melody in the process. I courted her for three months before she would go out with me. I wondered why she was playing hard to get, when she finally told me that she was married, but had been recently widowed. Her husband had only been dead a year or so, and she thought if she developed feelings for another man and slept with him, she would betray his memory. She had slept with one persistent suitor, a mate of her husband's, about three months after his death—more out of loneliness than any fervent desire for Mr Charm Offensive. After the one and only time they had sex, he remarked, 'That was sensational. I always wondered what you'd be like.' He went from 'charm' to 'offensive' in one brief sentence.

Taking advantage of the emotionally fragile is utterly cruel. So, rather than try to persuade her, I simply accepted her decision. I believe this impressed her more than anything, and we became good friends. She told me about the lack of love in her life and how she felt she had made a major mistake falling for the patter of the guy she slept with.

Shortly after that, we had a day at the beach, and Melody asked if she could have a shower at my place.

Of course, I ended up in the shower with her, then in bed, doing the wild thing.

It was like that for the next eighteen months. I walked around with a permanent boner hard enough to crack walnuts. We fucked like rabbits, on average five times a day.

Eventually I was evicted from the unit I was living in for a long list of transgressions, the last of which was 'bedroom noises'. I felt rather good about that. I wish I'd kept the real estate agent's letter. After receiving it, I took the letter to the agent's office on the following Saturday morning when the place had a line of tenants snaking through it, waiting to pay their rent. I stopped in the middle of the large lobby, waving the letter above my head.

'I'd like to speak with someone about my letter of eviction!' I proclaimed loudly. 'I know about the oil stains on the concrete, but I need clarification on the bedroom noises. Can someone explain what these bedroom noises are? Is it me moving furniture about, or perhaps playing my clarinet? And who made the complaint? Could it be the retired bank manager and his wife, or—'

'Please lower your voice,' said a balding, middle-aged, going-to-fat man I took to be a middle-level employee. 'You are embarrassing yourself.'

'Embarrassing myself? I don't think so, cobber. I'm quite pleased to be evicted for bedroom noises. I simply want to clarify what the noises were, and how they became apparent to the complainant. I imagine that's the people down below. Was she standing on his shoulders with a glass to her ear, pressed to the ceiling?' I left this last statement hanging in the air. Going by the winks and nudges I saw, the image obviously appealed to many people waiting in the queue.

The buttoned-up property bouncer bustled me to a quiet corner. 'Please, sir, stop this now,' he pleaded.

'No problemo. Simply write me out a cheque for a full refund of my bond and the week's rent I've got paid up, and I'll move out today.'

He couldn't get the chequebook out quickly enough. My problem was solved, and there were no hoops to jump through getting a full bond refund back.

I always rented furnished flats and travelled light: just a suitcase of clothes, no mementos. I was doing 'gone in 60 seconds' long before they invented the expression.

As I exited the agent's office, I was given a rousing round of applause and not a few come-hither looks from the ladies in the queue. I got the impression they wanted a fuller demonstration of what had caused the bedroom noises. I bowed from the waist and took my leave.

Melody saved my bacon on one memorable occasion. I was driving her back to the pub from the beach one afternoon after we'd had a few drinks. Without warning, Melody reached across and began fondling my wedding tackle. Up it rose like a soldier on guard. A hand job wasn't enough for the greedy little scrotum-licker: she decided I required the full treatment, so down she went with those magic ruby lips and little pink tongue of hers.

Fair dinkum, how I stayed on the road is a mystery. My eyeballs were pointing in different directions and disappearing into the back of my skull every few seconds. I could barely breathe. My legs were as stiff as the punters who backed Stainvita the day it was leading by a furlong, in sight of the post, and put a hoof in a hole. I was so hard a cat could have sharpened its claws on my love pole and done no major damage. As I was about to hit the gravy stroke, in the dim recesses of my mind I heard a siren. When both of my peepers were pointing in the same direction, I saw blue flashing lights in the rear-view mirror.

'Fuck! Cops!' I exclaimed. I jerked her head away from my rod of steel so abruptly I'm surprised she didn't chip a tooth. Without thinking I drove straight through a stop sign. I swung the car into a spot right in front of the Broadway Hotel. The coppers parked on my passenger side.

'Quick, get out and go into the pub *now*!' Melody urged me.

Without a backward look and my dick now completely deflated, I followed her instructions, fully expecting a hand on the shoulder. But it didn't happen. Five minutes later, Melody came into the pub, pushing that flashing smile ahead of her.

'What did you do?' I was amazed that the jacks hadn't come in after me.

'I hopped out and leant on the driver's windowsill with my hands dangling inside the car just over his crotch. I introduced myself and told them they were cute, all the time letting my fingertips lightly brush the driver's cock through his police-issue trousers. The driver started dribbling from the corner of his mouth and his partner was so keen to get my phone number they forgot about you completely. So, I gave them a bullshit number, and said I was a hitchhiker and that I'd be at the Family Hotel tomorrow night if they wanted to have a drink with me.' She turned to the bar. 'Hi, Lindy. Can I have a vodka and tonic please?'

'Make it a double, sis,' I said. 'She's earned it.'

It's amazing how the little head overrules the big head when the possibility of a root arises.

Time with the Gouger was always interesting. We were doing our usual thing one Saturday, drinking and punting with the local bookies. They were illegal but every pub had one. I'd just won a couple of hundred on that outstanding champion of the seventies, Manikato, and headed to the brasco for a slash. I no sooner had a foot in the door when the sight I saw there caused me to quickly wheel about and head back to the bar.

'Gouge, I've just seen a very disturbing sight in the shithouse, mate. Parker Pen Ray is leaning against the urinal, sobbing his heart out.' (There were several blokes named Ray who drank in the bar, so each had a personalised moniker. This particular Ray worked for Parker Pens.)

'No surprise there,' my piss-guzzling partner said. 'He always does that when Manikato goes around. He had first opportunity to buy, offered $3000 and wouldn't stump up when the breeder wanted an extra $500. Now the fucken horse never loses. You'd cry, too.'

We only remember the bad decisions we make, never the good ones. It wasn't the only unwise decision Parker Pen Ray made, either. He'd still be rueing the day he invited Gouger and me to his daughter's wedding reception.

CHAPTER 33

THE CAKE DESECRATOR

Parker Pen Ray's daughter's wedding party was held in the backyard of the family home. It was late Saturday afternoon; we had to get our punting out of the way first, so we didn't arrive until the sun was gently setting. Coming through the side gate, the sloping lawn ahead of us, I spied the mother of the bride eyeballing these two inebriated strangers intruding on her daughter's big day. I'm fairly sure Parker Pen Ray was pissed when he extended the invitation to what he now realised wasn't just his Friday night drinking buddy, but also an extremely pissed 150 kilograms of unstable lard.

As Parker Pen Ray extended an uncertain hand to the Gouge, his somewhat unwelcome guest spied the bride and made directly for her. Unfortunately, she happened to be standing in front of the trestle table upon which her wedding cake sat. The Gouge, a slobbering beast with lips puckered, did a crab-like stumble down the slope towards bride and cake, gaining momentum with the speed of Manikato. He went to plant a wet one on the girl of the moment just as she adroitly side-stepped, leaving only thin air and regret between our behemoth and the cake.

He hit that table at full steam and turned the cake into a pizza base, smashing plates, the table and whatever else was on there.

'Fuck!' cried the mother of the bride. 'Shit!' muttered her dad. 'Get that arsehole out of here!' screamed the now-traumatised woman in white.

It took all of my and Parker Pen Ray's strength to get Gouger the cake desecrator to his feet and, as quickly as we could, hustle him out to the car and away from the bride's personal disaster area. Fortunately, it was such a unique show that he'd put on that none of the wedding party had time to gather their wits and attack us before we fled the scene of the crime.

Oddly enough, we never saw Parker Pen Ray in the pub again. Perhaps the wedding party killed him, as Gouger had surely killed their once-in-a-lifetime celebration. Or maybe the wife just grounded him. Some wives are like that, I'm told.

The Gouger, for all his rough edges, had a heart of gold and a mind like a steel trap. He was respected and well-liked by all who knew him. And they were many, from the lowly to the famous.

We were sitting at the bar in our usual spot one midweek late morning when in through the door bowled Mick Young and Bob Hawke, union men both, yet to be elected to federal parliament, along with a couple of others. Bob embraced the Gouger like a long-lost brother. The affection and mutual respect were obvious. Because I was introduced to these blokes by Ray 'the Gouger' Harris I was immediately accepted and treated as an equal.

Bob was head of the trade union movement at the time, and very much enjoyed a drink. This was of course, well before he was prime minister and swore off the grog while in office.

'Come on, you cunts, we're off to the Port,' came the command from our fearless leader. So off to Port Adelaide we went, the Gouge and me following the others in my car. Drink driving wasn't given even momentary consideration in those days. We spent the afternoon in one of the pubs frequented by the Adelaide wharfies, drinking, laughing and bullshitting with Bob, Mick and an ever-increasing band of merry wharf plunderers. I think all of them approached Bob at some stage during our session, and he knew every single one by name, when they each in turn insisted on delivering a fridge/TV/lounge suite/washing machine or some other recently or soon-to-be-acquired item. He refused each one with grace and a laugh. I've never seen anyone control a room like Bob Hawke. When you were in conversation with him you had his full attention. And he was 100 per cent genuine.

CHAPTER 34

THE VIEW FROM THE BENCH

It was early 1976 and my time in Adelaide was drawing to a close. I knew I needed to get home and make some money.

Corky called me and said he had a guy, Michael, who had the connections to buy cocaine and smuggle it into the country. Did I want in? We needed $3000 in seed money, and that would bring in a couple of pounds. He reckoned it would sell for around $1500 an ounce, so we were looking at a profit of $40,000 after expenses. Shit, yes, I wanted in. I flew to Sydney to meet Michael and hand my $1500 over. I waved him bye-bye at Mascot airport and expected him back three weeks later. I figured that gave me time to get back to Adelaide and do what I do best for a couple of weeks, before heading home to sell the coke. I'd never seen or used the stuff, let alone dealt it, but how hard could it be?

After two weeks of drinking piss and punting with Gouge, and doing some horizontal dancing with Melody, it'd be time to kiss Adelaide goodbye. It wasn't so easy to do, though. My old flatmate JB paid me a visit, and we did a day at the wineries. We didn't actually sample wine—we quaffed it, in great quantities. By the time we got back to the Broadway we were blind. That's no reason to stop drinking, though, so we switched to beer. Eventually JB stumbled out to wherever he was staying to get some sleep before catching a flight back to Sydney the next day.

Not me, though. I slipped a few moon shots—the deadliest drink known to this seasoned pisspot, comprising of an ounce each of Tia Maria and vodka in a port glass—down the hatch. Around midnight I decided to drive home to Aldgate, in the Adelaide Hills, where I had moved after my eviction. I exited the hotel car park like a rock out of a slingshot, over corrected and neatly slid my old Holden into a gap between two parked cars, facing the wrong way and less than a foot from the bumper bars of the cars I was parallel parked between.

According to the court report, when the police arrived I was lying on the footpath, my briefcase open beside me revealing $1000 in cash. I was apparently addressing the assembled residents of the neighbouring properties.

'Who's going to open the bidding on this lovely little cottage? Come on, make me an offer. It's a lovely, quiet neighbourhood. Shout it out, make an offer . . .' I thought I was Arthur Tapscott back at the Gunnedah saleyards.

'Can you stand up, mate?' came the enquiry from one of South Australia's finest, who had seemingly appeared out of nowhere.

'I don't think I can, old mate,' I mumbled. 'Would you give us a hand?'

And he did. As I leant against my car he asked, 'Do you own this motor vehicle?'

'Never seen the fucken thing before.'

'Are you the driver of this motor vehicle?' the wily copper insisted.

'Well, no other cunt could have parked it this well,' was my proud rejoinder. (All this was read out in my later court appearance.)

With that, the police quite gently placed me in the back of their car and we headed off to a local station. I awoke the next morning, having no idea what had happened or where I was, to the sound of a cell door being opened. In stepped my mate from the night before, a breakfast tray in his hand.

'I'll just pop this down here,' he said. 'When you've finished eating you can stroll up to the front desk. I'll leave the cell door open. I don't have to worry about you bolting, do I?' There was a twinkle in his eye.

'No, mate,' I replied. 'I'll be up.' Incredulously, I noted the contents of the tray. Hot toast, butter, jam, a steel knife, an icy-cold bottle of milk and, unbelievably, the morning paper. I've had worse breakfasts in some of the pubs I've stayed in. I ate the tucker, checked the paper to see if my name was in it and duly plodded up to the office.

When I entered the room there were about eight coppers there. They all stopped what they were doing, stood and applauded me . . . then sat down and got on with their tasks.

'What the fuck is going on?' I enquired of my breakfast waiter.

Ignoring my question, he replied, 'How do you feel?'

'A bit woozy, somewhat confused as to why I'm here, and my jaw hurts,' I replied.

'Yeah, sorry about that,' he said. 'When we were driving you to the station you started telling us jokes. My mate who was driving had to pull over three times he was laughing so hard. When we got you back here, I asked you to tell the gags to the boys in the station. You had them crying. Because you had so much money on you, $1000 in notes and over $400 in change on the passenger's side floor of the car, I asked you to sign the property book. By the time we had finished laughing you had moved from the property book to the charge sheets. You crossed out your charges as well as those of the five blokes before you. I yelled at you, and you turned nasty, so I had to clip you. That's where you got your sore jaw from. Sorry about that.'

'No, mate. Fair whack. What happens now?'

'Well, you are on a high-range drink drive. You read 0.295. Nearly blew our machine up. You'll need a bloody good lawyer; the magistrate you'll be up before is a terror on the drink drives.'

How right he was. I made some enquiries at the Broadway and found the mouthpiece with the best reputation for drink-drive cases. I don't remember his name, but I do remember he charged me $200: a decent sum in the mid-seventies. I met him on Glenelg courthouse steps on the duly appointed day at 8.30 a.m. Passing the lawyer the cash with one hand, I shook his other and asked what the drill was.

'Well, Rod, I've pulled a few strings and organised us to be first case on after lunch. Meanwhile, why don't we sit in on the circus?'

The first case we saw was a drink drive, and the careless road warrior's reading was .09. Bearing in mind the legal limit was .08 you can imagine how I felt when the magistrate let fly at the defendant: 'Your behaviour is an absolute disgrace,' the red-faced, spittle-spraying judge declared. 'You are a menace on the roads. An abomination. People like you must be stopped. Fined $500 and disqualified for three years. Next!'

'Christ Almighty, mate, what the fuck? This bloke will put me away!' I hissed to my legal representative, who seemed to be taking the show in his stride.

'Relax, Rod,' he said. 'You're paying me the big bucks for my local knowledge. Just stick with me and never lose faith.'

After a few more tirades and unctuous lectures to those poor unworthy souls who had the misfortune to come up before the hanging judge, he abruptly called a break in proceedings and declared court would resume in half an hour. Considering it had only been an hour, I thought this most peculiar.

'What gives?' I asked my man.

'Stick with me and I'll show you,' he instructed. 'But be unobtrusive.'

We slipped out the courthouse door and swiftly made our way across Jetty Road and the tram tracks. We found a hidden possie near the side door into the Pier Hotel, and quietly maintained our post. After a couple of minutes, I espied the dispenser of justice making his way through the traffic and trams, escorted by the court clerk.

'What's happening?'

'Rod, he's a bigger pisshead than you. He drinks a bottle of scotch on the drive into court, then ducks over here for a couple of triples. Then he's back to work for an hour, then back here at lunch time. He sits in the Ladies Lounge where he's unlikely to be spotted by the public. He has another three or four triples, then heads back to court for the afternoon session. That's when we're on. I'm guessing you'll be the last case for the day.'

And that's how it panned out. The merry magistrate seemed to ease off a bit after play lunch, then came back in the afternoon quite obviously pissed as a newt.

'Righto, let's get this show on the road,' the pickled purveyor of justice declared. 'Who's next?'

The young police prosecutor said: 'The defendant's name is Roger John Halsted, your honour. He is charged with high-range drink driving. His blood alcohol showed a reading of 0.295.'

She went on with a description of the 'auction' I was running, the fact that I couldn't stand on my own two feet without help, and the rest of the sorry saga, finishing with, '. . . and, when asked if he was the driver of the car, he replied to the sergeant, "Well, no other cunt could have parked it this well," and then slumped over the bonnet of his vehicle, your honour.'

By the time she had finished, I'd shrunk to a height low enough to get me a part in *Snow White and the Seven Dwarfs*. I was about as short as the magistrate's attention span. He was away with the pixies, gazing out the courtroom window at the sun-drenched ocean only a couple of hundred metres away.

'Sir,' the petite prosecutor said to the now apparently non-present head of proceedings. '*Sir*, that's all the evidence, sir.'

The magistrate startled. 'Righty-oh. Well. That's a sad and sorry tale, isn't it.'

'This is one of the worst cases of drink driving . . .' the magistrate continued, but he was gone again. His gaze was drawn inexorably towards the window, through which a yacht could now be seen in the distance. He just kept watching as the yacht sailed into view from the left-hand side of the window frame before slowly drifting past the right-hand side. It must have taken two minutes which to me, in the confines of a silent court of law, awaiting judgement from a demented despot, seemed like a year.

As the yacht finally exited from view he snapped to, quickly glancing at the wall clock above the window, then to his right wrist and then, incredibly, to his left wrist. He had a watch on each arm. I've never understood what that was about. He must have looked at each of the three timepieces three or four times, his head rolling around in a clockwise direction, quickly gathering speed. He got so dizzy I thought he was going to tumble off the bench.

'Where was I?'

'This is one of the worst—'

'Yes, yes,' he impatiently interrupted the prosecutor. 'It's a shocking case which deserves the full weight of the law. How about six weeks' disqualification and a hundred bucks?' he benevolently asked of me.

'Ah, yes, your honour, thank you, your worship, very decent of you, your holiness—'

'Shut the fuck up!' my mouthpiece hissed.

'That's all. Court's done for the day.' And off the pissed protector of the peace staggered with the help of his clerk.

Local knowledge won again.

CHAPTER 35

OKIE DOKE

It was time to check on the coke. Corky called me and told me that Michael, our would-be international cocaine smuggler, had gone missing with the buy money. He was a month overdue and had been in Bali when he was last heard from. One of us had to go over to sort him out and, since Corky was heading off to India, the task fell to me.

I boarded the first Bali-bound flight I could get on, then booked into the Legian Beach Hotel before going out to look for Michael. He wasn't hard to find. In the seventies, Kuta Beach was the only place to find nightlife in Bali, and there were only a few strips of bars. I knew he was a booze hound so I felt confident I would track him down. Sure enough, in the fourth smoke-filled joint I walked into there he was, propping up the bar, bleary eyed, with a cigarette hanging out of his gob.

I walked up to him, took the fag from his mouth and dropped it in his drink. 'Hello cunt, where's the product?'

'Fuck, Rod? How'd you find me?' They weren't exactly the words of an innocent man.

'I'm staying at the Legian Beach Hotel. Be there at nine sharp tomorrow morning.' I turned to go, but not before nodding towards the well-built punk drinking with him. 'And come alone.'

The next day, right on time, in strode Michael, his drinking companion beside him. He was showing much more confidence than he'd exhibited the night before.

'Michael, thanks for coming,' I said. 'I asked you to come alone, and here I see you've brought along the Cisco Kid.'

'You didn't ask, you told me!' my quarry replied.

'Have a seat, Michael. We have business to discuss. If it doesn't turn out the way I want I'm going to feed you to the sharks.' And, turning to Mr Universe, I said nice and quietly, 'And you, too, cunt, if you want to get involved. Turn around now and fuck off.'

And he did.

'Now, Michael. What the fuck. Are they tears I see in your eyes? Buck up, man. Pull yourself together.' The wind had well and truly left his sails and he found himself becalmed with someone he had badly misjudged.

'Here's the plan,' I said, my voice just above a whisper. 'You're going to meet your commitment and go through with what you started. You're going to South America and you're going to return to Sydney with the two pounds of cocaine you promised Corky and me. And do you know why you're going to honour our bargain?' By this time he had gone white, which isn't easy to do in Bali, and he was shivering like a dog shitting razor blades. 'Because, Michael, if you don't deliver I'm going to hunt you down like the thieving dog you are, and I'm going to hurt you. You do believe me, don't you, Michael?'

'I'll do it,' he said.

'Good. Now fuck off and have a swim. Get yourself in shape and don't drink again until you hand me that package. You've got one month. Off you go.'

And sure enough, one month later he gave me a call and said he had something for me: two pounds of pure-as-you-can-get coke. My chemist mate Steve tested it and said if the crystals were any purer they would be liquid.

It was a major score, and since Corky was out of the country I would have to deal it myself. I hawked it around Sydney but, believe it or not, I couldn't sell it for the dollars I wanted. It was an unknown product in Sydney at that time.

I tried Gator but he had no use for it, so I decided to go back to Adelaide and use Andy, who had shifted a lot of smoko. He assured me he had a mate who could move coke so, what the fuck—back to Adelaide I went.

And it began to sell—more slowly than I would have liked, but it was moving. I took a liking to it as well. I started shooting it up and, on one occasion, I did a speedball (heroin and coke together). I knew the mix would produce a sensational high, and it did, but I vowed it would be the only time I would shoot up smack, and it was. It was also the only time I shared a needle, and I'm convinced that's how I picked up hepatitis C.

While in Adelaide I was back to drinking with the Gouger. We ran an SP book together on Saturdays and Wednesdays: Gouge in the Broadway, and me in my rented house in Aldgate, just in case the jacks decided to raid the pub. The Gouger would ring the bets through and I'd write them down. It became a nice little earner: in no time flat we had a bankroll of $10,000-plus.

Meanwhile Andy had managed to get rid of half of the gear, and I reckon I'd managed to use eight ounces myself. It was unfair on Corky, but when you are in the grip of an addiction it takes something massive to break it. I loved the high it gave me, but it changed my personality completely. The cocaine took my arrogance and self-belief into orbit. It also clouded my judgement.

When Andy suggested he introduce me to a guy he believed could tap into the top end of the market, I stupidly agreed. He brought Mark—a solicitor, unbelievably—over one Saturday afternoon. Andy rang the doorbell and left immediately before I could answer. My belief was that if there were any more than two people in a meeting your word, even if gospel true, meant nothing if the other two conspired against you.

I'd just had a shower when the bell rang, so I answered the door with a towel wrapped around my 100-kilogram frame.

'You must be Mark. Come in.' I showed him into the kitchen, where I had the coke sitting on the bench ready for tasting. 'Let's get this done quickly.' I was businesslike: there's no room for niceties in the drug world. Get it done and get out was my motto.

'It's there on the bench. Make up a fit. Be careful, mate: it is as pure as you can get. You don't need much.'

Naturally, being a drug-addicted glutton, he used way too much.

The phone rang. It was the Gouger, calling through bets. I began noting them down as Mark the moron stuck the needle into his arm. After that, all hell broke loose.

'Yeah, got that, $25 each way on Blarney Stone—what the fuck? Hold on, Gouge.'

Mark had overdosed. He'd no sooner got the needle out of his arm than he keeled over onto the kitchen floor. His eyes rolled back into his skull, and he'd swallowed his tongue. He was choking to death. Fuck me. He was going to die on my kitchen floor. I was going to do twenty years in gaol. Fuck! I leapt from the chair, depositing the phone handpiece on the dining-room table. I sprang across to Mark and stuck my finger inside his mouth, pulling his tongue back. I know now that's not the ideal response, but I didn't have a clue back then. The moment I pulled his tongue back he relaxed and began breathing normally, so I removed my finger. The second I removed it, he went back to his tongue-swallowing trick. Shit. I drove my digit back into his gob, not realising in the course of my first-aid administration my towel had fallen off. The crazed coke fiend looked up through watery eyes and, from his point of view, saw me—an overweight, extremely agitated naked man—straddling him, my finger down his throat and my wedding tackle inches from his face.

What was he going to do?

Bite down as hard as he could on my finger, that's what, and deliver as many punches as possible to my head—all this while vibrating across the lino floor. As he dragged me past the dining-room table I reached out and grabbed the phone with my left hand.

'Gouge, you still there?' I gasped.

'What the fuck is going on?' was the reply.

'Mate, no time to explain.' Numbnuts punched my tooth through my upper lip. 'Just get an ambulance here ASAP. I've got a bloke overdosing on coke.' I threw the phone away and, with all the strength in my body, prised Mark's mouth open. My intention was to hit Jaws hard enough to knock him out. The moment I extracted my finger he slumped. I grabbed him by his shirt front and propped him against the wall.

'Fuck, what just happened?' Fang enquired, wiping his hand across his face. 'Ah, blood!' he screamed.

'Yeah, blood—but not yours, Boofhead. Mine. You've spent the last three minutes working on my head like a jackhammer operator coming down from a twelve-hour shift. Lucky for me, you're more bantam weight than heavyweight. Anyway, no time for fucking about, mate. The ambulance is on its way, and the boys in blue will be hard on their heels. Time for you to make like a Russian ballerina and pissenovsky.'

'Sorry, mate? Pissenovsky?'

He was from Adelaide, so obviously didn't have the cultural sophistication of his Sydney-raised host.

'Yeah, mate, time to *fuck off* is what I'm saying.' All this was relayed to him with my family jewels swaying in the breeze.

And with that, Lockjaw did as I bid and removed himself from the scene in his dark blue Jaguar. I immediately set about burying the plastic-wrapped betting slips and cocaine in separate holes in my secluded backyard, still with my nuts swinging in the cold winter air, all the time attuned for the sounds of sirens—which never came.

I threw some clothes on and drove immediately to Aldgate hospital. After explaining to a very new intern that I had encountered a crazed and drunken patron in a hotel in the city, he set about cutting away jagged skin from my finger and sprinkling antiseptic powder onto the wound. He gave strict instructions to change the dressing every six hours.

I drove to the Broadway and asked the Gouger what he had said when requesting an ambulance.

'I didn't call one,' was his brief reply.

'Why the fuck not, mate? I had a digit-chomper dying on me and you didn't call an ambulance?'

'Well, he's not dead, is he?'

'No, mate, but you didn't know that at the time.'

'So, no harm done, no coppers involved. No problem. And if he had died and the jacks got involved, you'd get done for supplying a shitload of powder as well as complicity in a death. I imagine you would have got out after a decade in the slammer. With good behaviour. Rod, they call you the Silver Fox. Think like one. If the cunt'd died, we'd have disposed of the body and that'd be the end of that. One less arsehole sucking oxygen.'

In that moment I realised a number of things: the Gouger was as staunch as they came, I could trust him (as if I'd ever had any doubts), and I knew he was quite capable of disposing of a body. Me, too, probably. It would have bothered me for a while, but I imagine I'd have gotten over it. Maybe. In time . . . ah, bullshit, who am I kidding? I've known several men who have killed other men and every one of them, without exception, is haunted by the deaths.

I now realise how lucky I am that the bloke didn't die. I'm not the callous criminal I imagined myself to be. Not deep down. I am, however, more than capable of giving an exceptionally good imitation of one when called upon, as past and future events attest.

My cannibal mate came to a sticky end a couple of months later when he overdosed on heroin. Not before I went looking for him, though. He owed me $100 . . . the price I decided I would charge him for the taste he had that led to him chowing down on my finger.

He actually came around a month or so later to apologise.

'Mate, forget the sorry. What I want to know is, have you used today?'

Blithely he replied, 'Yeah, some smack to come down.'

'Smack. Mmm. Here's some smack for you.' I belted him across the gob with an open hand, very solidly. 'Listen carefully, you dense cunt: you would have died if I hadn't stuck my finger in your idiot gob. You have a wife and kids, and you used smack today? You, my moronic friend, owe me $100 for the taste. Lose my phone number, never come to my house again and I'll meet you tomorrow outside the GPO to collect my money. Be there at 5 p.m., and don't be a minute early or late. Now fuck off and start thinking of your family instead of yourself.'

He missed our appointment, so I went looking for him. I knew his house address and knocked on the door. It was answered by a woman who should have been in her prime but looked absolutely beat.

'Are you the police?' she asked.

'Why would I be the police?' I replied.

'Because my daughter's husband has brought the police into our lives,' replied Mark's mother-in-law, who had appeared behind her daughter.

I softened. 'No, ladies, I'm not the police. Unfortunately, your husband owes me money and I'm here to collect.'

'We don't have any money for you, and we don't know where he is,' the older lady replied.

'I'm not here to take your money, ma'am. It's only $100. But this bloke needs a lesson, so I'll chase him down for it. Does he have anything here that's not yours?'

'A few things in the garage,' the older woman replied. 'Follow me and I'll show you.' Leaving her daughter behind, she led me down the drive. I entered the garage and took the first thing I set eyes on: a shitty light probably worth $5 in a garage sale. But it was the principle of the thing. I was owed tens of thousands of dollars by others that I had written off; the drug trade's like that. But I was determined to get my pound of flesh on this occasion.

'I'll call this $50. He still owes me $50. Any idea where I might find him?'

'The only details I can give you are for his solicitor.' She gave me a name and address, before adding: 'One last thing. May I ask you a favour?' Her eyes were pleading.

'What's that?' I was by now having trouble keeping up the tough-guy act.

'When you find him, will you give him a hiding? Before my daughter met him, she was the happiest girl in the world. Now she's a shell.'

I took a couple of beats before replying. 'I will take care of that for you. Tell your daughter to forget him. He's forgotten about her, and her kids. I'm sorry to have troubled you.'

I drove straight to the solicitor's office. I walked through the front door, past the receptionist and through the only internal door I could see. The receptionist made a half-hearted effort to call me back, but my manner convinced her not to chase me. I bowled in, the solicitor glancing up with the look of a startled gazelle spotting a cheetah bearing down on it.

'Before you open your mouth, listen. Your cunt of a client, Mark, owes me $100. I want it and I'm not leaving this office until I get it. Call the arsehole and get him here. Now.'

The solicitor turned baby-shit yellow. Grabbing for his wallet, he extracted $100.

'Here's the money. I don't know how to contact him. He calls me. Please—'

'No problem,' I quietly replied, 'thanks for the dosh. You can get it from him. Tell the cunt that when I see him, I'm going to bash him. Leave the police out of this or you'll be next. Guaranteed. Do you believe me?'

I always asked this when issuing a threat. I found by receiving an affirmative reply that the threat became a real possibility. I guess it locked the decision into the conscious mind of whichever poor bastard was looking into my cold, crazy eyes.

I never saw Jaws again but, as I mentioned earlier, I did hear he died a couple of months later. At least the wife and kids were free of him.

CHAPTER 36

STEADY ON, MATRON

Take my advice: the drug game is a dirty business. The silver lining of my interaction with Mark was that it cured me of my cocaine addiction. It only took a couple of minutes and a chewed finger. Cheap, really, when I think of how powder has decimated the lives of so many people I know.

After exiting Aldgate hospital I went straight down the hill to the Broadway, where I got on the piss with my business partner. After a solid eight hours' drinking and passing out for another eight, I'd completely forgotten to change the dressing on my finger as the doctor instructed. I was reminded of this by the putrid smell that travelled through my nasal passage when I finally got around to removing the bandage the next day. As the last of the bandage came off, the rancid smell was overpowering.

I knew I was in trouble. I jumped in the car and drove myself to Flinders Medical Centre which, at that time, was the best medical facility in Adelaide. In no time flat they determined septicaemia had set in and my blood was poisoned. They prepped me and had me on the operating table in double-quick time. Another couple of hours and, they told me afterwards, I would have lost my arm at the elbow. It would've been a double tragedy, had it happened, as it was my drinking arm.

After the op the surgeon came around, a look of wonder in his eye.

'Mr Halsted, do you drink very much?' he enquired.

'What do you call "very much", Doc?'

'Well, how much do you drink?'

'Oh, on average 40 to 50 beers, and the odd scotch.'

'My God. Every week?'

'No, Doc. Every day. Bar Sundays when I only drink until mid-afternoon. No point being a glutton.'

His eyebrows shot up like a champagne cork. If he hadn't had a decent head of hair, I dare say they may have travelled over the top of his head and come to rest on the stethoscope strung around his neck.

'Well, that explains what just happened. Were you awake at any time through the operation?' His face had the look of David Attenborough discovering a new species of butterfly.

'Awake enough to hear you rabbiting on about your new Mercedes. Trying to impress the girls, were you, Doc?'

'Well, if I was, I didn't impress them as much as you waking up as I scraped the flesh from your finger bone. As I cut away the putrid flesh from the perimeter of the wound and scraped the bone clean, you groaned. Let me tell you, Mr Halsted—'

'Doc, please. It's Rod. Why so formal?'

'Let me tell you, Rod, that hasn't happened to any of us before. I stopped and asked you quietly, "Can you hear me?" And you groaned back, "Fucken oath." I immediately ordered more anaesthetic and got back to work. Five minutes later, buggered if—'

'Doc, language please!'

'Rod, I think we understand each other well enough now to dispense with the formalities. As I was saying, five minutes later, fucked if you didn't wake up again. Let me tell you, in the history of this medical facility no one, and I mean absolutely no one, has required as much anaesthetic as we used on you. I seriously suggest you have a good hard look at yourself and your alcohol intake. I'll call by tomorrow to see how you're doing but, somehow, I think you will be fine. It would take an axe to bring you down.'

With that, he was replaced by a ginger-haired nurse who wheeled me into a four-bed ward. I spent the next month in the company of an old Seventh-day Adventist who didn't drink; and a young motorcycle accident victim who never complained, even though he had a skin graft from his right forearm to his left shin and couldn't move. I can't imagine how uncomfortable he must have been, but he was always in the best of spirits. The fourth member of our merry band was a Scottish migrant policeman from the Northern Territory. He was continually moaning and calling for more pethidine. I don't recall what was wrong with him, but compared to my little mate, not much. He was forever bagging 'hippie drug users and Abo petrol sniffers' and anybody else who was slightly different to his own redneck self. The irony was, through his treatment he had become a drug addict. Every time there was a change of shift, not five minutes would go by without the arsehole breaking into a monotonous moan, which he kept up until the new ward nurse did her rounds.

'What's all the noise about, Mr MacArsehole?' she'd ask.

'Oh, nurse, the pain. I need a little jab.'

'Not yet, Mr MacArsehole. You're not due for more drugs for another six hours,' she'd reply, peeping over her chart at me and the Motorcycle Kid, a sly grin on her lips.

'Oh, nurse, I can't last that long. The pain, it's terrible.'

Often a teaspoon would hurtle across the room, thrown with unerring accuracy by the kid, usually hitting Constable Groan on the head or thereabouts. Fuck, he was thick. The kid would throw at least one spoon at him every day and still the idiot would forget to cover up. I guess it probably didn't hurt all that much, what with all the drugs coursing through his system.

Life wasn't so bad in the ward. The Gouger made sure I always had a slab of beer on hand, kept cold in the nurses' fridge, and a bottle of Southern Comfort in the cupboard next to my bed. I shared my grog with my fellow internees and even, on one memorable occasion, got the God-botherer pissed. It only took a couple of cans, but I was happy I set him on the right path. The young bloke enjoyed a drink, but I didn't include our resident drug addict. I've always been fussy about who I'll share my company with, even more so if it involves my beer.

I even worked out how to get the coin-operated phone, which was only set up for local calls, to ring interstate so I could call Gator and get the tips for each Saturday race meeting. I got an SP book going and picked up a few bucks from the porters and other patients. The nurses would bring me the money and patients' bets, neatly written on hospital stationery.

I regularly fell in and out of love with the nurses, but it was the ginger-haired nurse who finally brought my stay in hospital to an abrupt halt. She slipped into the ward one night when all the boys were asleep and pulled the curtains around my bed closed. Without preamble she pulled the bedclothes back and slipped onto the bed beside me, lifting her skirt to show her lightly fuzzed pleasure patch, unadorned by panties. She had the old boy out of my pyjamas and into her hot, wet mouth without so much as a nuzzle of the neck or a rub of the nuts.

'Jeeesus, fuuuuck,' I whispered. 'Slow down or I'm going to shoot my bolt in double-quick time.' I like to talk romantically when the circumstances are right. I could feel myself not just rising to the occasion, but ready to erupt. 'Not yet,' I grunted through clenched teeth, taking her abundant mane of auburn locks in my good hand and dragging her mouth away from my now-pulsating lighthouse. It was hard enough to hammer nails.

'I want to really give it to you, baby,' I said urgently. 'Can't do that here. Where can we go?'

'Come with me,' she ordered. She slid off the bed, taking me by the hand.

As we slipped through the darkened corridors I had no idea where we were going. Without a pause Ginger guided me into a section of the hospital that was being renovated. Silently she opened a door and locked it behind us. As I looked around it appeared we were in the matron's newly renovated office. Taking pride of place was her brand-new, never-been-used desk. Yep, you guessed it. We went at it hammer and tongs on the cool, slippery oak surface destined for the hospital head honcho's elbows.

As we were both rapidly approaching a volcanic eruption we heard voices approaching.

'I definitely saw someone come down this way before, Matron,' said a male voice, presumably a security officer.

'They must be here somewhere . . .' The handle to our little love nest started rattling. 'Have you got a key to this door?'

'I didn't think it was locked,' the male voice replied as we held our breath and position number 47 from the Karma Sutra. 'Oh well, the builder must have locked it before he left this afternoon.'

As their voices retreated we couldn't leave it at that; with a few giggles and a couple of plunging thrusts, we tipped ourselves over the edge and off the matron's desk. Somehow or other I managed to get back to my bed, and my romantic partner in crime slipped away before either of us was corralled by security or Matron.

Matron did come around the next morning, though, and without preamble threw my belongings—Southern Comfort included—out of the cupboard. With the assistance of a couple of nurses she then wheeled the bed out of the ward and down the corridor.

'So, Matron, how's life?' I enquired with all the sincerity I could muster.

'Not as good as it's been for you, Mr Halsted,' she replied with a tight smile. 'But that's all about to change.'

'Why Matron? Where are we off to?'

'You, Mr Halsted, are off to a place where you can't corrupt the morals of my patients or nurses. You have been nothing but trouble since you got here. Beer in the nurses' fridge, indeed, and invading spaces that are totally off-limits. Disgraceful. Leading my staff astray. Well, this is the end of the line for you.' She had the nurses wheel my bed through a doorway above which was marked, 'infectious diseases ward'.

'Okay, Matron, I've got the message. I'm signing myself out of here.' I immediately reached for my trousers.

She didn't argue, although I did get a wink from each of the nurses. I ducked back to say goodbye to the Motorcycle Kid and the God-botherer. I brushed off Mr MacArsehole, though.

CHAPTER 37

HIGH FINANCE

While I was in hospital, the Gouger headed to China with a bunch of his Labor Party mates and $5000 of our hard-earned in his pocket. Our intention was for him to buy teak chests, leather jackets and anything else we might sell for a profit. He left our mate Charlie with the remainder of our cash, some $8000, with the instructions to keep running the SP book but not take any risks.

By the time I signed myself out of the Cuckoo's Nest, the Gouger was back home with the goodies. He brought back some beautiful stuff but, having landed it and stored it in a vacant shop, we both lost interest. Spending so much time at the pub was not, in any way, conducive to the life of a businessman. If we'd played our cards right, with the Gouger's Labor Party contacts, we could have built the first serious import/export business between Australia and China. But after some procrastination, we sold what we could—plus some diamonds Gouge had picked up somewhere—to recoup our money, and let the whole thing fold. We did have a couple of the diamonds, both high quality (mine a one carat), made into matching gold rings, which we wore on our little pinkies.

To top it all off, Charlie lost our $8000. According to him, he hid it when he was pissed one night and couldn't remember where.

This was actually plausible, going on our own experience. Then one day as he was lounging in his favourite chair, his wife was vacuuming around his feet.

'Oh, don't trouble yourself by lifting your feet,' she told him. 'I'll vacuum around them.' Then she said, 'I think I'll wash the curtains.'

According to Charlie, the hiding spot came back to him in a flash. He leapt to his feet.

'Let me get them down for you.'

'Oh no, stay put, I wouldn't want to trouble you.' She stood on a chair, lifted the curtain rod from its pelmet and tilted it so the curtain rings would slide down, straight off the rod.

The curtains slid down, alright, along with a number of rolled-up bundles of $50 notes—eight grand's worth, to be exact—that Charlie had secreted in the hollow curtain rod.

The wife gleefully scooped them up and claimed them as 'lost treasure'. The next time I saw her, she was wearing a mink coat. She must have been the envy of all her girlfriends.

What are you gonna do?

CHAPTER 38

TRUE LOVE

I thought I'd stay for a bit in Albury on my way back to Sin City. Little did I know that while I was there I would meet the woman of my dreams.

It was 1979 in a little drinking establishment known as Maudie's Wine Bar that I teamed up with my future bride. Completely ignoring the doctor's sage advice, I'd been on the turps all day at the Star Hotel, punting big on the neddies and guffawing with my old drinking pals—so by the time I hit Maudie's I was as full as a butcher's pup.

I'd met Jane here a couple of weeks prior. She'd been standing at the bar with her girlfriend Kay—another rare beauty. I bowled up to them and my friend Gerry introduced us. 'Jane and Kay, this is Rod Halsted, an old mate of mine. Be careful of him, he's dangerous.' These were the key words that got Jane in, so she told me down the track.

'Which one's mine?' I had developed this smooth line in patter, spending all those hours at the bar with my old mate the Gouger.

'Mate, that's not very nice,' Gerry replied with the stutter that overtook him in times of stress.

'Fuck nice, let's get pissed!' I responded.

Gerry wisely removed the girls from my company and I, no doubt, found someone else to drain a bucket of cider with.

Then, on the fateful day a couple of weeks later, I was at the bar, drunk and howling like a demented wolf. Vivian, the owner, had no idea how to control me, so she sent my regular drinking mate Steve over to quieten me down.

'Mate, settle down, you're making a cunt of yourself,' he advised sagely.

I wrapped my right mitt around the pole at the end of the bar and rotated around, feet firmly planted but my body completely airborne. 'Mate, if I'm gonna make a cunt of myself I might as well make a *real* cunt of myself,' I roared. At this point my glowing face landed about two inches away from the horrified eyes of two old biddies, who apparently had decided to take a walk on the wild side and hobnob with the raucous crowd that Maudie's had a reputation for attracting. The whole joint came to a standstill for a long moment, then burst into spontaneous applause.

With an insane grin, I apologised to the two ladies, ordered up a bottle of champers for them and turned to the crowd and gave them a deep bow. As I stood upright I saw a vision of a woman, long golden-brown locks tumbling around the most beautiful face I'd ever seen. It was Jane.

'What's all the noise about?' she enquired.

I was tongue-tied. For the first time in my life, I simply couldn't find words.

'Ah, er, um . . .'

'Why don't we have a drink and talk about it?' my future bride suggested.

After that, we did everything together. We laughed all the time; we were in sync with our thoughts and words. We had the same values and similar Catholic-raised backgrounds.

It was the beginning of a beautiful love affair.

One day Jane invited me up to her parents' place, where she was living. It was midweek, in the middle of the day. I bowled up to the house with one of my desperado mates, Dave O. I parked my midnight blue Mercedes Coupé in the open garage up the top of a long, steep driveway. Leaving my mate in the car I was met by Jane, who walked me into the kitchen and introduced me to her mother.

'Mum, this is Rod Halsted,' she said. 'Rod, this is my mum, Dorothy. You can call her Dot.'

'I'm very pleased to meet you, Rod,' Dot said. 'Jane has told us a lot about you.' The greeting was warm and genuine; I liked her immediately. We settled down to a cup of tea at the kitchen bench and were getting along like a house on fire when into the party strode Jane's father, a scowl on his face.

'Dad, I'd like you to meet—'

'You parked your shitheap in my garage.' These were the first words addressed to me by my future father-in-law, or FiL, as I will call him.

'Rod Halsted,' I said, extending my hand—which he ignored. 'Pleased to meet you.'

'Didn't you hear me? You've parked in my spot.'

'Dad, please.'

'Really, love. How important is it?' said an embarrassed Dorothy.

And that was the start of it. FiL was the boss. He knew best and, as long as he got his way, the ship stayed on an even keel. Over time it became apparent to him that Jane and I were in love and there was nothing he could do about it, so he put up a pretence of acceptance; but all the while, as it turned out, he worked on dragging us apart.

I was to learn years later from a cop I regularly drank with that FiL visited the Albury police station and requested to see Inspector M, head of detectives. According to my mate, M summoned two detectives to his office, where he introduced them to FiL. Without waiting for handshakes to take place, he said, 'Would you like to tell my detectives what you just suggested?'

'Certainly,' FiL replied. 'A bloke by the name of Rod Halsted has been seeing my daughter and it looks like it's serious. I'm told he's a drug dealer and I want him out of our lives.' He paused.

'Go ahead. Tell the boys what you put to me.'

'I just suggested if you could find some drugs on Halsted, enough so he goes to gaol, then I'd be more than happy to contribute $5000 cash, which you blokes could direct on to any charity you like. I don't need to know where it goes, if you get my meaning.'

'So what do you think, boys? Do we have enough to charge him?'

'Absolutely,' replied one of the detectives. 'Open and shut.'

'Wow, I didn't think it would be this fast,' FiL replied. 'Fantastic.'

'I don't mean charge Halsted, you fuckwit,' M said. 'I mean charge *you* with attempted police bribery. It's an extremely serious criminal offence, punishable by gaol.'

'We've got more than enough to charge him, Boss. You want me to process him now?'

'Wait! I can't possibly go to gaol!'

'Why not?' M responded. 'You were prepared to send someone else there. You're a fuckwit. Stay out of your daughter's life and mind your own business. Now get out of my office. I don't want to hear from you again. And if you decide to go to any other copper in New South Wales, I'll hear about it, and we will charge you with attempted bribery. Now fuck off!'

CHAPTER 39

BHUTTO AND THE TURTLES

While I courted Jane I continued to deal with Gator, driving to Sydney and making smoko runs to Melbourne. One day he asked me to take some money to London. I was to deliver it to a man named Bill, who I would then accompany to Pakistan.

Gator had been doing business with the family of Pakistan's President Bhutto for a few years; but since Bhutto had been deposed in a violent coup by General Zia, Gator was no longer safe in Pakistan. The last time he was there was when the coup was taking place and he only escaped from the presidential palace by the skin of his teeth, having to shoot his way out with his bodyguards. So, it was up to Bill and me to get the money to Bhutto's representatives so the profit wagon could continue to roll on.

Thus, I found myself on a London-bound flight, $20,000 taped to my legs and wrapped around my mid-section. It wasn't an ideal way to spend 24 hours on an aeroplane.

I was only in London for a day and a night, but it was memorable. At our first stop Bill introduced me to a mate of his who turned out to be Buster Edwards, one of the Great Train Robbers, who was now selling flowers. We had a cup of tea together and then Bill asked me to take a walk; they had business to discuss.

That night we went to a pub that Bill's brother-in-law owned. It was in what appeared to be a run-down area in the East End. But it was only rough on the outside—inside it was spacious, classy and had six beautiful women working behind the bar. They were not only gorgeous, but boy could they work. The place was jam-packed with some of the best-dressed people—mainly gangsters and their wives and girlfriends—I'd ever seen.

I got a couple of hard looks when we walked in, but once it became apparent that I was with Bill and his wife, the attitude changed immediately. Bill was obviously highly respected.

The place was rocking with gales of raucous laughter and some serious drinking. The only people who didn't seem to fit in were half a dozen hard men in suits who were drinking in a small side bar. The publican went over and had a couple of words to them. In unison, they drained their glasses and left through a side door. When he returned I asked him what the story was.

'Well, Rod, that was the Old Bill. I told them we were intending to have a party and they may not feel comfortable. I suggested they come back tomorrow night and I'd buy them a drink.' As he was telling me this, a couple of the boys went around the doors and bolted them.

That's when the party really kicked off: top-shelf booze, joints of primo hash the size of Cuban cigars, and jokes—lots of jokes, not a few from me. I've found if you can tell a gag well, you can travel in any company.

We finished up in the wee hours, and Bill and I were on a plane to Pakistan early the next morning. This time Bill was carrying the folding. We landed in Karachi and checked into what had once been a palatial British Raj hotel: all marble floors and walls, and ornately carved wooden banisters. Now it was a faded rose, but it still had the fittings. Bill and I had a two-bedroom suite with a marble bath big enough to accommodate a football team. And the joint was dry: no booze. The only place you could get a drink was the Hilton, about 500 metres up the road, where all the airline crew members stayed. So that's where we spent the first four days of our trip, while waiting for the other side to make contact. There was a curfew in place from 8 p.m. to 8 a.m. due to the coup; we had to get home from the Hilton before the witching hour, or into the watch house we would go.

We were staggering home one night—it was pitch dark and there were no street lights—when we heard a whirring noise behind us. We were on a narrow footpath, just wide enough for us to walk side by side, with parked cars on one side and a three-metre-high stone wall on the other.

The noise came rapidly, growing ever louder until it was almost upon us and we still couldn't see what it was. Then the whirring was joined by a loud scream.

Fuck me! I came close to shitting myself. I flung myself onto the bonnet of the nearest car while Bill started climbing the wall. Even with absolutely nothing to grip onto he almost made it to the top, arms and legs going like pistons, a guttural, sustained grunt of terror emitting all the way from his slammed-shut clacker to his wide-open mouth.

The noise whooshed past and quickly dissipated, leaving two pissed Westerners lying on the footpath wiping beads of terror-induced sweat from our brows.

'What the fuck was that?' my feared gangster mate enquired.

'I'll tell ya what that was, Billy, my fearless leader. That was a bloke with no legs going past us on a mechanic's trolley at a speed that would overtake most six-cylinder cars. I saw the fucker as I came rolling off the bonnet of that badly dented car behind me. That cunt knew exactly what he was doing. He had the look of a demented getaway driver in his one good eye. No legs, an eye patch and arms like Popeye—I'm told his name is Lucky.'

That was it. We broke into howls of laughter, trying desperately to keep a lid on it until we found the safety of our hotel.

'I think I shit myself,' my man Bill declared.

'Only think? I can one-up that. I *did* shit myself!' And away we went again.

By now we were on the floor trying to hold our guts together. Just another day at the orifice.

The following night we were picked up by two of Bhutto's finest in a medium-sized sedan. As we climbed into the back seat, I noted the headlights were taped up so only a sliver of light emitted. It was just like London in war time. Odd, I thought, then worried as we headed out of the city that there wouldn't be enough time to return us within curfew hours.

As we drove on, at least two hours of road behind us, I whispered to Bill. 'What the fuck is going on? Evidently neither of these blokes speaks English. Do you know where we are going?'

'Mate, I haven't a clue,' was his less-than-reassuring reply.

'Bill, for all we know these fuckers are going to shoot us. When the car stops, get out fast and find some cover. If they go us, we each deal with our man. Okay?'

'Okay,' came the firm reply.

The car did stop. We immediately threw our doors open and leapt from the vehicle, rolling off into the only cover available: 30-centimetre-high dry grass. Both our escorts stepped from the car and removed from their jackets . . . torches. It took them about two seconds to locate two very embarrassed Westerner gangsters. Communicating in sign language, they indicated we should follow them.

The first thing I noticed was the sound of rolling surf.

After a few minutes we spotted moving lights below us. We wound our way down a sandy track to the high-water mark of a beach lined by tall palms. As the waves came rolling in, massive green sea turtles, weighing up to 150 kilos each, would regularly ride the foam in. Once on the sand they used their huge flippers to haul themselves up the beach.

We concentrated on one particular beauty. We were riveted from the moment she emerged from the surf, through her laborious trek up the beach, past the high-water mark, through her labours digging a hole I would guess to be over a metre deep. Through all this she paused, for up to five minutes at a time, to regather her strength. Eventually she was deep enough and began laying her eggs; perhaps 100 in total. One of our tour guides reached in and took one. He bounced it off the old girl's shell and caught it like a tennis ball. When she was finished laying her eggs, she began the task of covering her future offspring with the sand she had dug from the hole. I estimate the entire process took somewhere around five hours. By the time she had finished, the area where she had left her eggs was indistinguishable from any other part of the beach. Her task complete, she then hauled herself back down the sand and, without a backward glance, disappeared into the waters of the Indian Ocean off Sandspit Beach, just out of Karachi.

It remains one of the standout moments of my life. To this day, we have no idea why two tough guys took us sightseeing.

I left a couple of days later; Bill stayed on to hand over the money. The day after I left, Zia's troops had a running gun battle with Bhutto's boys. Billy told me they actually took the fight into our hotel, with some of the Bhutto gang firing from the internal balcony into the lobby. Billy shoved the wardrobe across the door then lay in the bathtub with a mattress pulled over himself for cover. And they reckon making a quid out of the drug trade is a giggle? Bullshit!

CHAPTER 40

OUT OF THE GAME

The trip to Pakistan was the last business I did with Gator. I caught up with him in the Golden Sheaf Hotel where we had first made our acquaintance. We found a quiet spot.

'Mate, I'm done,' I told him. 'I'm moving to Albury and going straight. Do we have a problem?' The drug trade is not usually a career you can retire from.

Gator looked me in the eye for a very long time, then a grin slowly spread across his face.

'No, Rod, no problem at all,' he said. 'You are one of the very few I trust. Have a good life, mate. And best not to stay in touch. It's a shame, though. I've just had a meeting in Queensland with a very high-powered bloke who is not only going to finance container-loads of gear, but who also has contacts at the highest level in both customs and the cops. Are you sure you don't want to stay in?'

I asked him who it was, and after a bit of back and forth he told me. I won't name him; I want to keep on breathing. Let's just say he was, at one time, publicly implicated in the drug trade and stared the authorities down.

'No, mate, that bit of info just confirms my decision. And I want you to know I've forgotten it already.'

We shook hands and went our separate ways after 30 beers. I haven't seen the bloke to this day, but would love to bump into him again. I really enjoyed the man's company and, oddly or not, I trust him.

As planned, I moved back to Albury and was living and working at the Star Hotel in no time. I'd finally figured it was time to settle down and try my hand at an honest trade: bar work first to learn the trade, then buy a pub. That was the plan. I picked the right pub: it was the centre of the town's social life and the Mansell brothers, Bill and Peter, were easy people to work for from the start. I resided upstairs in Room Four, and was quickly made manager of the garden bar, where all the action took place.

Living and working in a pub is paradise for a budding alcoholic. After every shift we would have staff drinks. On one occasion we got so pissed I left the entire day's take for the whole pub on top of the lounge bar, forgetting to put it in the upstairs safe. If that wasn't careless enough, not only did I neglect to lock the door into the lounge from the beer garden, I left it wide open. The bag was still there the next morning when Bill did the rounds.

Jane and I did the courting thing and set the date for our wedding: November 1980. It was a church job followed by a reception attended by friends, family members and ancient relics. The reception got off to a bad start. Jane and I arrived to a packed room. As we entered, we were besieged by people wanting to kiss and shake hands, hug and so on. We were both incredibly happy until my new father-in-law pounced.

'Jane, over here. We've got the whole family together for a family photo.' Jane's paternal grandparents were there, along with her mother, her three brothers, and her paternal aunts, uncles and cousins. 'Up here with us,' he ordered.

Jane stepped onto the dais, holding me by the hand. As I made to step up I was greeted by the back of FiL's hand. He shooed me away with the words, 'Not you. This is just family.' It was a clear demonstration of several things, which should have sent me bolting for the door, taking Jane with me: first, he had no class; second, I knew exactly where I stood with him; third, he was a control freak of the highest order; and fourth, the worst of the lot, he intimidated his daughter.

Two of my sisters were standing with me and saw the whole thing. As soon as FiL was satisfied with the photo, Lindy called Jane over for a 'Halsted family photo'. 'After all, Jane,' she said, 'you're a Halsted now.'

After that we had a good time, regardless of FiL literally pulling the plug on the band because he considered the music too loud. No big deal. I turned the power back on.

CHAPTER 41

THE HONEYMOON

Jane had booked a holiday for us at Club Med Tahiti. We hopped onto the plane in Sydney, looking forward to relaxing on the sand—but not so much the ten-hour flight.

Shortly after take-off my seat back was wrenched backwards and a bearded head appeared. A guttural Germanic voice boomed: 'I zinc ve hav honeymooners here, have ve not?'

'What the fuck?' was my response.

Jane is far more socially adept than me. 'Why, hello, yes, you guessed correctly. My name is Jane, what's yours?'

'Hullooo Jane, I am Helmut and zis is my vife, Brunhilda.'

'Hullooo!' cried Brunhilda as she peered over our head rests.

'Und hoo iz zis handsome gentleman?' asked Helmut, indicating yours truly.

'Oh,' said my new bride, 'this is my husband, Rod. Say hello, Rod.'

'Hello Rod,' I duly obliged.

'Don't take any notice of him, Helmut. He's usually really funny but he's got a big hangover from the party last night.'

That's all it took for Helmut to decide he and his Nordic spouse would team up with us at Club Med. Yes, the fuckers were going to the same destination as us. But I had other plans.

We landed at Papeete airport and were directed to a bus, which then took us to a boat. I thought, when we landed, we would catch a cab to the resort and be free of these two pests. But no, there was more pain in store. Jane and I boarded the boat with the pair. The babbler just wouldn't shut the fuck up, giving a running commentary from travel brochures he had read in preparation for their 'trip uf a lifetime'. Stuck on a plane with him for ten hours, then a boat for another hour, I felt like I'd been given life. (Of course, a year or two later I was locked in an actual prison cell and got a little perspective on the situation.)

The boat docked at a wharf backdropped by swaying palm trees and tranquil waters. *Beautiful. We are finally here*, I thought. Not bloody likely.

'Okay, everyone onto the bus, please,' our Club Med representative instructed us.

A further two hours over bumpy roads and our bus eventually pulled into what I freely admit looked like paradise. As we exited the bus, beautiful Tahitian women approached us and put frangipani leis around our necks. One of them pressed a cold glass containing a colourful blend of booze and mixer, a straw, a swizzle stick and a lump of pineapple into my hand. I nearly took an eye out getting the stuff into me. I'd have preferred a beer, but booze of any kind out of an old sandshoe would have done me at that time.

'Okay, everybody, pick up your bags and follow me,' said our guide.

'Fuck me, seriously? You don't have porters to carry the bags?' I brusquely enquired.

Helmut to the rescue. 'It vould be my pleasure to help viz your bags, Rot,' he cheerily announced.

So, I let him, much to Jane's disgust.

The pudgy little fucker carried his bag and mine, too. As it should be. Well, we won the war, didn't we?

That was the start of the honeymoon, and it didn't get much better.

We discussed divorce at one stage, which brought me to my senses. Sort of.

CHAPTER 42

DON'T GIVE ME ADVICE

We put divorce on the backburner, bought a house and settled into married life. At least Jane tried to. I didn't realise I wasn't still single. Not that I chased girls; far from it. I'd always been a one-woman man and, as far as I was concerned, I'd found the love of my life. I believe Jane thought the same. Trouble was, it was a massive shift for me to go from drug dealing, with the huge financial benefits and very short work hours that honourable profession delivered, to working behind a bar. And we both enjoyed a party.

I'd moved on from the Star and now had a job at Brady's Railway Hotel, with another set of brothers. Lionel, with his brother Geoff's help, ran a good operation, catering to the working class of the town. On occasions when a fight erupted, the brothers, although well into their fifties, would take care of the bouncing themselves. They weren't short of backup from some pretty tough men, but the policy was they did the chucking out. It didn't hurt that, both being former quality rugby league players, they enjoyed a scrap.

On one Saturday, when Lionel was locked away in his office, a dozen blokes turned it on in the back lounge. Huey, the head barman, bellowed for help, so the front bar brigade sprang into action. Led by Geoff's sons Les and Ray, plus Dybie, Butch and whoever was ready, willing and able (including yours truly), we made short work of all bar one of the amateur pugilists. The last one, a long, rangy beanpole, jacked up in the doorway exit. He grabbed hold of the door jamb with his hands and knees and couldn't be budged no matter how hard we pushed.

Then along came Lionel. He'd heard the commotion and came rattling down the corridor, took the situation in at a glance and pushed his grimy glasses back to the bridge of his nose, as was his regular habit. 'Out of the way, you useless pack of drongos,' he said. 'I'll show you how to get rid of the cunt.' And with a solid knee into the base of the unfortunate's lower spine, he popped the fool out the door like a cork out of a champagne bottle. The dunce hit the ground, gripping his arse bone and writhing in agony. Never one to give a sucker an even break, Lionel followed him out, lifted his right foot and aimed a massive kick at the beanpole's rib cage. Before he could launch the killer blow, a couple of uniformed cops came bursting around the corner. Lionel espied them, gave a couple of small movements with his leg as if to follow through, then thought better of it. As he placed his foot back on terra firma he was heard to regretfully mutter, 'Ah, fuck it.'

He was a good bloke to work for. Unfortunately, he sacked me. He had no choice, really. He's still, to this day, the only boss I've worked for who gave me my marching orders. (Rex Mitchell, from my *Border Morning Mail* days, would argue otherwise, but remember, I got my resignation in before he could say, 'You're fired.')

What happened was a confluence of events that led to my downfall and, after surviving the fires of hell, my ultimate redemption.

Those events unfolded thus.

I was working the bar on my own one quiet evening when a bloke named Col Bottrell, who had worked with my old man, came in.

'G'day, Col. What can I get you?' I said. It seemed like a friendly enough greeting, and I'd always got on well with him.

'Just a seven, Rod,' was his abrupt reply.

Odd, I thought. Bit grumpy. Must be having trouble at home. I served him the beer and went back to the other end of the bar to serve the next thirsty customer. Each time I glanced Col's way he was staring at me, his beer untouched. It got too much for me. I walked up to him and asked what the trouble was.

'You are the trouble. What did your old man ever do to you for you to put him through the sort of shit you're hitting him with? You've got all the brains in the world, come from the best blood, yet the way you live your life is a disgrace. Get off the piss, stop doing whatever the fuck it is you do to earn a quid illegally and get a proper job.' And with that, he turned on his heel and walked out. Left his beer on the bar, undrunk.

Fuck you, I thought. *Who the fuck are you to tell me how to live my life?* I immediately dismissed his unsolicited advice.

CHAPTER 43
DOG TURDS

The next event, following hard on the heels of my uninvited character assessment, was a phone call from an old mate, Brian, whom I'd last seen at Hawthornden. He was from up Kuranda way, north of Cairns, and he had a proposition for me. He had grown some of the best dope ever produced, so he claimed. And, once I'd tried the sample he sent me in the post (no sniffer dogs or X-rays in those days), I agreed. It was mind-blowing. He picked the flowers from the heads of the female plants and hand-rolled them into fat, cigar-shaped, half-ounce deals. They were individually packed in plastic bags and were the thickness of a fat man's thumb, tapered to a point at each end. Every type of dope has to have a marketing name, so I christened these Dog Turds. All you needed to do was shave a little off with a razor blade and mix it into tobacco. One joint was enough to send half a dozen people off to Disneyland for a few hours. Incredible.

I gave a brief moment's consideration to the fact I'd retired from the dope trade and immediately dismissed it. I was bored and wanted the money. I contacted Rex in Melbourne and offered the Turds to him for $200 per deal. That translated to $3000 per kilo when the going rate for Aussie grass was less than half that. He laughed and asked if I was serious.

'Have I ever not been serious when it comes to business? Furthermore, when did you ever not make big money when dealing with me?'

'Very good point. How much have you got? Doesn't matter, there's a drought down here so I'll take the lot.'

Brian brought the first shipment to Sydney, where I picked it up. I'd flown up to Sydney with my golf clubs and brought the initial five pounds back packed into the base of my golf club bag. I got clever and flew into Wagga airport and had a friend pick me up. Jane was with him and, although she didn't know anything specifically, she knew I was doing business. That was what attracted her to me in the first place. I was a dangerous man, and she liked that.

I did everything wrong setting the deal up. There were too many phone calls. I'd brought a mate in as a partner when I didn't know his form and, frankly, I didn't need help from anyone. My generous nature was overruling my street smarts.

I took it to Melbourne and did the deal with Rex in a motel on the northern outskirts. That was another no-no. Never meet indoors. It's best to meet in a park where there are multiple avenues for escape, but it all went swimmingly. I collected the cash. All up, it was close to $30,000: a $7500 earn for very little effort.

Naturally, the call came the next day from my little Melbourne pal.

'Mate. I need more. Now. Fucking mind-blowing. How soon can I get as much as you can put together?'

'Leave it with me.'

Brian wasn't at all surprised to hear from me so quickly. He suggested, rather than bring it to Sydney, he'd pack it in plumber's PVC tube with a cap at either end, sealed with glue. The only way to get at it would be to saw it open. He intended to send it by air courier to a bogus company. Stupidly, I agreed. The reason I hadn't been busted in the past seven or eight years of dealing was because I had done all the legwork myself: always picking up the goods and delivering by car. That way no one knew my movements, and I had the choice of changing direction and delivery times on a whim.

Why the hell I agreed to bring an airline into the scheme I'll never work out. Probably because I was working at the pub and didn't have time to drive. And yes, I was getting sloppy.

A parcel duly arrived addressed to my name at Albury airport. Unbelievably, it came through unchecked, and weighed 5 kilos!

Off I went to Melbourne, this time taking my new partner with me for the experience. (Another amateur move.) I had to leave him in a pub when I did the drop to Rex because, wisely, Rex said he didn't want a third party involved. In fact, he questioned why I would have a partner when I never had in the past. I really had no answer for him, and put it out of my mind.

We pocketed $22,500 between us and I arranged to take up the third shipment. This time I got really cute and had it sent to Wagga airport to a fictitious name and address.

Unfuckingbelievable.

CHAPTER 44

BUSTED

I had Jane ring the airline, from our home phone no less, and ask if a package was waiting for 'Buttfuck Pty Ltd' or whatever bullshit name I was using. They kept her on the line while they checked, and came back and assured her it was there. Off to Wagga I went, planning on being back for my afternoon shift at Brady's. Well, that didn't happen.

I went into the airline office in town and nonchalantly asked for a package addressed to Buttfuck. All my instincts told me something was off, but I ignored them. Living and working in a country town, rather than fast-paced Sydney, not to mention the different types of people I was associating with, had dulled my instincts. In the old days I wouldn't have entered the office, let alone stuck around while they made me wait five minutes for the package.

Out the bloke came, no doubt on reflection a copper, and handed me the parcel. No request for ID, just a 'sign here' and I was out of there. I took half a dozen steady paces to my ute, opened the door, tossed the PVC package onto the seat with my blue heeler puppy Bo Diddly, and put the key into the ignition.

Next minute there was a gun to my head, and a very strained male voice saying, 'Hands on the wheel, very slowly. Open the door and step out of the vehicle.'

'So, which first, mate? Hands on the wheel in which case I can't open the door, or the other way around—hold onto the wheel while I'm standing outside the car?'

I gave the game away there and then; shouldn't have been such a smartarse. It was another mistake piled on top of the others that led to this fucked-up situation.

Off to the station we went. It was the usual routine: good cop, bad cop; cajoling, threats, standover tactics and so on. Water off a duck's back. I dropped my Albury copper mates' names, which bought me a bit of time. I remembered the advice I'd received from Charlie Waterstreet and every other criminal lawyer I'd had a drink with over the previous decade: *say nothing*. And I stuck to it, until I got a call from Detective Sergeant C in Albury saying that they had showed up at the hospital Jane worked at and took her back to our house. Jim M, another Albury detective, was part of the crew that searched our house and found a dope-smoking pipe on the coffee table, along with a small amount of Turd. Jim and I didn't see eye to eye, and he was salivating at the opportunity to see me go down.

Then the Wagga boys played their trump card. They had a recording of Jane when she made the phone call to enquire about the package. They intended to charge her as well if I didn't play ball. My immediate response was, 'How far do you want me to kick it?'

No way was she going down as well. She always knew what I did for a quid, but never actively helped me—apart from that one phone call. She didn't even smoke the bloody stuff, apart from one memorable occasion when she became convinced she was stuck in a puddle of glue on our living room floor. That gave us a few chuckles over the years.

I gave Detective M my word I'd work with them and was released by the Wagga jacks, minus of course my package. I was charged and it became news immediately, but information about the size of the bust and the quality of the gear wasn't released until the case went to court quite a few months later.

It didn't take FiL long to hear about the disgrace I'd brought on his name. 'Did you know he was dealing in drugs?' he roared at Jane as he prowled around his living room, kicking holes in walls and screaming. Naturally her defensive mechanisms kicked in, which I fully understand, and she denied it all. 'No, Dad, honestly. I thought he made his money from gambling on the horses.'

That satisfied him. So long as he heard the answer he wanted, the truth simply didn't matter.

The deal I struck with the cops, both the local police and the Sydney drug squad, was that I would set up a cocaine bust for them in Sydney.

CHAPTER 45

THE GLENSYND FUCK-UP

This is how it went down.

I contacted Dave O, an old Albury mate I'd introduced to dealing a couple of years before, who was now living in Sydney and moving some cocaine with a gang of cobbled-together international types. I didn't give a rat's arse who was involved or who got busted as long as my mate didn't end up in cuffs. That was the agreement.

I found myself at Drug Squad HQ in College Street, Sydney, being introduced to my contact, Mick Drury. I'd never heard of him before.

The deal was, Mick was the buyer and he and his 'girlfriend', an undercover policewoman, were ensconced in a room on the second floor of the Glensynd Motel in Randwick, just down the road from the racecourse. I was to take Dave to meet them and he, in turn, would call his people, let them know he had counted the cash, and that it was all good to go. It was a substantial deal, well over $200,000, so a hard one to pass up. Once the suppliers had the nod from Dave, they were to drive into the motel car park and wait. When everyone was happy and they adjudged the situation good to go, they would bring the blow to the room where it would be weighed, and the cash exchange would take place. Why anyone would agree to have both the goodies and the folding in one location was beyond me, but to that they surely nodded their collective empty heads.

I took Dave to the room, introduced him to Mick and the girl, and he sighted the cash. He left to make the call. Once he was out of the room, I took to Mick.

'What the fuck are you doing, mate? What's with the kissing and cuddling? No one behaves that way doing business. For fuck's sake, you look too relaxed and cool. Knock it on the head.' The girl backed me up. 'Yeah, Mick. No more.'

A couple of minutes later, we had Dave back with us.

'They've gone cold on it,' he said.

Thank Christ, I thought.

'But I reckon I've talked them around,' the greedy fucker said. 'They want to put it off till tomorrow.'

'No problem,' Mick readily agreed.

It was another amateur mistake that Dave didn't pick up on. When you have the cash, you are king. He should have called it off, given himself some cred. If I'd been in it for real, I'd have run a mile well before this, but both sides were so greedy they weren't thinking straight.

We agreed to do the business the next day, sticking to the same time. Dave and I left together and, as we headed to our cars, I asked him how he felt about the situation.

'Mate, it felt a bit suss, but all good now. It's a big earn for me, for all of us.'

'Yeah, mate, but you can't spend it if you're locked up. If you have any doubts, any at all, you should walk away,' I urged him.

I all but told him it was a set-up, but when those dollar signs are big enough they blind the best of us.

There we were the next day, same motel room, looking out to Alison Road and over part of the car park. Some good had come of deferring the deal, because the jacks had tailed Dave back

Dad as Ordinary Seaman, RAN. Also the best salesman I ever knew!

Mum as Assistant Teleprinter Operator, WRANS—she is the most astute person I have ever known.

Flying Officer R.H. Halsted RAAF. I hope I've done you proud.

Mum and Dad's wedding, 25 June 1949. Clearly my genes are excellent!

My kindergarten class at St Xavier's, Gunnedah, in 1957. I'm in the front row, second from the right.

The Halsted Kids, Christmas 1960. *Left to right:* me, Bill, Chris (holding Karen), Helen and Madeline.

Dinner's on Dad! Good mate Geoff Romero (centre) and me at the Summit Restaurant with Dad, 1970.

Always biting off more than I can chew!

Our getaway driver, Chris.

Michael and me outside 4 Longdown Street, Newtown. Michael was probably muttering 'Get over yourself.'

Dr Mike and Chris at their wedding, 1970.

The groomsmen, me and Al (right), at Tim and Marianne's wedding, 1975. (Courtesy Hawthorndenites)

All banged up. One of seventeen cars I've written off or had a tangle in.

The Hawthornden era, 1970s. (Courtesy Hawthorndenites)

My sister Chris and me, 1978.

Two years into a sober life, in 2001.

My Fair Lady, by the Albury Wodonga Theatre Company in 2014. *Left to right:* Nicky Pummeroy as Eliza, Tim Bishop as Higgins and myself as Pickering. (Courtesy Rob Lacey Photography)

With my generous friend, actor John Wood (left). (Courtesy Megan Rigoni)

Myself as 'Nev' from *Heroes*, a 2015 AWTCo production. (Courtesy Megan Rigoni)

to the stash and they now knew what car the lads were using. The plan now was that the police would top and tail the loaded vehicle. When they were in light traffic, the rear car would run up the arse of the car carrying the gear, the front car would stop so they couldn't bolt and there would be a passing police car that would stop to investigate the 'accident'. Not a bad plan; it would let everyone off the hook.

Pity they didn't do it that way.

For some unknown reason, the guys running the operation allowed the gang's car into the car park, at which time they surrounded it with guns drawn, bellowing, 'Hit the ground, motherfucker' and other such bullshit they'd heard on television.

We heard the commotion and I quietly said to Dave, 'Get the fuck out of here. Take the back stairs and don't look back,' and I pushed him out the door.

The rock-solid agreement was he wouldn't be busted.

Yeah, sure.

I pulled the curtain aside and looked out the window in time to see two plain-clothes coppers with guns drawn corralling Dave, one of the half-dozen dopers they arrested that day. I turned to Mick and said, 'Thanks, mate, you've just signed my death warrant.'

He was all apologies, but what does that mean when it was obvious that I was the one who set the whole thing up? Dave was arrested, and probably a good thing, too. If he hadn't been, he'd have been the prime suspect in the set-up.

I have to acknowledge later events showed that Mick had enormous courage and integrity, evidenced by the way he stood up to the bent, murderous and disgraced copper Roger Rogerson. He took a bullet for standing on his principles. And for that alone, he has to be admired.

I had the cops drive me to the airport and got on the first available flight to Albury. I wanted to be in town when the news broke.

It made no difference. The next day it was all over town that I'd set up Dave, that I was a dog, a give-up, a grass, a lagger. Not that any of the people spreading the word understood anything about the drug world or how it worked. Only one friend had the balls to front me and tell me what was being said. That was Head. He didn't judge, just told me what he'd heard. I thanked him without commenting further.

I was reminded of a conversation I once had with Gator about how tight our crew was, how we'd go to the wall for each other. He gave me a deadpan look and said in that inimitable way of his, 'Mate, this is a dog-eat-dog game. You're kidding yourself if you think anyone would do a single day inside to protect you. This is every man for himself.'

And that's the way it is, the way it's always been and always will be. The criminal code of silence is something the syndicate heads invented to keep the dumb, loyal soldiers silent. And in the main, it works.

I was persona non grata and I kept it that way by avoiding the pubs and keeping my head low. All those 'friends' I'd kept supplied with free smoko dropped off and perpetuated the story that I was a grass.

Life was tough for both Jane and me. She had to endure the whispers around her work and pressure from FiL to leave me. To her credit, she stuck with me.

Lionel sacked me quite matter-of-factly. 'Rod, this is a working-man's pub. They hate drugs. I don't give a rat's arse how a bloke makes his living but my business will suffer if I keep you on, so you're gone, son.' Ah, for the good old days when you could actually tell someone the truth about their termination.

I always admired Lionel, Head and Col for being direct

with me. I remember with great respect and affection those blokes and others who were straight-up.

We knew my court case was coming up, and in the end it arrived in a rush. I was working as a brickie when I got a message to go home immediately. I was to be in court in Sydney the next day, 24 September 1982. My oldest friend, whom I'd met when I arrived in Albury at age thirteen, was Geoff Romero. He had graduated as a lawyer some eight or so years before and was practising in Albury. He came to Sydney with me. I asked Jane to stay at home. I knew I'd get some time in the slammer; it was necessary to give a bit of cover to the coke bust involvement. I didn't expect what I got, though.

CHAPTER 46

THE BIG HOUSE

Through my dad I met a supposed top barrister who agreed to appear for me. It was a guilty plea so should have been easy; but the useless prick spent most of his time in court mumbling into a handkerchief, sneezing and half-heartedly speaking on my behalf. He forgot my name at one stage and failed to play up the fact that I was a cleanskin.

The prosecution, which was supposed to go easy on me, pointed out that the drugs I was busted with had the highest THC content of any marijuana analysed in the New South Wales government laboratories. Ever. This is not what we wanted to hear.

Throughout it all Mum, Dad and Geoff endured watching this person they knew to be a decent man painted as a commercial drug dealer.

When both sides had finished the judge decided that, since I'd pleaded guilty and saved the court time and expense, I should be sentenced to six years' incarceration with eighteen months to be served before I'd be considered for parole.

We were stunned. Anything over a year before parole consideration and you went straight to maximum security.

I don't know who organised for a second plea before the judge, but the next day there I was again, this time with a different man appearing for me: a young up-and-coming barrister my old man found through a judge he played golf with. I won't name the barrister because he's gone on to bigger and better things, and I doubt he wants to be a bit player in my life's story—but I will say he was a bloody sight better at the persuasion caper than the first bloke.

His argument worked, and my time to be served before consideration for parole was reduced to a year, which meant I was off to medium-security Silverwater Gaol rather than the hellhole of Long Bay. I'd spent the night in Long Bay waiting for this result and what I saw there wasn't pretty. The howling at night was what got me: inmates being raped, bashings by both screws and inmates, and a general sense of anarchy. Not for me, thanks.

I was led from the dock into a set of cells designed a century before for five-foot-tall convicts. Alone I was locked in a cage about 2.5 metres square by less than 1.8 metres high. I had to keep my head bowed to avoid hitting the ceiling. One of the court clerks eventually led my mum and dad to see me. Christ, I used all my willpower to hold it together. I was an instant away from breaking down. My parents were visibly upset, too, but we all managed to hold steady. I have no recollection of what was said, but I know when my folks left I was in no doubt of their unconditional love and support for me. There was no judging, no kicking of walls, no 'How could you do this to us?' Just affection and a smidgen of humour. There was no doubt in my mind about the quality of blood I came from.

I was loaded into a New South Wales prison transport wagon, along with half a dozen other guilty parties, and trucked off to Silverwater. I was held at Silverwater for around six weeks with the plan to then be transferred to Mannus prison farm near Tumbarumba, which was the closest holding facility to Albury.

The first person I met at Silverwater was an armed robber named Phoss. He was connected to Albury: his uncle had owned a well-known restaurant there for many years. When Phoss heard

I was from Albury, he adopted me. He was a few years older than me. Even though I was 30 and had years of criminal experience behind me, prison is an entirely different deal when it comes to age.

It is very easy to extend a short sentence into a long one in gaol. Your freedom date rides on your split-second responses to others' actions and words when everyday situations arise. There is always some loser with no family to go home to who will bait and niggle and outright attack another individual for any number of reasons—boredom, machismo, fear, wanting to build a rep, cowardice—or no reason at all.

Phoss included me in the group that ran our section. Most of them were decent people, I found. In fact, the one positive out of gaol is that I met some bloody good blokes in there. I was left alone and spent the time getting fit.

One day, Phoss instructed me to stay in my cell all night and not come out until breakfast. In those days our cell doors were left unlocked as we shared a common ablutions block. It made it easier for the blokes who were rooting each other to get together, too. I think the screws worked out if those who wanted sex were getting it, the whole population was easier to control.

I didn't ask Phoss why I should stay in my cell that night: best not to have too much information in case you're questioned. As it turned out, five of our boys decided they needed a night on the piss, so they got hold of a pair of wire cutters and cut a hole in the back wire fence. A car was waiting for them, and off they went to a favourite watering hole in Balmain.

It went well until one of the boys spotted his wife sitting on a stranger's lap. He belted the human armchair and dragged his wife out of the pub by her hair. The remaining four escapees, including Phoss, thought it wise to bolt back to Silverwater.

When the count was done the next morning, as it was every day, our fifth musketeer was found to be missing. He handed himself in the next day, having spent a loving night with his wife, who explained nothing serious had been happening between her and the now-hospitalised would-be Lothario. Our boy told the screws he had missed his wife dreadfully and, after finding a pair of wire cutters, he impulsively decided to let himself out for the night. It wasn't a bad story, but not good enough to stop him being shanghaied back to Long Bay.

The price we pay for romance.

My first visitation was scheduled for the following weekend. Jane and my folks turned up and, a little later, my old mate JB arrived. Immediately upon seeing Jane and my parents JB said he'd come back another day, but I insisted he stay. I value mates who stick regardless of circumstances, and JB has always been one of those.

Before I knew it, I was being transferred from Silverwater to Mannus with an overnight stop at Goulburn Gaol. I shared the transport with a dozen men, some obviously terrified and others old hands. One particular loudmouth shouted about how he was going to fuck up everyone in the wagon given half a chance. I kept my head low and didn't make eye contact until finally, after one abusive tirade too many directed straight at me, I looked up. What I saw was a skinny, would-be gangster with more tats than IQ points. I made eye contact and maintained it steadily, no expression on my face. All the communication was done with my eyes.

He kept raving: 'What the fuck you looking at, cunt? I'll stick you first chance. I'll make you my bitch, I'll . . .' Then he slowly petered out when I didn't give him the cowering response he had got from the others he'd targeted. Since we were all handcuffed and chained to individual points no one could actually do anything to anyone else, other than what Motormouth was doing: offering up empty threats.

When he finally stopped, I broke the heavy silence by saying, very quietly but with much intent, 'I don't know you and you don't know me, but now you have an enemy to deal with. The first time you get close enough to me I'm going to bite your nose off. Then I'm going to rip your tongue out. Clear?'

It seemed to do the trick. There was total silence for the rest of the trip to Goulburn.

Into C Wing I went for the night, supposedly to be transferred the next morning. That didn't happen. As fate would have it the screws decided to call a snap strike, so everything was shut down with a skeleton staff manning the stations. Instead of being transported the next day I ended up spending four days in a zoo. I have never before or since seen humans behave the way some of the C Wing inmates did that first morning.

At around 7 a.m. we were fed porridge and toast, with everything consumed using plastic utensils. When breakfast was over, the long-term lags headed off to their cells and the sweeper, who is the head prisoner, in our wing went off to do his cleaning. I was herded, along with 60 or more other cons, through a gate the size of a regular doorway into C Yard so we could fill in the next four hours with a spot of exercise.

The gate was at the narrow end of a funnel set-up, and the yard itself spread out broadly, meeting at a high stone wall about 50 metres away. I stepped away from the others smartly and made for the end wall. Very quickly the men teamed up in pairs or groups, as they would every morning. There were maybe 40 Aboriginal prisoners mooching about in groups of anything from three to seven or so. There were half a dozen white guys all hanging together, no doubt for safety, and in the far-right corner was an exercise set-up with weight-lifting equipment, a couple of bench presses and a shower. Standing around it were maybe ten tattooed body builders. Near the exercise equipment were three skinny white boys, still in their teens. They were naked. The muscled-up Mr Universe types were alternately pumping iron and sexually assaulting the boys. It was hard to watch.

My blood was boiling as I reached the far wall and turned on my heel to walk briskly back. I didn't look again, but couldn't escape the sobbing sounds of the kids being abused. I had a nice steady pace going when three of the Aboriginal guys stood in my way. When I was about ten paces away, one of them asked the question that is taboo in gaol: 'What you in for, Bud?' I didn't break stride and was quite prepared to walk over the top of them. As I bore down all three leapt out of the way, one of them saying, 'Stay out of his way, that fucker's crazy. Did you see his eyes?'

Good, I thought, *I've got them fooled.*

I had pulled the 'don't fuck with me' cloak on in the wagon to Goulbourn, which served me well in gaol—but unfortunately, I didn't know how to take it off until many years later. I wore it through my marriage, my kids' births, the building of businesses, when I employed people—indeed, every moment of my life. The only reason most people didn't see my hardness was because I was a consummate actor, able to become whoever I needed to in any situation.

During the lunch break I sought out a screw, otherwise known as a prison warder, and very politely requested he put me anywhere but with those animals. 'If I go back into that yard, mate, I'm never going to be released. I'll kill those grubs raping those kids. Or as many as I can before they kill me.' Thank God I was talking with a decent man. 'Take this note to the library and hand it to the head man there,' he said. 'Go there every day until you are put on the transport to Mannus.'

After another three days, all spent in the library, I was finally transferred to Mannus.

CHAPTER 47

UMPIRE PLEASE

What a difference Mannus was to the human zoo I'd just been released from. I'm not sure being incarcerated with multiple murderers, child rapists and other psychopaths is the most effective road to rehabilitation—particularly for non-violent offenders, most of them doing time for drugs or traffic offences.

At Mannus I was put into a ten-bedroom box. There were no locks on the internal or external doors so you could basically come and go as you pleased. I concentrated on getting fit and staying away from anything that might see me returned to Goulburn or Long Bay. A few of the blokes I spent time exercising and swapping bullshit with had organised regular drops of beer. I was offered in but, as much as I wanted a drink, I was not inclined to spend my full sentence of six years back in the zoo for the sake of a couple of cans.

A contact of one of my fellow inmates would deliver a box of 24 cold cans to the fence line, and one of the lads would slip out after lights out and collect it. Half a dozen of the men would then demolish the grog and dispose of the evidence within the kitchen refuse. The system worked a treat, but I asked myself what the point of it was. To risk years, all for a few cans of frothy. Even then, but more so on reflection, I realised it was all about machismo.

One of the inmates reminded me of the thief Steve from my Boulder Block Hotel days: big, blond, muscles in his shit, walking around like he had a tennis ball in each armpit. He had set his sights on a little bloke named Billy, who was in for killing his mother. It was clear the Steve lookalike had romantic designs on Billy. I fully intended to tune the big prick up when one of the boys took me aside and pointed out two salient things. First, the offender was soft and would drop me in to the screws as the bloke who bashed him, and then off to the big house I would go. And second, maybe Billy was up for it.

This last point stopped me in my tracks. It had never occurred to me that someone might actually enjoy being the receiver of swollen goods in this prison version of hide the sausage. Then I reflected on a few of the relationships I had witnessed during Her Majesty's Tour over the previous three months or so. I realised I had turned a blind eye to the way some of the inmates had lovingly gazed at their partners or would-be partners. It was no different to what happened on the outside, really. So I pulled my head in, looked the other way when Billy was being goosed by the goose, and concentrated on the gym. After all, I knew there would be a day of reckoning to come out of the Glensynd fiasco, and I wanted to be ready.

I had visits every weekend, mostly from family. Jane came up regularly, always with lots of home-cooked goodies. The guy I was in business with when I was busted came to see me with another drinking pal and brought oranges injected with vodka. The moment they told me what was in the oranges, I signalled the screw to come over and asked him to escort them back to their car, and to take the stuff they had brought in. They couldn't believe I wasn't grateful.

'Let me put it to you this way, boys. If I'm caught with booze in any form I'm straight back to maximum security, and likely to do the full six years. Don't come back. I'll see you on the outside. Now fuck off.'

I stayed fit by running, using weights and, on one memorable occasion, umpiring a game of Aussie Rules football. I'll never do that again. Without doubt it was my most dangerous two hours in prison. No matter who I blew the whistle on, they raged. No one could accept a decision given against them or not given against an opponent. I honestly believed on a dozen occasions I was going to have to fight for my life. I don't know why I thought people who couldn't live within society's boundaries would change for a game of footy.

Another time we played a game of cricket against the local townspeople. My little sister Karen had driven down from Sydney to say hello and was a spectator at the game. It was in Tumbarumba on an oval with dense bush around about a third of the boundary fence. One of the opposition team members hit a massive six straight into the bush. Half a dozen of our fielders immediately made a dash for the fence—ostensibly to find the ball, but if the screws hadn't blown the peas out of their whistles pulling them up, it was a certainty that fewer would have come out of the scrub than went in. The drive to escape is in some cons' DNA.

CHAPTER 48

WELCOME HOME

Finally it came time for my release. It was March 1983, six months earlier than my supposed earliest release date. I'd been behind bars for six months.

I rang Jane and told her I would be released at 9 a.m. the following day. She didn't arrive to collect me until 11 a.m. I was coldly furious. *Keep me waiting for two hours? How fucking dare you.* The fifteen-year-old boy in me was alive and on the rampage. I didn't give her a chance to explain that she'd been up half the night cooking food for my homecoming; that she had to stop on the side of the road for a nap, otherwise she would have crashed. That she was here. For me.

I was being totally unreasonable. I now know my response was designed to push her away, because I knew I was unworthy of her love. I still had the 'don't fuck with me' cloak on. I felt lower than shark shit, but I didn't know it. What I needed—what all prisoners need upon release—was counselling and guidance, preferably from someone who has been through the system. Of course, there wasn't any.

Just because you are released from gaol doesn't mean the sentence is over.

We arrived back at our home on Hanel Street and tried to reconnect. And we did, too, for a while. We ate the food she'd been up all night preparing, made love and tried talking—but I was restless. Around 6 p.m. I said I wanted to go to the Star Hotel, where I knew all my mates would be—those who had stuck by me and those who had talked behind my back. When Jane and I walked in there was momentary silence, followed by a load of backslapping. 'Mate, great to see you.' 'A beer for my old mate, Roddy.' 'How are you, mate? I was going to come up this weekend to visit you.' (Yeah? Really? Why not last weekend or the weekend before?)

I shook hands all round and got to my co-conspirator last: the bloke who walked scot-free, and who thought it a good idea to bring me booze in gaol. The one who contributed nothing to paying my legals. He was baby-shit yellow and had the look of a stunned mullet on his drooping face.

'Mate, you look shocked to see me,' I said quietly. 'Did you think I'd stay in there forever? Your cheque must have been lost in the mail, mate. Haven't seen a penny towards my legal bills. I also hear you've been chasing Brian to keep doing business. Don't look so shocked, mate. Word travels. Brian and I are old mates.' Then I turned my back on him.

I bump into him every now and then. We get on fine. He eventually did his own lagging for another deal gone wrong, so he knows what I went through. People change. I did, so why not him? Anyway, resentment gives you cancer so it's water under the bridge.

I had always trusted Jane and didn't believe for a moment she had cheated on me while I was inside, but that came into question one night shortly after my release. We walked into a crowded party when some pretty little blond-headed boy greeted her with, 'Babe, where ya been?' He moved towards her with the obvious intention of getting closer. She immediately gave him the cold shoulder, but not before I took it all in.

'Who's your little mate?' I quietly enquired.

'Who do you mean? Richard? He's no one,' she blithely replied and neatly slipped away to chat with one of her girlfriends.

The seed of doubt had been sown. That's normal for an emotional cripple.

I was no sooner home and trying to make a go of our marriage than I had a visit from my old mates Inspector M and Detective Sergeant C. They were in a sweat. In my experience, cops don't get nervous unless there is a possibility of violence or they are going to get caught doing the wrong thing. These two were as jumpy as skydivers with badly packed chutes.

The cocaine gang had all been convicted and their sentences weren't on the light side: between four and ten years, from memory. Dave's was one of the lighter ones, although I'm sure he didn't see it that way. The cops and I were always aware that word would get out in the prison system that I was a grass. That would make it open season on me.

When I first went into Silverwater I was offered protection. That is, I could choose to do my time among those most in danger in the prison system: paedophiles, grasses, cops who'd been caught and anyone else who felt fearful for their life. I knocked that idea on the head. I'd rather take my chances than spend a day in the company of those lowlifes.

So, having made it out of the system intact (physically, anyway), I kidded myself that life could go back to normal. Not so, according to Albury's finest. M delivered the bad news. 'Mate, there's been a fuck-up in Sydney and two of our bad boys have escaped. The Israeli and the German; the most dangerous and smartest of them. Word is that there is a contract on your life.

C and Mick are under threat as well. I'm suggesting you take off and lay low until we either catch these arseholes or we know the threat has at least abated.'

'I know I'm fucking off, mate,' added C. 'This is as serious as it gets.'

I thought about it for a bit, but made my mind up pretty quickly. 'There's no way I'm leaving Jane,' I said. 'If they come I'll deal with them.' Just how I'd do this I hadn't really thought about, but to leave my wife so soon after getting back was not an option.

'Your call, mate, but if you change your mind, come to me straight away. We'll give you all the help you need to disappear. And Jane, too, if that's what you want.'

I thanked them and put the idea of running out of my mind, but I did prepare for a possible confrontation. I got myself as fit as I could in case one or more of these fuckers arrived. I really didn't think it likely, though—they were drug dealers, and in my experience not many dealers were killers. In fact, most of them couldn't throw a punch hard enough to bruise a peach. So, my level of concern was low, until I got another visit from M two weeks later. The situation had quickly escalated to red-flag level.

In June 1984 Mick Drury, the undercover cop I'd set the bust up with, had been shot. It happened the night before M came to see me for the second time. Mick was in his home when, in police lingo, 'a person unknown' lined him up through the kitchen window and shot him in the guts with a heavy-calibre weapon. He wasn't dead but it obviously wasn't from want of trying on the shooter's behalf.

Well, that got me moving. I packed a small carryall with a few clothes and my passport in case I needed it. Jane wanted to know what was going on.

'Jane, the less you know, the safer you will be. I've got to take off, and I can't tell you where to. In fact, I don't know where I'm going myself, but even if I did, I couldn't tell you. My life is on the line. If anyone comes looking for me, all you say is, "He's left me. I have no idea where he is or if he's ever coming back." You got that? Stick to it, but it's highly unlikely anyone will come around.'

Naturally enough, Jane was baffled, scared and fearful I wouldn't ever come back. Mostly I think she was very worried that I would be killed or badly damaged.

'You are coming back, aren't you? You're not leaving me?'

'Jane, I'll never leave you. I'll be back as soon as I can. These people mean business, but they made the mistake of shooting a copper. Every cop in Australia is looking for them.'

Then I left.

CHAPTER 49

HIDING OUT

I got into M's car and he drove me to the airport. I caught a flight to Sydney and headed by train to my parents' place in Wahroonga, in the leafy northern suburbs. I caught a cab from Turramurra railway station to the street one over from my folks' place. It was evening so by cover of dark I slipped through four or five neighbours' backyards and made my way to my folks' back door. It was never locked, so I quietly let myself in and walked into the kitchen. I nearly gave my mother a heart attack.

'Good lord, Rod, why didn't you come to the front door?'

It seemed like a reasonable question deserving an honest answer.

'Ah, I'll answer that in a second. Is Dad here?'

'I certainly am,' Dad said as he entered the kitchen with his hand outstretched for me to shake. 'It's good to see you, son. What's going on?'

'We better sit down and, without being dramatic, we need to close the curtains. Don't want anyone to be able to look in.'

Without question my parents did as I asked, and we sat at the dining-room table.

'Well,' I began, 'the deal I set up for the cops has taken a twist.'

They were both aware of me setting up the bust for the cops and the reason why. They knew if I didn't do it Jane would have been charged along with me and, convicted or not, her nursing career would be over—and that would be the best of it. They knew I couldn't do that to her, so they fully understood why I set the coke bust up and, as through my entire life, despite all the shit I put them through with my wild and unpredictable ways, they supported me. They didn't necessarily agree with my decisions, and the old man often went off at me, but at the end of the day, they backed me 100 per cent.

The great lesson they taught me was to never let the sun go down on my anger. In other words, don't hold resentments. I forgot that lesson at different times and held grudges for the most minor things. I've since learnt that's not a good way to live. The ability to forgive is a beautiful thing.

I explained there was a contract on my life, that one guy had already been shot so the threat was very real, and I was just calling in to say goodbye for a while. I had it in my head I'd go to Cairns and see if I could hide out at my old mate Corky's place. After all, his property comprised 10 acres of rainforest backing on to a massive national park, most of it jungle. There were plenty of places to scarper to if the fuckers came looking, and I knew I could rely on Corky to back me up.

My parents wouldn't hear of it. 'You'll stay with us, Rod. For as long as it takes for the police to straighten this out.' I didn't really want to argue with them. I knew I was placing them in danger, but when I explained the peril they may be in they dismissed it out of hand.

'I'll set the pool room up for you,' Mum said. 'There is a door in and out which you will keep locked and only use if necessary. There is a toilet and shower. Keep the curtains closed, and don't play snooker during the day or until Dad comes home so if anyone happens to listen they won't hear anything out of the ordinary. The rest we can sort out as we go.'

Incidentally, when I asked the old man decades later if he had anything to do with my very early release, he said he had a meeting with Rex 'Buckets' Jackson, then the new minister for prisons, later to be a guest of the same organisation.

'What did it cost you?' I asked.

'A bottle of Johnnie Walker whisky,' he replied.

'Red, black or blue?'

'Red,' Dad replied. 'Rex is no snob.'

What brilliant parents I had. When the Mum and Dad Sweepstakes was drawn, my siblings and I won first prize. They kept my presence so quiet that none of my siblings, as they came and went, knew at any time during my stay that I was downstairs.

So that's how I lived for the next five or so weeks: slipping out the window at night on the blind corner of the house, dodging through hedges and over neighbours' fences until I reached a safe distance away, and running. Running to stay fit. Running to stay sane. Running for my life. And running to the bottle shop. (I had started drinking cask wine.)

I had no contact with Jane. I don't know what I thought—maybe that my would-be assassins were able to tap my phone. Insanity. But when a thought takes root in an already disturbed mind, fucked up even more by drinking four litres of wine a day, it's only a shuffle to believing the impossible is reality.

And so I stayed in my hideout for over a month, slowly going mad.

Towards the end of my stay, Mum was admitted to hospital to have her varicose veins operated on. All her life she had trouble with the veins and ulcers on her ankles. She put up with constant pain; I don't think I ever truly appreciated how much. She was home from hospital after about ten days, but probably should have been in there for four weeks just to have a break. She had spent every day of her adult life looking after people: first the old man and six kids, then her father, Pop Brewster, came and stayed with us. He alternated between Mum and her sister, Auntie Jeanne, three months there and three months with us. Pompa was a great old man and was at pains not to be a burden, and I'm sure we all loved having him with us, especially Mum; they were great mates. But it's still someone to care for. No sooner had he died than Dad's mother, Dinnie, moved in with us. The load mostly fell to Mum and Dad. We all believed that the older generation shouldn't be shuffled off to a nursing home.

The day after Mum returned home from the hospital, I got a phone call from C.

'Mate, the coast is clear. Turns out Mick Drury was shot by a bloke from Melbourne. We reckon the two escapees are long gone. Probably having a drink in a Mediterranean bar talking about the war. Anyway, mate, it's safe to come home.'

CHAPTER 50

MUM'S DEAD

My imminent homecoming was excellent news. I was as pissed as a newt—never the best time to make phone calls—but I thought I'd give Jane a bell and tell her.

'Hello?' came her familiar, beautiful voice.

'Hey, babe. How ya doin'?'

'Hey to you, too. How fantastic to hear your voice.'

'You, too. What are you up to?'

'Just getting ready to go out with Annie. She's been staying with me.'

'Oh yeah? Who are you meeting? How often you been going out? Having a nice time without me?' And off on a rave I went. My immature imagination had kicked in and I built myself into an alcoholic rage. 'Who are you fucking?'

'Rod, calm down. It's Friday night, I'm going out with Annie and the girls . . .'

But it was no use. I wasn't listening. There was no point in telling her I was coming home, so no need for the phone anymore: I smashed it onto the lounge room floor and watched it shatter into dozens of pieces. When the red veil of rage lifted from my eyes I looked up, and there was my beautiful mother, standing at the top of the stairs with tears flowing down her cheeks.

'Oh, my son, my son. What's to become of you?'

'Well, I can tell you one thing: I'm going to Albury to sort this out once and for all!'

With that I went down to the pool room, grabbed my wallet, ran back up the stairs and, without a backward glance at my distraught mother, I was gone.

All that running practice had come in handy. I was at Turramurra station in no time and headed to Central, where I boarded the night train to Albury. I stocked up on supplies, first buying two large bottles of Smirnoff vodka. After all, it was a ten-hour journey, and my daily four litres of wine wouldn't get the job done.

By the time I stepped off the train in Albury I was in a cold fury. I walked straight across the train tracks to East Albury rather than taking the long way around via the Dean Street bridge.

It was around 5 a.m. when I knocked on the door. When Jane answered it she had a look of shock on her face, put there not so much because it was me but because of the state I was in. (Four litres of wine and two bottles of vodka tend to show on your face.) I stepped inside and pushed her up against the wall. I accused her of all the usual stuff a doubting husband imagines, raving and scaring the shit out of her. Then Annie stepped out of the spare bedroom and brought me to my senses.

She called her boyfriend who came over and took on the duty of babysitting me while Annie drove Jane up to her parents' house. I played doggo for my babysitter but, when he turned his back, I bolted up to the family home. I prowled around for a while trying to get in, but all the doors were bolted. I learnt later that FiL had positioned himself near the back door with a loaded shotgun. If I'd come through the door he would have shot me, no doubt. He'd deal with the consequences later.

Fuzzy though the next hours were, I know that Jane came home that evening and we attempted to talk it out. I can't speak for Jane, but I certainly didn't have the maturity or wisdom to understand the problem was far deeper than jealousy or trust issues. It took me years to understand what was actually going on with me.

We eventually went to bed, each on the far side of the mattress. We did our best to sleep but it was difficult. At last, I drifted into some sort of rest when the ringing of the telephone woke me at 5.45 a.m. I was up and answering it in the dining room before the third ring.

'Hello.'

'It's Dad. I've got some bad news. Are you sitting down?'

'No, Dad, I'm standing up. I just answered the phone. What's the bad news?'

'Mum's dead.'

'Your mother?'

'No, son. Your mother.'

'What happened?'

'I think she had a heart attack.'

'I'll be there as soon as I can.'

And I went back to bed.

Jane must have sensed the gravity of the situation because normally she would sleep through an earthquake.

'What is it?' she asked as she rolled towards me.

'Mum's dead.' Then the tears and snot welled up and, when she put her arms around me, I almost started to howl. But I didn't. Not a tear was spilled, and the snot never made it to my top lip. I sucked it all up.

Next thing Annie was at our door, asking what she could do. She put the kettle on. *Thanks, Annie.*

Jane and I found ourselves in the car and on the road to Sydney within the hour. We arrived at my folks' house early afternoon.

Most of the family were there by then, plus a few friends, Uncle Des and Aunty Les, and my sister Karen who was with Dad when Mum dropped to the floor. She bore the brunt of the death. She was the youngest of the six kids and the last to leave home. She and Dad had to endure watching Mum go.

When a death happens in the family, one as pivotal as the matriarch, everyone has their own way of dealing with it. We did have a common anaesthetic, though: scotch. Between us we managed to empty fourteen bottles of scotch and countless bottles of wine and beer that first afternoon alone. True Irish Catholics.

We were all stunned that we would never again hear or benefit from Mum's laughter, wit, wisdom, empathy or protection. Most importantly, we would miss her ability to unify us siblings, to help us find common ground, to bring us back to reality during a disagreement, and to remind us to ask, 'How important is it?'

The only good thing that came out of Mum dying was that it helped Jane and me to get through the hard times and reunite.

The funeral was awful. My brother Bill was so distraught he had to be supported by a couple of our sisters. I, on the other hand, being the emotional cripple I had become, showed no emotion at all.

CHAPTER 51

HONEST LABOUR

Out of Mum's ashes I remembered her advice to me: 'Get a trade, a qualification, Rod. Whatever you turn your hand to, you will be successful. And remember, it's *never* too late.' She suggested I look at something to do with plants, as I was an avid veggie grower when I was a kid. When I was eight years old, I was growing cabbages and selling them for sixpence (about five cents in today's terms) to the neighbours. The old man was somewhat horrified when he heard what I was up to, but Mum encouraged me, and must have settled him down as she was always able to do.

I can't blame my adult behaviour on my upbringing, which was ideal. I never once heard a cross word between my parents, and only ever saw a loving relationship. Not to say they didn't have their issues, like every couple since Adam and Eve, but we kids never saw anything to cause us to fear that the family unit was in trouble.

Sadly, I can't say the same about the way my kids were raised.

Jane and I moved to Sydney. She got a job at St Vincent's Private Hospital, and I signed up for the Landscape Technicians Higher Certificate at Ryde School of Horticulture. As we began to build a new life together, I found employment with an upmarket landscape business operating on the North Shore. I discovered a natural aptitude for building gardens, which was enhanced by guidance from the main designer of the business, Trisha. She became a lifelong friend to both Jane and me.

We were working on a job one day, raking out a massive area of soil and prepping it for turf. My workmate Scott and one of the other boys were throwing clods of soil at each other's backs. It started out with a few giggles, but as the clods got bigger and were thrown harder, the fun went out of the game. Eventually the inevitable happened: Scott got belted hard in the back of the head. 'That's it, you arsehole!' he roared at his opponent, launching himself at the projectile thrower, fists up and ready for action.

Fortunately, the foreman, John, had seen the whole thing unfold and used his very large frame to great effect, keeping Scotty away from his tormentor.

'Before you go off tap, Scott, it might be worth noting that you stepped on that rake lying on the ground. It was the handle that smacked you in the melon, not a clod of dirt. Might be a good time to concentrate on your work, you blokes. The fun's over.'

Pretty funny to watch, really.

CHAPTER 52

DON'T FORGET MY LAWNMOWER

Moving away from Albury was the smartest thing Jane and I did. I carried so much guilt over setting up the bust and the only way I knew to deal with it was drinking. We needed to get out of town if we were to have any chance of making the marriage work.

We found ourselves in a nice rented semi on Victoria Road, Drummoyne. Our neighbours were a bunch of pisshead no-hopers. They didn't last long, and when they were evicted the landlord moved in to fix up the mess they had left behind. His name was Geoff. Nice bloke; architect by trade. Wouldn't say boo to a goose.

One day Jane, our friend Peter 'Doc' McGrory and I went to an AFL football game at the Sydney Cricket Ground. Doc and I had plenty to drink, and Jane did the driving. After the game, as we headed up Renwick Street to the back of our house, just on dusk, I noticed a utility loaded up to the gunnels driving off from the back of Geoff's place. The ute was piled high with all sorts of furniture—or so it appeared—but what caught my eye was my push lawnmower tied precariously at the top of the pile, like the angel on a Christmas tree.

'Thieving pricks. They've knocked off my lawnmower!' I said. 'Let me out, Jane. You and Doc go after them and get their plate details. I'll see if anyone's still inside.'

There wasn't anyone there, and it appeared the only thing of mine missing was the lawnmower. I learnt later that the rest of the stuff was from Geoff's house. They stripped the joint of everything, including the fireplace mantles and light fittings. They took all his clothes, his extensive range of electrical tools, his furniture. Everything.

When Jane and Doc returned with the plate details we called the cops. While we were waiting for them, Jane related her excellent adventure with my mad mate Doc.

'Rod, I nearly crashed,' she told me. 'I was following the car, but Peter asked me to drive up on the driver's side. When we drew level, Peter was leaning his whole body from the waist up out his window trying to grab the thief by the throat. "Closer, Jane, closer. I'm gonna drag the prick out!" he bellowed. Honestly, all the blood drained from the driver's face. I've never seen anyone so terrified. His eyes were as big as dinner plates.'

By now we were all in fits of hysterics. Then Geoff knocked on the door, shortly followed by the police. The cops took our statements and promised to get back to us. And they did—that night.

Turns out the idiot borrowed his mate's utility to do the job. He didn't tell his mate, either, so he was happy to finger the bloke. The police told us they booked him, but he wouldn't admit to anything and certainly wouldn't say where all the gear was. I asked one of the cops where the bloke lived, and said that I may be able to persuade him to hand the stuff back.

His reply, after a quizzical look, was, 'Rod, if I told you the bloke lived at 4 Smith Street, Balmain, do you know how much trouble I'd be in?'

'Yeah, mate. I see your point. Forget I asked.'

Once the cops left I had a word with Geoff.

'Mate, have an early night. We're leaving at sparrow's fart. Gonna get your stuff back.'

He looked a little perplexed, but agreed. Being a professional man, he had lived a different life to me. I think he imagined we were going to knock on the thief's door, have a chat and explain the error of his ways, after which he'd see the light and willingly hand the stuff back.

Well, it sort of went that way, with a couple of minor variations.

We arrived at 4 Smith Street at 6 a.m. It was a Sunday morning. I had guessed, correctly as it turned out, that our boy was a pisshead or doper, and that early starts were something in which he didn't engage. I knocked on the back door so lightly I'm not sure my knuckles would've bruised a banana, at the same time muttering, 'Anyone home?' Not getting a reply, I eased the screen door open. It was the middle of summer and the security door was wide open.

'Are you sure we should be doing this?' Geoff whispered.

As we entered the kitchen, he quickly changed his tune. 'The bastards,' he said. 'Those are my best gabardine trousers!'

'They *were* your best,' I replied. 'Now they are a mop for the floor of this cesspit.' I picked up his daks out of the greasy mess where they had been used as a dishcloth.

'Follow me and watch my back,' I told him. I headed up the staircase to the bedrooms. The first one I entered had a long streak of pelican shit stretched out on a single bed. He was lying on his back, a pair of jeans and a T-shirt on. He looked to be nearly two metres tall, but was as skinny as my bank balance back when I was collecting Coke bottles in Newtown. I threw my right leg over him and lifted my left up, pinning his arms to the bed, at the same moment putting one hand over his mouth and pinching his nose closed with the other. The poor, simple prick's eyes shot open, glazed, showing pure panic.

I let him suffocate for 30 seconds, or a year in his view, then removed my fingers from his nose, lifting my free index finger to my lips to give the universal signal for silence. If he could have nodded his head, he would have. I had his head firmly shoved into the pillow so he did his talking with his eyes, and they said, 'I will do anything you ask as long as you let me live.' There's no point fucking around with arseholes. They need to know who's boss.

I removed my hand from his mouth. 'You the cunt who burgled my crib yesterday?' That was another nice touch: using the gaol term 'crib' so the silly prick thought he was dealing with a criminal. (Well, I suppose he was.)

'No!' he urgently whispered. 'He's in the next room.'

'Okay, now you pull the covers over your head and forget we were here. I don't want to have to dispose of another body.' He was shitting himself by this stage. I could tell by the smell.

So I hopped off Stretch and went next door where I observed a bloke about my own size, but with his blubbery guts making him fifteen kilos heavier. He was lying on his side, his belly hanging over his jocks. I took a quick look at Geoff and decided he was with me: he didn't seem entirely convinced that this was something he wanted to be involved in, but was now committed. I gave him a little smile then quickly sprang on my prey, roaring like a banshee. I began slapping him around the head with my left hand and grabbed a handful of his nut sack with my right. The poor simple fuck came out of a pleasant dream and emerged into his worst nightmare. I could see it in his eyes: a mixture of intense pain as his scrotum was being tugged in a different direction to his body, and deep puzzlement about who this lunatic might be who was visiting these atrocities upon his person. He remained silent for a goodly length of time, finally entering the conversation with a sobbing, blubbering plea for me to stop assaulting his corpulent, jelly-like body.

By that time I was snarling like an enraged hyena. I learnt early in my gaol term that if you wish to engage with a criminal or lunatic it's best to out-insane them. I have been known at times to bark like a dog and drool at the same time. It's very disconcerting if you're the one staring into those insane eyes. It's all an act, of course, but tell that to Fatboy. You reckon he's gonna believe you? Not fucking likely!

I dragged him off the bed by his hair and pushed him down the stairs. He half-staggered, half-fell and, as his feet hit that putrid kitchen floor, I was all over him. Geoff was right behind me. I put my left forearm against Fatso's throat and said, in a very quiet voice, 'I want every item back that you stole. By 5 p.m. today. If you don't deliver, and think carefully about my next words, when you go to gaol, I will see to it that you end up with your head in a vice and ten cocks up your fat arse. You do believe me, don't you?' I drove a hard right hand into his guts. 'And don't forget my lawnmower. Cunt.'

Geoff and I swiftly left and headed home. Not much was said but I could tell that, even though that type of behaviour went against the grain, on this occasion Geoff was quite pleased to have been present to see a little justice delivered.

At 5 p.m., up rolled the ute. Everything came back bar one power tool—my mower included. I rang my copper mate and informed him. He gave a chuckle and replied that he wasn't surprised. He also asked if Jane and I would be witnesses in Chubby's case. I asked Jane and we both agreed we would. The cop replied that, more often than not, people got cold feet and often didn't show on court day. I assured him we would be there.

'You know what, Rod? I believe you. We'll be in touch.'

A couple of months later, Jane and I each took a day off work and found ourselves in the waiting room of the local courthouse. Jane was called in first, then I was called five minutes later.

When I walked into the court I had to walk by Jane to get to the witness box. She was white as a ghost.

'Are you okay, Jane?' I quietly asked.

Immediately the magistrate said, 'Silence! No talking to the witness.' I replied, 'I'm checking on my wife,' and turned back to her. 'Are you okay?'

'He's frightening me,' she said, referring to Blubberguts. 'He keeps staring at me.' I gave her a wink and proceeded to the witness box.

After the swearing in I noticed our two detective mates up the back of the court.

The prosecutor began the show.

'Mr Halsted, I'm going to ask you some questions. Please answer "yes" or "no". Is that understood?'

'Yes.'

'On the day of the theft, did you see who was driving the vehicle that was loaded with the stolen goods?'

'Yes.'

'Is the person in the court today?'

'Yes.'

While this was going on, Porky was giving me the evil eye—trying to intimidate me, as he had Jane. He must have forgotten it was me who gave him the flogging at his filthy dive, or maybe he simply didn't recognise me. You can't blame him: the day of the touch-up he was woken from a deep sleep by the madman from hell dressed in shorts and a singlet. Today he was looking at a besuited gentleman.

'Would you point him out, please?' the prosecutor said.

'Sure. That mug in the dock, the one who's looking hard at me, and that I'm looking back at real hard. Drop your eyes, arsehole . . . now!'

The bloke running the show was now repeatedly banging his gavel and demanding 'Silence, silence in the court!' He continued:

'Mr Halsted you will answer "yes" or "no". No more comments. Is that understood?'

'Yes, your worship,' I replied, catching a look up the back of the court at my new best mates, the arresting detectives. They were grinning from ear to ear.

The case droned on, but Jane and I were allowed to leave. Our copper mates met us outside the court and insisted on buying us lunch.

One of them remarked: 'Rod, mate, I thought at one point you were going to jump into the dock and give that flea a smack in the mouth.'

'I would have if he hadn't followed instructions and lowered his gaze,' I replied.

'And you can take that to the bank, gentlemen,' Jane said.

CHAPTER 53

LATE NIGHT FOOTBALL COACH

Jane and I decided it was time to put roots down and buy a house. After looking at countless properties we settled on a three-bedroom house in North Rocks. Our neighbours Kevin and Julie and their two kids Brook and Melanie were a gift from heaven: beautiful people with big hearts and great humour. One time, Julie related an encounter she'd had with her eight-year-old daughter.

'I was standing on a stool reaching into the back of a cupboard when Melanie chose that moment to say, "Mum, did you know there are rings around Uranus?" I nearly fell off the stool.' Melanie had studied the planets at school that day.

Always impatient, I had completed two of the four years of the horticulture course in which I was enrolled. I had my job, but decided I needed to make better money than I could earn as an employee. I opened Halsted Landscapes, and my hunch proved to be correct.

Life should have been rosy, but my inner demons took hold. I found it hard to live with myself after the bungled bust and my role in Dave's incarceration—even more so when he contacted me after his release.

I arranged to meet him at North Rocks Shopping Centre and, once I'd checked the area for an ambush, I picked him up and drove him to our house. We made small talk in the car but, once he walked through the door and saw Jane, he broke down. Sobbing, he wanted to know why I'd set him up. So I told him.

'Mate, I was given no choice. If I didn't give them a coke bust they were going to charge Jane, and I simply couldn't allow that to happen. You had the coke connections, so it had to be done through you. You were never supposed to be busted.'

'Yeah, well, it's a bloody good thing I was. If I'd walked they'd have had me killed for sure.'

'Dave, I did everything I could to persuade you to drop the deal,' I told him. 'When we had the fuck-up on the first day, I did everything but tell you it was off, but you simply weren't listening. Mate, all you could think of was the cash, the payday.'

'Yeah, I realise that now,' he said. 'I've had time to think about it. The second day, that copper, the way he was carrying on with the sheila, I said to you that it felt suss and you said, "Mate, if anything feels wrong, walk. Walk right now." You even led me to the door and told me to walk to the end of the hall and take the back stairs. I remember, mate.'

'It was a fuck-up from the moment the coppers put the thing together,' I said. 'Trouble is, they have no real idea of how a deal goes down. Believe me, I'm sorry. I know that doesn't mean much but mate, it's time to move on. The guilt I've carried over this has haunted me from day one. I'm drinking every day, I'm impossible to live with but Jane has stuck like glue. I'm putting it behind me from this point on. All I can suggest is you do the same. What do ya reckon?'

I offered him my hand, which he took.

He was done three times more in the coming years. Three more laggings.

Jane and I did the best we could. We were actually very happy in North Rocks. I cut my drinking right back after clearing the air with Dave and never went to the pub.

We would do crosswords in bed and laugh heaps. The business was solid and growing. We were happy—even happier the day Jane announced she was pregnant. We decided to take a week off over the Christmas break and have a holiday.

When we got home, our next-door neighbour, on the other side from Kev and Julie, couldn't wait to speak to me (a rare event).

'You're going to have trouble getting to sleep tonight,' he announced fretfully. 'The neighbours at the back have been away for the past week and their teenage son has had a party every night. The music starts at midnight and goes till dawn. And they have been throwing their empty stubbies onto the driveway of the old man across the road from them.'

'Right,' I said. 'And what did the young bloke do when you confronted him?'

'Oh, none of the neighbours have been to see him,' he whined. 'There is always a gang of them. It's a very dangerous situation.'

That night, right on cue at midnight, the noise started: some shit that generation called 'music' blaring out. Jane and I both snapped to attention.

'What the fuck?' I muttered to my better half. 'Well, we know it's not going to stop, so I may as well take care of the problem now.'

'Be careful, Rod. Why don't you take Skeeter with you?' she suggested.

'Yeah, right, Jane. I'll take our savage blue heeler. She can lick them to death.'

I pulled a pair of jeans on and marched around the corner with my faithful protector. The first thing I noticed was the glass glinting on the driveway of the house across the road.

Walking into the front yard of this upmarket house I was struck by two things. First, the area was littered with empty cans and bottles; second, there was a youth of around seventeen sitting on the steps leading to the front door in a puddle of his own vomit. He was aware enough to heed my advice that he should fuck off if he valued his life.

The music was so loud as I approached the front door that there was no point in knocking. I entered and found myself on a landing overlooking a sunken living room. Seated around the place in varying stages of drunkenness were around twenty late teen boys doing their best to enter adulthood.

Skeeter had stuck to my heels and was now sitting at my feet, tongue lolling out, looking with interest at what her master might do next.

'Right, you cunts, turn the radiogram off. Fucken *now*!' (Yes, I did use the ancient word 'radiogram'.)

One young fella, more alert than his pisshead mates, acquiesced immediately.

'Right, that's nice. Now we can all hear each other. Who's the cunt who resides here?'

There was no immediate response, just 40 saucer-sized eyes staring at me with a mixture of fear and wonder.

'Fuck me, lads. We're back to the shouting . . . *Who lives here?*'

One of the boys, who must have been sitting on his nuts his voice was so squeaky, said, 'He's in the bedroom.'

'Well, lad, *get him*!'

He scurried away and returned shortly after. 'He won't come out. He's scared.'

'Okay. Well would you mind delivering a message to Mr Scaredy Pants? Would you tell him I expect to see him on my doorstep at 5 p.m. tomorrow? That's five sharp. Around the corner, where the truck is parked. Would you mind doing that for me, old mate? And meanwhile, if I hear one more sound from this house any time before school goes back, I'll come back in here and clean the lot of you up. The ones I miss, the dog will rip apart. Got it?'

And I swear, just like if it were a classroom, the boys said, 'Yes, sir.'

As I exited I roared, 'And clean this yard up. It looks like a tramp's camp.'

When I got home Jane was lying in bed, crying with laughter. 'Well said, Rod. Succinctly put. You should be a football coach.'

At 5 p.m. the host of the evening's shindig arrived, like a puppy, tail between his legs. He knocked on the door and Jane answered.

'Hello, how can I help you?' she said in a far more friendly manner than her raving lunatic of a husband would have.

'Um, er, ah, that is, urgh.' At this point I thought he was going to swallow his tongue so I stepped forward.

'You must be the arsehole from around the corner,' was my friendly greeting. 'What's your name?'

'Barry,' came the all-but-inaudible reply.

'Barry! And you are the son of . . .?'

'Ah, Mum and Dad?' Barry replied.

Before I could humiliate the poor little prick further, Jane took pity on him.

'What's your surname, Barry?' she enquired of the quivering mass of jelly.

'Thompson,' he replied, shooting Jane a look of thanks, his eyes begging for protection from this monster in front of him. Besuited in my normal work gear of shorts and a blue singlet, muscles bulging, I must have looked to Barry like his executioner.

'Well, Barry my boy, last night was your last party. If I hear any noise from your house after 9 p.m. on any night between now and when your parents return, I'll be around to sort you out. You get my drift?'

'Yes, sir. I'm sorry, sir. It won't happen again, sir. I promise, s—'

'Enough of the sirs, Barry. My name is Rod, and this lady is my wife, Jane. Now off you go. Oh wait, one last instruction. Your next port of call is your neighbour across the road. The old bloke whose driveway you and your idiot mates have been chucking bottles onto. You're going to humbly apologise, then you're going to sweep and vacuum his drive clean of glass. Understood?'

'Understood, s— Rod. I apologise for my behaviour. You won't tell my parents when they get home, will you? Please?'

'Do the right thing, mate, and life tends to turn out okay. By the way, you showed some balls turning up here today. Don't let the idiots lead you astray.'

I offered him my hand. And he took it, looked me in the eye, glanced over to Jane and said, 'It was nice meeting you Mrs . . . um, Jane.'

Pretty impressive overall!

CHAPTER 54

THE MEANING OF LIFE

By early 1986, I built up Halsted Landscapes and our child's birth drew closer. We'd been blown away to discover a few months earlier that we were expecting twins. About two months out from the predicted birth date I came home from work at 5 p.m. on a Friday to find Jane in the bathroom, bleeding heavily. I didn't think about an ambulance. I scooped her up, rushed her to the car and placed her in the passenger seat. I ran back inside and rang my sister Chris who was also heavily pregnant. As soon as she picked up, I said: 'No time to explain. Ring the hospital and tell them I'm bringing Jane in. She's bleeding.' I hung up.

I was out the drive and doing 80 before I hit the first corner. I put the hazard lights and headlights on, held a handkerchief out the window, kept my thumb on the horn and drove as fast as Sydney traffic would allow on a Friday night. I drove on the wrong side of the road, through red lights and over double lines, and arrived at Baulkham Hills Private Hospital in record time. The usual trip in light traffic was about half an hour; we were there in fifteen minutes.

Jane was basically immobilised for the next two months. She had lost one baby with the bleed, so the safety of the remaining child was paramount—certainly to us, but also to the hospital staff.

She was bed-bound for those two months, besides one occasion in February. By then, Chris was in the same hospital and had given birth to her second child. Complications arose with the baby, so Jane got out of bed and went to see how Chris was faring. When Chris asked her if she wasn't supposed to be lying down, Jane replied, 'I don't care.' As Lindy said at our wedding, Jane was family.

Our obstetrician decided that 21 March 1986 was the date he wanted to perform the caesarean. I was seated on Jane's left and she had a tent covering her lower half. I'm sure we were both frightened, but we were looking into each other's eyes and operating as a tight unit.

'Congratulations! You have a beautiful baby girl,' the doctor said over the squalling of the newest member of our small family.

My gut dropped through the floor. I'd been asked many times whether I wanted a boy or a girl and I'd answered, completely honestly I thought, 'I don't care, as long as the kid is healthy.' And here I was, deeply disappointed. But that lasted all of a nanosecond. The nurse took the little girl from the doctor and brought her around the tent to show us.

My gut, which had fallen to the basement a split second earlier, rocketed back up, through my head, through the ceiling, through the hospital roof, and soared into the heavens. I fell instantly and forever in love with this perfect little girl. That deep paternal love has never wavered through all the ups and downs a parent and child experience.

Each day, I couldn't wait to get home from work to be with my two girls. I thought my life was complete. Then, less than a year later, Jane announced that she was pregnant for a second time.

There had been a number of child abductions and murders in Sydney around this time, so we decided we would leave Sydney and raise our kids in the country, which was not only safer but cleaner. We discussed where to go and thought about the coast, but finally settled on going back to Albury.

Take my advice: never move back to the town that your parents or in-laws live in, unless you have an exceptional relationship with them. Especially not if one of those people can't accept you—which is how my father-in-law felt about me. Another good reason to avoid moving back to your hometown is having mates there who are big drinkers, meaning you will give less attention to being a good father and husband and more attention to gargling the liquid amber.

Still, the first few years were good. A house on Elm Street became our new home. We ended up at Albury Base Hospital for the birth of our second child and, bingo: deja vu. Another little miracle arrived in October 1987. My stomach didn't plummet to the basement this time, though: it went straight to the stratosphere. Now I had a beautiful wife and two beautiful daughters.

What could go wrong?

CHAPTER 55

HOW TO WRECK A FAMILY

Head down, arse up, I kicked off Halsted Landscapes in my hometown. For a while it felt pretty good. I was tendering for decent-sized contracts and getting my share of them: such as paving around the Albury Entertainment Centre and landscaping the new local police station.

Then I was cheated by the contractors on a couple of jobs to the tune of just over $40,000: a huge sum of money back then. Rather than deal with my problems as an adult I chose to drink more.

It all came to a head at a ball we attended along with Jane's friend Jan and her partner Pretzel, who was my good mate, and some other friends. One of them was a travelling salesman named Chris, who boarded at Jan's house when in town. I'd suspected something was happening between Jane and this arsehole for some time. Whenever I raised the subject, though, Jane looked me squarely in the eye and flatly denied it.

I'd sworn off the grog six days before the ball, knowing innately it was destroying not only my life but my kids' lives as well. So there I was, drinking water while the others socked back the wine and beer, when Jan in all her wisdom said, 'For God's sake, Rod, have a drink. You are so boring when you don't drink.'

Remarkably, this was followed swiftly by Jane agreeing with her.

Fuck me. This was from the woman who bore the brunt of my alcoholism. She dealt with me emptying money into publicans' tills that should have gone on our family. She lived with the hangovers and the self-loathing, not to mention the stink an active drinker and smoker gives off. And here she was, urging me to have a drink as Chris made eyes at her across the table.

'Is that right? I'm boring? Okay, watch this.' I picked up Jane's glass of wine and downed it in a swallow. Then I walked around the table, picking up each glass and stubby, drinking them all. I left Pretzel's beer and another mate's drink alone but downed nine other drinks, including Chris's, with nary a word of protest from the weak prick. When I arrived back at my seat I reached into the centre of the table, picked up both bottles of wine, red and white, and necked the contents.

The mood had changed. At first our friends were somewhat curious about the tense dynamic that had developed between the Halsted couple. Now there was stunned silence. I sure as shit wasn't boring now.

I don't remember a lot of the rest of the night except that Pretzel followed me to the toilet as I tracked Chris the Grub. My intention was to fuck him up, but Pretzel grabbed me in a bear hug and pulled me away. It was a pretty fair effort considering the mood I was in.

I won't go into detail about what happened next, other than to say that was the last night we were a family unit. Jane took the girls to live at her parents' place. The next day I attended an AA meeting, and kept going back. I held out hope that we could repair our broken family, more so when FiL came around and assured me he would do everything possible to assist. 'We are Catholics, Rod. We don't believe in divorce. Just be patient and give Jane some space and time,' he suggested.

I took him at his word and diligently stayed sober, attending AA meetings as often as possible. Jane brought the girls around to see me; she said she was proud of the fact that I was sober.

I lived in hope.

CHAPTER 56

BAYONETING THE WOUNDED

I lived each day hoping Jane and the girls would come home. Then one day, the phone rang.

'Rod, it's FiL. Do you have a ladder?'

'Yes, of course. What's up?'

'Can you meet me on the third tee at the golf club? I need you to bring the ladder.'

So off to the golf course I went, taking my mate Corey with me.

Arriving at the course, we were greeted by FiL, who showed us a tree littered with golf clubs. His driver was in the uppermost branches. The tree, an average-sized liquidambar, was without foliage as it was autumn.

I laughed and said, 'So, what happened here?'

'I hit a bad shot and meant to throw my driver down the fairway, but it came off the end of my thumb and landed in the tree. I threw all the other clubs trying to knock it down.'

'All eight of them? Well, you certainly are persistent. We don't need a ladder.' With that Corey boosted me into the lower branches. I steadily climbed the tree, dropping the clubs down to FiL as I got to each one. When I finally reached the driver I threw it over his head, and said, 'Sorry, mate. It came off the end of my thumb.' We all had a good old chuckle over that.

'Follow me round home. I've got something for you.'

'No, mate,' I said. 'I don't want anything.' (I should have added, 'Other than that family get-together you mentioned five months ago,' but I held my tongue.) 'I'm happy to help.'

'No, come round home. I insist.' He was speaking somewhat forcefully now.

So, I drove my truck around to his house, Corey beside me, and parked at the bottom of the steep driveway. A few minutes later, down the driveway he walked, a bottle of red wine in each hand. 'Here you go. Thanks for helping me.' He thrust the alcohol towards me. *What the fuck?*

'No, mate, I'm an alcoholic. I'm going to AA meetings. No alcohol for me.' I was stunned he had offered it to me, and further shocked when he insisted I take it.

'No, it's okay. It's just wine. Doctors say it's healthy to have a glass with your meals.'

'I don't want it.'

'Take it.' By now he was forcefully thrusting the bottles through the truck's window.

Corey reached across me, grabbed the two bottles out of my father-in-law's hands and said, 'Thanks, mate. I'll drink every drop.'

At the time, FiL's look of absolute disappointment didn't register with me. I was, frankly, in shock. But much later, probably twenty years on, the penny dropped when I was mowing a lawn around a tree with a very similar shape to the liquidambar I'd climbed all those years ago. It came to me in a flash: all the golf clubs I had retrieved on my way to his very expensive driver were old and worn. He had set the whole thing up so he could have me do him a favour, which he could then, rightfully, reward me for—with two bottles of booze which would break my sobriety, get me back on the grog and, hopefully, in his eyes, I surmised, result in his daughter abandoning all hope of reuniting us as a family. It's akin to bayoneting the wounded.

Jane didn't come back, my kids continued to live under their grandparents' roof, and I lost the hope I'd been hanging onto that Jane would see me as a changed man. I couldn't give a fuck about FiL, but I knew Dorothy—or Mother, as I called her—liked me. She was a beautiful woman and I'm glad my girls had her in their lives. However, the damage FiL did to us is incalculable.

I determined the only way to get Jane and our girls back home was to vacate the house on Elm Street. I informed Jane I was leaving town to go to Far North Queensland where I'd see if I could clear my head.

CHAPTER 57

THE SOUND OF TWO HEARTS CRACKING

My great mate Geoff Romero acted for me in tidying up the loose ends of our marriage. I agreed to sign over my interest in the house to Jane. I'd keep the truck and equipment and take the tax debt, and I would give support money when I could. Jane agreed to this, but I still had a matter of $12,000 outstanding to my creditors. Geoff asked FiL to help with this, as I was being more than generous and helpful in the terms of separating from Jane.

FiL contacted me and said I should go to each of my creditors and offer them 50 cents in the dollar. I did this and reported back to him that they had all accepted.

'If they will take 50 cents, they will take 25. Offer them that.'

I was incredulous, but only momentarily. I'd known for a long time he enjoyed humiliating people, so why would I be any exception?

'You know what? Go fuck yourself.'

I went to each creditor and told them what had happened. They all responded similarly: 'Mate, pay me when you can. FiL is well known for this type of behaviour.'

George B was the staunchest of them all, and he was also my biggest creditor with $6000 owing. He said, 'Rod, you are a good bloke. You've hit a rough patch. Don't worry about the money. Just go, and take care of yourself.' And he offered me his hand.

Some twenty-odd years later I called in to see George, after I'd been sober for several years, and I offered to pay him back through a regular bank payment. His response? 'Fuck off. Mate, I'm just so pleased to see you back on your feet. What you've done, getting sober, is so very rare. I'm delighted for you.' And now, whenever I bump into him, Georgie insists on telling anyone within shouting distance how his mate Rod got sober in AA and is a living marvel. (I've tried explaining to him the second 'A' in AA stands for 'Anonymous'. He doesn't listen.)

On the day of my departure in 1993, Jane brought the girls around to see me before taking them to school. It was all I could do not to bawl in front of them. Instead I smiled, held them tight and explained Daddy was going away for a long time. I told them I would write to them and ring them at every opportunity. I handed Laura a junior dictionary which had an adult bent to it. I said, 'Darling, I'm going to write to you the way we speak. I'll use big words the way we do now, but I won't be here to explain them to you; but you can look them up in this book. It's called a dictionary. And you can use it when you write back to me. And, Brigitte, your sister will help you read my letters, too. Won't you, my beautiful girl?'

'Yes, Dad, of course I will,' Laura replied. 'Where are you going? How long will you be away?' She was the most inquisitive child, and nothing has changed. Both my girls swallowed a thesaurus. The first big word I taught them was 'cooperation'. It was when they were fighting, as siblings do, and I had them sound it out and then spell it. At the time, I think Laura was about five years old and Brigitte three and a half.

I was just holding it together and Jane was choking up. Meanwhile, the ever-present FiL was hovering.

Dorothy drove the girls to school while Jane and I said our goodbyes. I don't think either of us wanted to part. I actually had to ask FiL if he would mind leaving the room so we could have some privacy.

Reluctantly, he retired to the front porch.

Jane sat on my lap and started to kiss me. Talk about confused; both of us.

Eventually we parted. I hopped into my truck and, driving north, my heart cracked in half.

CHAPTER 58

THE LONG AND WINDING ROAD TO NOWHERE

What a lonely ten months I had ahead of me without my girls. I started drinking again as soon as I left my family in the rear-view mirror. I wasn't capable of thinking straight and had no plan. I arrived in Cairns and shortly afterwards sold the truck and equipment for half its value. I needed the money to live.

I got a job selling real estate. Unfortunately I started just as a national pilots' strike began. Cairns, being completely reliant on tourism, was exactly the wrong place to be in any business, let alone selling houses.

I rented a flat in Clifton Beach, just a kilometre's walk along the beach to the snazzy little beach bar at Palm Cove. I'd do my day's futile labour at the office, then get home, change into shorts and a T-shirt and stroll to Palm Cove—like I was a man of leisure out to seize the moment whenever it arrived. I'd get a skin full then reel my way back to my decrepit digs. It was like living in heaven with hell ever-present.

It wasn't all bad, though. My luck held firm one night when I was exploring the coastline on foot. I'd crossed a stream that emerged from the dense bush and flowed across the sandy beach to join the Pacific Ocean. By the time I was on my way back, the stream had turned into a powerful, knee-high torrent, through which I trudged, emerging sopping wet. The following night, a German tourist followed the same path at the same time of night and was taken by a crocodile.

Someone up there was looking after me.

CHAPTER 59

HOW TO LOSE TEN KILOS IN TEN DAYS

I'd been away from Albury and my beautiful girls for close to a year. I couldn't bear not being with them for a second Christmas, but even though I was still working, it was commission only, so I was broke. What to do?

I saw an advertisement for a deckhand position on a prawn trawler. I had no experience in the caper, but when has that ever stopped me? I resigned from my real estate job and was immediately employed. We sailed from Cairns Harbour the following day: the skipper, the first mate and the deckhand (yours truly). I figured the ten days we were out would return me enough cash to buy a flight home.

I'd stayed in touch with Jane and my babies as often as I could. Working in an office I had a phone at my disposal and, although he must have been aware, my boss never questioned my phone calls home, nor did he ask me to pay for them. He was a truly decent bloke.

I'd call home and after speaking with Jane I'd ask for the girls. Without hesitation Jane would put them on. She only ever wanted us to have the best relationship. On to the phone would come a little voice: 'Hello, Daddy. Are you okay?'

'Yes, Laura-Lou, I'm fine, darling. What about you? What have you been up to?'

The conversation would go back and forth, before I said, 'Put your sister on please, darling.'

'Hello, Daddy. Are you coming home soon?'

And my heart would break a little bit more. Until the day I said: 'I'll be home in two weeks, darling. I can't wait to see you, Brigie Boo.'

The little voice at the other end of the phone would break into delighted laughter, and she would say: 'Got you again, Dad. This is Laura. Brigitte was on before.'

And I'd play the game and say, 'You pair of rascals. Just you wait till I get home.'

They imitated each other so well I often couldn't tell them apart.

Out into the wild blue yonder we chugged. For the next ten days I got out of my bunk four times every night, standing at the boat's stern to sort through a pile of dumped sea creatures under the soft glow of an overhead light. My job was to group the prawns into banana, tiger and whatever other types there were. I used a thin, stiff board about the dimensions of the book you are reading now.

The seafood was dumped from a net onto the waist-high table with a six-inch edge around the perimeter. A chute led from the table down to the trawler's rear port side. As I sorted the prawns I'd slide all other living things down the chute and back out to sea, where the trailing sharks and dolphins would gratefully accept the offerings. And it wasn't just fish that went back to Neptune: there were large turtles and manta rays, one of which decided to give birth while I was pushing it down the slide.

On one memorable occasion I was sorting away, pretty bloody quickly if I'm to tell the truth, the mate opposite me putting the prawns into their respective holds, when the mass of sea life in front of me started to move. I first saw the movement in my peripheral vision but quickly gave it my full attention. It happened in a split second. Out of the fish, eels and prawns emerged a sea snake as thick as my wrist. Its colours were so incredible—iridescent blues, pinks and purples—that I can still see it in my mind's eye today. And it had eyes only for my eyes. It reared up and struck with lightning speed, intending to bite me in the face. I moved faster, though. In a flash I brought my right hand up in a sweeping motion, the sorting board striking the snake in the neck, just below the head. And overboard it slid, down the chute.

The mate turned deathly white.

'Did it get you? Are you bitten?'

'No, mate, all good.' I went on sorting prawns.

It was at the end of the shift that both he and the skipper told me if the snake had bitten me I'd be dead. Even on land there was no antivenom that would work quickly enough to counter the sea snake's attack.

Prawns were all we ate for ten days. We boiled them in seawater taken directly from—where else?—the ocean. I've never eaten anything so tasty, and I still love a good feed of prawns. I did have trouble ridding myself of the waste, though. I couldn't take a crap for the first three days at sea. When I did finally use the onboard dunny I was in there for so long the skipper said, when I emerged, 'Fuck, mate. I thought the fucken thing musta corkscrewed ya to the ceiling.' Funny bugger, the skipper.

By the time we landed back in Cairns I was the most flexible I'd been for decades. I was ten kilograms lighter than when I'd boarded, and I could lay the flats of my palms on the deck beside my feet.

It was a tough way to get fit, though.

CHAPTER 60

HOME IS THE SAILOR, HOME FROM THE SEA

The day I arrived home, a good mate put me up. Jane brought Laura and Brigitte around to see me. As soon as I opened the door the girls leapt into my arms. I was overcome with joy which, in an instant, I turned into a cold stare when I looked up at Jane. The emotional, grudge-bearing cripple was alive and well. I knew she had started a new relationship and it ate at me.

If I could take back any moment in time, it would be that one. I was filthy on FiL and, rather than addressing that with him, I directed my hurt at my wife. I was emotionally shattered and should have considered what Jane had been through, too.

Things weren't great for our girls, either. While I'd been away, Brigitte had been showing lots of anger. She was only six and by nature a fun-loving little girl, sharp as a tack. And I realised Laura was suffering, too. My leaving so abruptly had left both of the girls feeling I had abandoned them.

And I had. Regardless of others' influence, that is my responsibility to carry to my grave.

A few days after I arrived home from Cairns, all four of us were sitting around the kitchen table at Elm Street when Jane mentioned in passing that my lawyer mate was in trouble.

'What kind of trouble?'

'He and his partner are being investigated over missing money from their firm's trust fund. Dad has a lot of money invested with them as well,' she said.

'I have to go round and see him,' I said, starting to rise from my chair.

'But Dad,' my brave and incisive older daughter said, 'you only just got home. Is he more important than us?'

'No, darling,' I replied. 'Nobody is more important to me than you and Brigitte.'

'Well, why are you leaving now?'

'Because, darling, he is my mate. He stuck by me when I was in trouble. Now I need to give him some support.'

'What trouble were you in?'

Well, there it was: the question I always knew was going to come up at some stage. I decided better the truth comes from me than her hearing a twisted version from one of her school friends, who would have heard it from their parents.

'Darling, a long time ago I broke the law. I sold some marijuana, and the police caught me. He stood by me. True friends stick by you no matter what you've done.'

'What happened next?'

Both girls' eyes were totally focused on me.

'I went to gaol, Laura.' And there it was, the secret out. Thank Christ. Her next question floored me.

'Did Mum know you were doing it?' All this from a kid of eight.

'No, darling, Mum didn't know.'

It's very important to state here that in the end the partner went to gaol and my mate was exonerated. No surprise to me.

It came to me again that I am the person my parents raised me to be, and the same is true for all of us. My parents explained to us kids the value of truth, and I'm sure Jane's mother explained the price of telling a lie.

The girls were quiet for a few moments before I asked if they were okay. Brigitte was the first to respond; like her sister she was also courageous, and direct, which I now understand showed her trust in me.

'Well, Dad, you left once—are you going to leave again?'

It was a fair enough question, I reckon.

'Darling, if I ever need to go away again, I will speak with you both and explain why. If you don't want me to leave I absolutely will not. Is that okay?'

'Yes, Dad. That's okay.'

In that moment I became a dad again. I took the girls for outings and we spent time together. We went to see *Free Willy* at the movies with the girls' two best friends. At the end of the film, when Willy the whale makes his dash for freedom and leaps over the breakwater into the open ocean, the whole theatre erupted in cheers. But I sat there with tears rolling down my cheeks, broken-hearted. As the lights came up, I couldn't get my hanky out of my pocket quickly enough before Brigitte saw the state I was in.

'Dad's crying!' she bellowed out, a big grin on her face.

Wiping my eyes I said, 'I'm just happy Willy is free, darling.' With that I blew my nose and wiped the tears from my face, not realising I was also wiping the last of a united family life away.

After only a short time back in Albury, I decided I simply couldn't stand to be around Jane while she was with her new beau, Brick.

On Melbourne Cup Day, I spent the day in nearby Corowa, catching the last bus back to Albury with the Blomeley boys,

Mick and John. There were only a few other people on board. John and I were standing in the aisle chatting away—probably about boxing, which we both loved watching together—when I noticed Jane and Brick sitting up the back. I hadn't seen them together before, and I was stunned. Jane was making out with Brick, who had obviously seen me and was doing his best to shrink out of sight. Johnny saw my gaze move over his shoulder, turned and surmised the situation in a blink. He gently but firmly took me by the shoulders and turned me around so I was now looking the other way.

When I think about kind acts others have done for me over the years, that simple one from John stands out. He later died of cancer, in his early sixties. The planet is short an incredibly good man.

That moment on the bus kept replaying in my mind every time I saw Jane with Brick. I soon realised that living in Albury and seeing them together would be intolerable.

Once I'd made up my mind to leave town, I was gone within three days.

Things weren't great between Jane and me, but she agreed that I could come around and speak with our girls before I left again. We sat outside on the front steps, me in the middle and my girls either side of me. Brigitte and Laura were both very tense.

Following advice my sister Chris had given me, I said: 'Girls, you know Mum and Dad love you both very, very much, but we realise now we don't love each other.' I paused. 'But that's not your fault.' And with those five simple words they both, in unison, relaxed into me.

I realised then that, in my immaturity, I'd not only allowed my father-in-law to come between my kids and me, then abandoned them, but I'd inadvertently allowed the girls to carry the blame for the break-up of our family unit for an entire year. How could I have been so insensitive?

I went on to explain to my daughters why I was leaving them again, so soon after I'd come back home.

'Girls, I can't see a future for me in Albury,' I said. 'I need to move to Melbourne and start working again. It's only a few hours away and I'll come back lots to see you. But I won't go if you don't want me to. How do you feel about that?'

Brigitte immediately piped up, 'That's okay, Dad,' and Laura said, 'I think you will be happier away from here, Dad, and we know you love us, so you should go. And we can come visit you in the holidays, can't we?' What a wise little soul she was.

'Of course you can, darling. There is so much to do in Melbourne. Thank you both so much for being with me on this.'

And I hugged them tightly, like I wanted the imprint of them on my heart.

Take my advice: avoid the pain of a broken marriage if you can possibly find a way. It's not just the marriage that gets broken, it's the family, their hearts, life itself.

CHAPTER 61

BACK TO THE BAR

Stony-broke, I caught the train south and headed to my mate Brian 'Wrecker' Leahy's pub, the Hydehurst, near St Kilda. It was a broken-down affair with a slim bar trade due mostly, I was to discover, to a gang of thug bank-robbers deciding to make it their local watering hole. Their trick was to give every new customer the evil eye. The head man tried it with me but, because of my association with Wrecker and another old mate, Mark 'Jack' Esler, he eased up on the intimidation routine.

When I walked in the door Wrecker, laconic as they come, said, 'Welcome to my castle, Roddy. What'll you have?'

'A middy thanks, Wreck, and a bed if you've one spare.'

Pouring the beer, he muttered, 'You're in Victoria now, son. Call them pots. You don't need these cunts to know you're from north of the border.' He gave a slight tip of the head to the five hard nuts sitting at the end of the bar; well, one hard nut and four hangers-on. One of them was an older, grubby bloke who looked like he could have been the leader's father.

Out of the blue and without any warning, Grub backhanded the young bloke sitting on the stool next to him. He hit him so hard across the side of the head that he came off his stool and landed half a metre away, his nose bleeding and a massive red welt growing deeper by the second on the side of his face. I made a move to come off my stool, but Wrecker gave me a look and I eased back down. The other three men didn't blink. As I came to know them through observation over the next two months, I understood this kind of behaviour was to show other patrons who ran the joint.

Wrecker was a bloody tough bloke himself—he played in a VFL premiership for Melbourne in 1960 at age eighteen—but he was well past his prime, and recognised this particular gang leader as a psychopath quite capable of killing. This left him in a tough position. His pub had a TAB licence, and his location was ideal for the St Kilda and Prahran lunch trade, but his hands were tied because of this gang of arsewipes driving potential customers away. I offered to speak with my contacts in Sydney but he wouldn't have a bar of it.

I turned back to Wrecker as he started speaking again. 'It's your lucky day, my son,' he told me. 'The bloke in Room Four overdosed last night. He's brown bread so the room's yours if you want it. Best outlook in this fine establishment, as it happens.'

Room Four became home for the next few months. Next thing needed was work, so I went back to what I knew best: bar work. Wrecker suggested I try South Melbourne as that's where the Grand Prix action was, and the race was only a month away.

I walked across Albert Park, around the lake and down Clarendon Street. The second pub I walked into was the Emerald Hotel, owned by the Lewis family. I asked for the boss and was introduced to Gerry Lewis. He introduced me to his son Andy and, bingo, I had a job. They were terrific people to work for. Their head barman, Russell, and I became pretty tight, both loving a laugh.

One night, when the bar was packed during Grand Prix time, Rusty came bursting into the main bar from the street where he'd been collecting empty glasses. He yelled to the young casual washing glasses behind the bar. 'Duncan, for fuck's sake, Duncan, get on the phone and ring the RSPCA. A cat has been hit by a car. *Now*, mate, do it now!'

Young Duncan—private-school educated, the son of a family friend, heading off to uni to study archaeology or arseholes or some bloody thing now his schooling was complete—was infected with the panic Rusty had so cunningly roused. 'What do I say?' the patsy pleaded as he searched the phone book for 'RSPCA'.

'Get the RSPCA on the line, tell them a cat has been run over in Clarendon Street, and tell them we need a pussy stretcher. And we need it now!' His tone further added to the callow youth's panic.

There must have been a hundred people in the bar. Every single one of them went silent as a mouse, waiting. Straining to hear our man, Duncan, in his big moment.

'Hello, is that the RSPCA? A cat's been hit. *We need a pussy stretcher!* Sorry for yelling. We need a pussy stretcher to the Emerald Hotel. Sorry? I'm not being rude. Hello? Hello?' Turning to Russell, he said with a quizzical look, 'They hung up on me.'

The bar erupted, and I mean *erupted*, in howls of laughter.

'What's so funny?' Duncan asked.

Gerry, wiping tears from his eyes, responded, 'It's all right, son, I'll explain later. Just go back to washing glasses.'

The Emerald was like that. A lot of fun to work at.

CHAPTER 62

MY TRUE CALLING

I was enjoying my time at the Emerald but I needed more income. One day I responded to an ad for telephone workers at a company on St Kilda Road, halfway between the Hydehurst and the Emerald. The hours suited me, being 6 p.m. to 9 p.m. Monday to Friday with Saturday morning work available to the highest earners. The task was to cold call householders, engage them in conversation and sell them raffle ticket books for organisations such as The Blind Leading the Blind, Riding for the Disabled and Seeing Eye Homing Dogs for Drunks. (I made that last one up. The first one, too.)

There were a hundred people working the phones, crammed in like bunnies in a warren. The guy next to me used a pseudonym so I thought I'd do the same. His pitch was: 'Hello Mrs Thomas, it's Yellow here, Yellow Marker from Riding for the Disabled. How are you this beautiful evening?'

I liked Yellow's approach, so I decided to go with, 'Hello Mrs Thomas, this is Sunny here, Sunny Climes calling on behalf of Riding for the Disabled. Do you have a moment for me, please?'

It worked a treat. I got the occasional rebuff, sometimes quite strongly; but by and large my sales instincts kicked in and my bloodlines benefited me. We were measured on how many raffle ticket books we got out in a shift, and how many came back with payment. I was always in the top three of both categories, and therefore one of the top earners. That got me the right to work Saturdays, where we picked up a higher commission. We were also calling at a more acceptable hour, so the targets were more receptive, ergo the returns higher. But not every call was friendly.

One morning I rang a number and the woman of the house answered. I launched into my pitch: 'Hello, Mrs Leathernuts, how are you this glorious—' She cut me short.

'I don't know who you are or what you're selling, but you can piss off right now, you arsehole. I'm sick and tired of you mongrels calling looking for money. DO I make myself clear, prick?' And she hung up. Frankly, I was appalled—not just at her tone but the language she used! I went into a state of shock, which lasted a full three seconds before a plan formulated in my mind.

An hour later I gathered a few of my co-workers and, asking for complete silence, I rang Mrs Leathernuts back. I put her on speaker.

'Hello, who is this?' she answered in a deep, threatening tone. 'I am so sick and tired of—'

'Hello, Mrs Leathernuts? This is Sergeant Jackson from St Kilda police station. I want you to listen very carefully to me now, Mrs Leathernuts. Your life may depend on your next actions.' I said all of this in a deep, gruff voice, getting quieter as I spoke. By the time I finished I was talking in a whisper. Mrs Leathernuts, now docile as a lamb, responded in a high-pitched whisper bordering on panic.

'What do you want me to do, Sergeant?'

'Go to the window. Tiptoe now, don't make a sound. Have you got blinds or curtains, dear? Come on now, answer up, blinds or—'

'Curtains, I've got curtains!' she said in a strangled, sobbing whisper. 'What is it, Sergeant? Am I in danger?'

'I'm afraid you may be, Mrs Leathernuts, but not if you do *exactly* as I direct you to do. Alright?'

'Yes, Sergeant, anything you say.'

'Right! Now, there is a lunatic in your street with a high-powered rifle. He could shoot you from 100 metres away. So I want you to ever so gently, *gently now,* pull the curtains back a tiny bit and see if you can spot the lunatic outside. He could be on the street or he could be right outside your window. Do it *now*, Mrs Leathernuts, then come back to the phone and tell me what you see.'

The members of my audience were, by this time, rolling around on the floor holding themselves together, hands over mouths. One less controlled individual had to run to the toilet from where muffled howls of laughter emanated.

'I'm back, Sergeant,' came a whisper from the phone. 'I couldn't see the lunatic. I couldn't see anyone. What do I do now? I'm terrified.'

'Don't worry about terrified, Mrs Leatherjacket—'

'Leathernuts.'

'Yes, Leathernuts.' Another of the audience members ran for the dunny. 'You have every right to be terrified. If this crazed gunman gets into your house, God knows what horrors he might perpetrate on your person before he shoots you.'

Hearing sobbing from the other end of the blower, the thought flitted across my mind, *Am I going too far with this? Nah.*

'So what I want you to do, Mrs Leathernuts, is tiptoe over to the window every fifteen minutes. If you see anything out of place, such as a body in the street or the gunman himself, I want you to ring St Kilda police station and ask for me, Sergeant Jackson. Okay?'

After a sniffle and a sharp intake of breath, she said, 'Alright, Sergeant, if I see anything I'll call you immediately.'

'Good woman, Mrs Leathernuts. But absolutely do not call unless you have something concrete to report. There may be a bravery medal in this for you, madam. Just keep checking the window, and easy with the curtain, okay? I have to go now.' I had to hang up quickly; I couldn't hold myself together any longer.

I've often wondered how long she went back and forth to the window before reality intruded. Who fucken cares? Rude bitch.

We all had plenty of interesting conversations, but the nasty responses were the ones that stuck in our memories. When we finished work, a hardened few of us would often go out for a drink. Which is what we did one night, after I'd received a particularly nasty response from a bloke I called.

'Hello.' It was a terse greeting, but I launched into my spiel nonetheless.

'Hello Mr—'

'Listen, arsehole. I don't know who you are or what fucken organisation you are ringing up for. I'm not interested. Got that, cunt? Now fuck right off and don't ever call this number again.' The line went dead.

That's a bit rude, I thought to myself. *Best note Mr Grumpy's number down*. Which I did, and I took it with me when we retired for a drink at 9 p.m. A couple of hours into drinks I asked one of the girls to call the number from the phone at the pub. I gave her a rough script to follow.

'Who is this? Do you know what time it is?' Grumpy asked as he picked up the phone.

'Sorry, mate. Can I speak to Barry, please?'

'There's no Barry here, love,' Grumpy said. 'You've got a wrong number.'

'Well, when he gets in would you tell him Sally called and I'll see him tomorrow? Thanks.' She quickly hung up.

Midnight rolled around and one of the lads made the next call.

'Fuck me, *what*?'

'G'day, cobber, is Barry there?'

'For fuck's sake, there is *no Barry here*. This the second—'

'Let him know Crackers called. I'll meet him at the footy. See ya.'

Fifteen minutes later, another co-worker called Grumpy and received the same pissed-off response.

I gave him time to get to sleep. No doubt he lay in bed, a tense ball of muscle, waiting for the phone to ring again. I let him slumber for an hour or so, then around 2 a.m. I called.

'Fuck me, what at *this* hour?'

'Hey, champ. Barry here. Any messages?'

There is simply no excuse for rudeness. Not even under the most trying of circumstances.

CHAPTER 63
GOTCHA, FRANK

Alone and carrying a heavy heart, I had been drinking heavily. The only way I could deal with the pain I felt due to the separation from my wife and two babies was to dull my thinking with booze. Working nights got in the way of my drinking, so I changed jobs.

I changed my accommodation, too. I'd been wanting to get out of the pub since I arrived there, but could never save enough money to pay a bond and the first month's rent. The catalyst for change happened one morning when I walked into the shared bathroom, pulled back the shower curtain and saw a huge turd winking at me from the middle of the shower floor. Jesus. I've got a strong stomach but that had me over the porcelain bowl in a flash, emptying my stomach, tears rolling down my cheeks and thoughts galloping through my mind. *What the fuck am I doing? My kids miss me. My kids need me. But not the way I am. I have to change.*

So I did. I stopped drinking and smoking. I saved like fury and within two weeks I had enough to rent a two-bedroom apartment in a block on St Kilda Road. It was just a stroll from the offices of Radio 3AK, which also housed the Variety Club Special Children's Christmas Party—where I worked my next telephone job.

The gig involved working with a dozen other 'blowers', calling up businesses that had contributed to the event in the past. We asked for $200 to support one special child, 'so they too can enjoy Christmas, just like your kiddies, Mr Smith'. We earned 10 per cent of what we raised. Basically, I needed to get donations for ten kids per day to make $200, which, back in the nineties, was very good money.

The 'special children' got to attend a Christmas party at the Melbourne Convention and Exhibition Centre—Jeff's Shed—at which they would get lots of lollies, ice-cream and, yes, Mr Smith, presents. Big, colourful presents worth, wait for it, Mr Smith, $120 per child. Of course, there were costs that took up the remainder of the $200 but, Mr Smith, to show our deep regard for your generosity, we will mention your business twice on Radio 3AK. So, Mr Smith, how many of our special kiddies' faces would you like to put a joyous smile on? Two, three? Tell me when to stop. Four, five?

'Okay, stop,' Mr Smith would invariably say. 'I'll sponsor two kids this year. So that'll set me back $400. Correct?'

'Yep. And all tax deductible!'

Another $40 went into my pocket. *That'll cover the booze tonight*, I thought.

Yep, I was back on it already. I didn't want to be. It was as though an invisible hand took me by the elbow and steered me left towards the Emerald instead of right towards my unit when I exited the 3AK building. I actually had no control over my drinking. I realise there are scoffers out there who will be muttering, 'Grow a spine, show some control'; but equally there are alcoholics and some family members of alcoholics who understand the power of alcohol addiction; the siren call of oblivion.

As much as I missed my family, and suffered a constant, deep and abiding pain, I simply couldn't pull myself out of the spiral of losing myself in the bottle. It was the only way I could live with the self-hatred I had for abandoning my family: my beautiful baby girls and the love of my life. What sane person would choose booze over blood?

I upped the ante at work. Hitting up previous donors for one or two kids was easy, but didn't put enough of the folding in my pocket. So, after considering where the big money was, I decided to open up new territory and began calling stockbroking firms, banks, law and accountancy firms and other big businesses. Getting through to the decision-maker was the challenge; it was that aspect of the job I enjoyed most.

Whenever the secretary who answered the phone asked why I wanted to speak with the CEO or MD, rather than take the standard approach—'That's something I'll explain to Mr Bloggs'—I'd launch into a long, technical, jargon-filled explanation. 'Ah, good question, Mary. I've got the figures here that Bill will need to make a decision on the outlay towards the Variety Club's annual event dealing with the numbers of kids your company is sponsoring for the Special Children's . . .' I could hear Mary's eyes spinning as she tried to keep up, and of course my language implied the company was already involved in this—what was it? A variety of needy kids? Not to mention, I called Mr Bloggs by his first name so I must know him. 'One moment please,' Mary would say. 'I'll put you through.'

'Bill Bloggs here.'

'G'day Bill, Rod Halsted here, mate, from the Variety Club of Australia. I'm trying to get some of Melbourne's special needs kids to a Christmas party and I was hoping you might like to get involved. But Bill, if this is an imposition, I'll hang up now . . .'

Rarely did they ask me to hang up. Who calls up out of the blue, gives a brief spiel then says they will drop off? No one. The trick with telephone sales is to be respectful, honest and, most importantly, funny.

There would usually be a brief pause, then: 'No, that's okay, Rod. Tell me more.'

And away I'd go, always finishing with, 'So Bill, how many kids do you personally want to be Santa Claus to this year? Apart from your own family, I mean—who, by the way, we encourage you to bring along on the day.'

'So we can come to see the kids enjoy themselves? My own kids included? And maybe some of my staff?'

'My oath, Bill. Think about the positive effect on those you bring along. And I'm not talking about how they will view you; I know that's not why you're doing this. It's about giving, mate, about sharing, about showing your own kids and staff what the true spirit of Christmas is really about. So, Bill, the crunch question is, how many kids' faces do you reckon your firm can put a big grin on? Ten, twenty? Fifty?'

'So how much to sponsor a child? You didn't say.'

'Two hundred bucks, mate. And we need all the help we can get.'

Then I'd stop talking. Say nothing. Wait.

'So to sponsor ten kids will cost us two grand?'

'Yep, and that's all tax deductible. And if you can manage more than ten, I'll organise it so your kids can hand some presents out. Could you see your way clear to sending twenty or even 50 kids to the party, Bill?'

'Fifty may be over our budget, but we can manage, say, 35? How's that?'

'Mate, that is so bloody generous of you. Thank you so much. I'll get the paperwork to you if you put me back to Mary. I know you are busy. And Bill?'

'Yes, Rod?'

'Why don't you bring Mary along on the day? She's got a tough job fielding calls from buggers like me. She sounds like a lovely girl.'

'Thanks, Rod, I'll do that, and I'll bring my two kids along as well.'

'Find me on the day, mate, I want to shake your hand. And I'll organise for your two kids to hand presents out. What are their names?'

'Jim and Sally. I look forward to meeting you too. Keep up the good work, Rod.'

I'd put $700 into the old skyrocket and Bill, Jim, Sally and Mary into my little black book so I'd be fully prepared on the day of the party. There is nothing like remembering someone's name to get them onside and have them sponsor again next year. Remember their kids' names and you'll be invited to their home for Christmas lunch.

It was this approach that put me in contact with Frank Dunphy from Colonial Stockbroking, one of the first firms I called. By the time I finally got Dunphy on the phone, Colonial was one of the last firms I had an answer from. My usual approach to get to the decision-maker worked in all cases except for Colonial. Each time I rang, his secretary would answer the phone.

'Hello, Colonial Stockbroking, how may I help you?'

'G'day Sheryl, it's Rod Halsted again from the Variety Club Special Children's Christmas Party. How's my timing today? Is Frank available for a word, please?'

Each time I'd hear Dunphy in the background: 'Tell him I'm out.'

This happened four or five times. Enough. At 5.30 p.m. on a Friday, when I thought the secretary would have left, I called again, hoping the boss would answer. Sure enough:

'Hello, Dunphy here.'

'Gotcha!' I said, triumphant and jocular. We both burst out laughing.

'You are the most persistent fucker I've ever come across, Halsted.'

'How did you know it was me?'

'Who the fuck else would it be late on a Friday?' my quarry said. 'What are you doing right now?'

'Having a beer with you, I suspect. And finalising how many kids you are sponsoring. Ten, twenty, tell me when to stop . . .'

'Stop. I'll give you four grand; that's twenty kids, right?'

'Yep. Now, where's your watering hole? The paperwork can wait till Monday.'

And so was born an unlikely but enduring friendship.

CHAPTER 64

THAT'S NOT A BUNGALOW, THAT'S A GARAGE

In 1997, the Variety Club Special Children's Christmas Party moved offices, well away from South Melbourne, so I moved from my St Kilda Road apartment to a boarding house in Camberwell. It was owned and run by a widow, who had bought the worst house in the best street of one of Melbourne's top suburbs. She was obviously struggling financially after the death of her husband, so had rented out every room in the large two-storey house to alcoholics. All the bedrooms were taken, so she showed me to the 'bungalow' that I'd seen advertised. It was quite obviously a garage, not a bungalow, but, because it had a square of carpet on the concrete floor, and an ironing board and iron, I went along with the lie.

I was still calling the girls daily, and visiting occasionally when I could get a ride back to Albury. But I was miserable. I missed family life so much. Having grown up with five siblings and parents who were loving and humorous I simply couldn't reconcile how I had ended up living in a garage in Melbourne, alone and drinking myself to death.

Jane was great as far as my access to the girls went. I suggested she bring them down so I could show them where I lived—in a bungalow, by a pool, in a garden.

The minute they stepped out of the car I realised what an error I had made. To get to the 'bungalow' we had to wade through knee-high grass and past the pool, which was covered by a slimy green scum.

My bright eleven-year-old Laura asked, 'Where's your bungalow, Dad?'

'There it is, darling,' I said, pointing at the grubby white structure surrounded by weeds.

She gave it the once-over and stated, 'That's not a bungalow, Dad. That's a garage.'

I'd never felt so humiliated in my life. I rushed them from the property and tried to get them back into Jane's car as quickly as possible.

'Wait! I left my new wallet on the back steps. I'll go back and get it,' Laura said.

I went with her. When we arrived at the steps, the wallet was gone. One of the low-life drunks from inside the house had taken it.

'That cost me $10, and it had another $10 in it!' Laura cried.

I brushed it off. 'We'll get you another one, darling, exactly the same.'

I had $40 in my pocket. I could have handed her the $20 replacement money right then, but I didn't. I needed the $40 for booze.

CHAPTER 65

BACK TO THE EMERALD CITY

No matter how much money I made in commissions, I spent all of it on rent and alcohol. I couldn't stop drinking. I needed a circuit breaker. The Variety Club had an office in Sydney, so I asked for a transfer.

Surely a change of scenery would help me turn my life around? Back then, I didn't understand the concept of 'wherever you go, there you are': the alcoholic geographical. Of course, nothing changed in Sydney. I drank just as heavily, simply in a different location: this time the Blues Point Hotel in McMahons Point. I'd scraped together enough to rent a unit in a waterfront block just down the road. It had a pool abutting the harbour and a view to Luna Park, the Harbour Bridge and the Opera House. I figured I needed something a little more upmarket than my Camberwell bungalow to show Laura and Brigitte. It was a high-end area for a low-life drunk; a bit like putting lipstick on a pig.

And when they saw it, they were impressed. However, when you are in active alcoholism, it really doesn't matter whether you are living in the penthouse or the outhouse: if you're blind drunk, there is zero point to having a scenic view in front of you. Drunks don't look outward, but inward. And they always look back to the dark past, not being able to envisage a brighter future.

Still, I was back in Sin City, and of all the places I'd lived, it was my most preferred.

It wasn't long before I heard my old Hawthornden friends Al and his wife, my dear friend Lesley, were back from the US and living in Vaucluse. I made contact and they were as happy to hear from me as I was to be in touch with them. Al asked me to meet them at Milsons Point Wharf the following Saturday for lunch.

I was standing on the wharf, only a ten-minute stroll from my unit, at the appointed hour when I heard a robust female voice behind me. 'Ahoy, Rod!' I turned to see a beaming, mid-teens girl beckoning to me from the deck of a very impressive Halvorsen motor cruiser. Ginnie, Al and Lesley's middle child, reached out her hand and welcomed me with an enthusiastic, 'Welcome aboard, matey!' The massive grin never left her face. Behind her I could see Lesley and Al, at the vessel's controls.

I got a big hug from Les and a strong handshake from Al and off we went, cruising across a sun-drenched Sydney Harbour and into Darling Harbour. Our destination turned out to be one of Sydney's finest seafood restaurants. Our roles were reversed from the Hawthornden hippy days, when I had plenty of money and Al was often broke. He had hit the big time on Wall Street and was delighted to be able to share with me.

Lesley and I drank at lunch but, to my surprise, Al didn't. I genuinely believe this was the day hope entered my life: hope for a turnaround in my thinking. I had no idea then that such a pivotal moment was taking place, but that's what happened on that beautiful, sunny Sydney day.

CHAPTER 66

WASH YOUR HAND, POS

After a short stint in the Special Children's Christmas Party Parramatta office I parted ways with the Variety Club. I didn't like the bloke who ran the show, and I questioned his ethics. I received a payout and went looking for a job—working the phones, preferably.

I applied and was given a date and time for interview with a mob named IPI.

The IPI offices were on the first floor of a building on Chalmers Street, on the eastern side of Central station. When I exited the lift, I was greeted by a severe, older woman seated at a desk opposite. She turned out to be the boss's firewall. Her name was Helen.

'Wait here while I see if Mr Farrington is ready to see you,' she barked.

I gazed around the office and saw it was comprised of partitions, each with a desk and chair, and sound-baffle walls either side rising above head height. Most of the booths were occupied. As it turned out there were more than 40 reps working the phones: 30 of them in this office and another ten from external locations as far afield as Brisbane and Melbourne.

Helen marched me towards the only glassed-in area in the entire space, inside of which sat a very upright bloke with tight, curly, greying hair. He was dressed in a coat and tie; everyone else that I'd glanced at was dressed in casual jeans and shirts or even shorts and singlets. I hadn't seen any women working the phones, but there were three or four young girls performing secretarial duties. They seemed to be overseen by a slightly older woman who I later learnt was named Natalie. She was a terrific scout, as it turned out.

I arrived at the office door and was met with a slight smile—not warm, but not threatening, either—from a lanky guy, probably 190 centimetres tall. He stood and extended a rather large hand.

'Richard Farrington,' he said in an upper-class British accent.

'Rod Halsted, Richard. Very pleased to meet you.' I gave him a warm smile and a strong handshake, never breaking eye contact. I saw his opinion of me in his eyes, in the way he first assessed me, then softened as I shook his hand and looked him in the eye. Respect. Got him. He motioned for me to sit down.

'Well, Rod, tell me: why should I employ you?'

'Well, Richard, if you are looking for an "order taker" you shouldn't. But if it's a fearless, hardworking bloke you're after, someone who knows how to close and equally knows when no is no and moves on to the next target, that's me. If you are looking for persistence, good humour and someone who is a team player, you'd be a mug to pass me up.' I waited a beat, gave him a grin and said, 'Not a bad pitch, was it?'

We both laughed.

'You're hired. Jolly good pitch, Rod. Are you at all interested in what it is we are selling?'

'It doesn't really matter, Richard. I like you, you like me, but hey, why not tell me anyway?'

'I must say, Rod, this is one of the more interesting job interviews I've conducted,' he chuckled. 'Righto. IPI represents a few dozen business information publishers from around the world—most from England, America and Australia. Those publications come in the form of newsletters and special reports on diverse subjects such as “Oil & Gas in the Caspian Sea”, “3G Mobile in Singapore” and “Logging in Brazil”. Our clients are companies and individuals who benefit from up-to-the-minute knowledge in those and many other areas—people such as stockbrokers, bankers, investors and the like. The material is delivered by hard copy or through the internet. Are you familiar with the internet?’

‘Not this morning, Richard, but give me until this arvo and I shall give you a rundown on it.’ It was cheeky, but accurate. I learn quickly.

‘Jolly good. Call me RF. Pronounced *Rouf.* We have a number of traditions here, Rod. One is that new chaps come to a welcome lunch with me on the first available Saturday. That happens to be tomorrow. Meet me out the front of the office at 11.30 a.m. sharp, would you? Dress decently, old chap. We always go upmarket. Welcome to the IPI family.’ And with that he stood and offered me his hand.

The next morning I was standing in the appointed spot with two other new guys when a sparkling, older Rolls-Royce pulled up, with RF behind the wheel. ‘Hop in, chaps!’ he instructed us.

We headed to Catalina restaurant at Rose Bay. In a previous lifetime it was the Caprice Restaurant and Nightclub and had been the scene of a dive into the water I’d taken for a bet one night in the seventies when I ran out of money. I’d left my cowboy boots and jocks on and handed my clothes to Popeye to hold. When I surfaced, somehow avoiding the underwater pylons and therefore certain paraplegia, and swam to the private dock—federal property, as it turned out, patrolled by an armed guard—my jocks had gone but I still had my boots on. The guard took one look at me, shook his head and unlocked the gate so

I could return to the Caprice. Popeye threw my clothes to me from the balcony, and I wandered in through the front door, somewhat perplexing the doorman.

I figured twenty years had passed and surely none of the Caprice staff would be at Catalina to remember me, which left me comfortable that I wouldn't be outed to RF as the idiot naked diver from the past.

The four of us enjoyed a slap-up lunch with plenty of booze, and I was never so grateful for my upbringing. While the other two new boys broke every dining regulation in the book, eating with their mouths open, using incorrect knives and forks and the like, I matched RF's excellent table manners.

Body language or a slight glance convey far more meaning than mere words—and I knew by the time we exited the restaurant that RF and I were going to get on famously. As we approached the car, one of the other lads made a dash for the front seat only to hear RF say, 'No, Barry, that's Rod's seat.'

Ah, the thrill of courtship, the exhilaration of victory—and I hadn't even made a call yet.

The following Monday I was shown to my cubicle and then invited to the Monday meeting, where the three new chaps were introduced to the old hands. Each employee was designated a 'company name', which was their initials with a vowel inserted in between—all except Richard, who remained RF. Peter S, the top-dog salesman, was POS, Dennis S was DOS, George D was GUD, Ray S was RAS, and so forth. I became RAH.

It was an exciting job, working commission only with bonuses available if we met certain targets. I took to it like a duck to water. My time listening to my old man on the phone at home, seeing him in action at the Gunnedah saleyards, going out with him as a boy when he visited farmers and charmed them, and listening to his advice to 'always talk the other man's language' all helped. My time dealing dope, reading body language, assessing people by listening to changes in their voice and inflections over the phone, negotiating the zoo that gaol was, relying on my selling skills to make my landscape business successful, then coming to phone work via the ticket placement job and the Variety Club—all of it had prepared me for this, the toughest sales gig available.

The job involved cold-calling busy executives around the world, navigating past their tenacious secretaries, getting their attention in the first ten seconds then holding it so I could get my pitch out. It isn't everybody's idea of a fun way to make a living, but I thrived on it.

I quickly realised the decision to buy or not is made during the fifth call. It's much the same as letterbox pamphlet delivery. The first pamphlet is delivered on a Monday and gets thrown in the bin after a quick glance; the second is delivered the following Tuesday and gets their attention, but still goes to the bin; the third is delivered eight days later and gets a full read, then sits on the bench for a week and goes in the bin; the fourth is where they recognise the business name, and it often finds its way under a fridge magnet; and the fifth, delivered on a Friday, prompts the family to discuss the offer over the weekend and call the company on the following Monday.

It was much like taking on an institution over a bill, too. It's the fifth letter you write that incites the response: 'We admit no liability, but you don't have to pay the charges,' or, more succinctly, 'Fuck off, you are too costly to continue to correspond with.' That said, it wasn't unheard of for me to get the sale on the second, or even first, call.

My aim was always to make them laugh in the first ten seconds, whether they were in the UK, the UAE or the US. With the Yanks I'd often open in the broadest Aussie accent I could manage: 'G'day Hank, its Rod here from Australia. How ya goin' t'day?'

'Rad from Austria, did you say?' I'd hear puzzlement and curiosity fighting with his urge to hang up.

'Nah mate, Rod, that's R-O-D, from Australia. You know, Down Under. Ah geez, hang on a minute, will ya?' I'd leave the line clear for ten or so seconds, then: 'Sorry, cobber, I'm back. I rode me kangaroo to work and the bloody thing got loose.'

Incredulity won out: 'You rode a kangaroo to work? Really?'

'Nah Hank, just pulling your leg, mate. I left the roo at home today. No, the reason I called you today—by the way, it's midnight here in Sydney. What time is it in New York?' I knew full well it was 10 a.m. and Hank was comfortable in his chair with a coffee in front of him.

'It's ten in the morning, Rod. You're working at midnight? Really? What are you selling?'

Ah, the magic question. I had his attention; and I *never* replied, 'I'm not selling anything' or 'I'm selling success' or any of those trite lines. My reply, almost without exception, was, 'I'm selling knowledge in your area of expertise, Hank,' and then shut the fuck up. Let it become a conversation. I'd also use his name as often as he used mine.

'What exactly does that mean, Rod?'

'Well, Hank,' I'd say. 'If my detective work is correct, you head up the research department for ABN AMRO in oil and gas, and possibly mining. Am I correct in that?'

'Yep, that's correct. How did you know that?'

'I read about you in a newsletter my company places subscriptions with to interested parties. Usually stockbrokers and investors. It was a publication called "Oil and Gas in the Caspian Sea". Are you familiar with it?'

'A buddy of mine mentioned something about that publication some time back. Are you able to send me a copy? I'm happy to pay for it.'

'Yeah mate, happy to, no cost. Let me have your email and I'll shoot off the issue I'm referring to and a couple of others in the same area of interest, if you like. Do you—'

'Absolutely, Rod, this is my email address. Would you get that to me ASAP, please?'

'Sure thing, Hank, I'll do it now. And I'll send the subscription cost and so on as well. I can tell you now the annual costs of these publications is usually around the grand mark, but let's talk about that tomorrow. I'll call you back at 10 a.m. your time, sharp. How's that sound, cobber?'

'Sure thing, Rod. By the way, what is this copper you called me?'

'It's "cobber", Hank. Same as "buddy". Friends use it to address each other here in Australia. Same as "mate".'

'Okay, cobber, I'll hear from you tomorrow.'

Sold.

The job was exciting to me; a bit like dealing dope. The rewards weren't as big as ganga, but the thrill of the chase felt very similar.

It was late on a Friday, and there were lots of people milling around the office. Our quarterly 'do' was on that night, and the out-of-towners and those working from home, such as POM and RIP, had arrived, and were enjoying a beer while a couple of us were finishing up. That week I'd made a sale into each of Africa, Europe, America and Australia, and I was currently on the phone closing a client in Asia. There were probably twenty reps standing around my desk, totally silent, waiting to hear if I'd achieve what I wanted.

'So I can take that as a firm order, Wun Hung Lo? Excellent, I'll have my secretary send the paperwork through now. And Wun Hung Lo, thank you for your business, it is appreciated.' I hung up the phone to raucous cheers.

'Chaps, chaps!' RF said. 'I want you all to know that RAH has done what no other rep has been able to achieve: made a sale into each of five continents in the same week. It's rare air, lads.'

They all congratulated me in their own way, besides POS. He was top dog, and took it as a personal challenge as well as an insult that RF had lavished praise on the new boy while he remained in the background.

Poor old POS: driven by ego, suffering low self-esteem. If only he knew I was in the same boat.

I did take the piss out of him during one Monday meeting when, in answer to RF's question about training a newcomer, he replied:

'Give me five minutes with him, RF, and I'd have him in the palm of my hand.'

To which I quickly retorted: 'If not him, then certainly yourself, POS.'

Cue outbursts of laughter all round.

CHAPTER 67

PUT THE MINISTER ON, PLEASE

One day, one of the better-earning co-workers, MOH, issued me a challenge. 'You reckon you're pretty hot on the blower, don't you, RAH?' he said. 'If you're so good, get a government minister on the line.'

'What government?'

'Fuck, I don't care. Sweden.'

'Which ministry?'

'Smart cunt! Defence.'

'$20?'

'You're on.'

Three minutes later I was talking to Admiral Dick Bjornson, Swedish Minister for Defence.

MOH had taught me how to use a computer to research, well, anything. At the time I started at IPI, there was only one computer. It was available to anyone to use, but only MOH saw the benefit. He was a visionary. Everyone else was relying on renewals and researching via the newsletters. I asked him one day to show me how the computer worked.

'Sure,' he replied. 'Sit in this chair. See that key on the keypad? Hit it and that turns the computer on.' And with that, he turned and walked away.

That was my first and only lesson in computers and how to use the internet, but I learnt quickly. It wasn't long before RF could see the benefit and put a computer terminal on every desk.

On the day MOH issued his challenge, I looked up the general number of the Swedish Defence Ministry, called it and waited for an answer. I had absolutely no idea what I was going to say. I'd learnt long ago not to rehearse. You don't want your opening spiel to come out sounding like a script.

'Hulloo, Svedish Defence Ministry, how may I direct your call?'

'Put me through to the library, please,' I answered.

'Hulloo, library here.'

'Library? What the hell am I doing talking to the library? I'm calling the minister from Australia.'

'Oh, I'm so sorry, sir. One moment.'

I waited briefly on the line before a baritone voice spoke.

'Bjornson here.'

'Bjornson?' I asked. 'What's your role in the operation?'

'I am Admiral Dick Bjornson, Minister for Defence in the Svedish Government. Who am I speaking with, please?'

I stood up and saluted.

'Rod Halsted here, sir, from Australia.'

Bjornson lowered his voice as he spoke to the people in his office: 'You will have to leave the room now, I have a very important call from Australia.' Then to me: 'How can I help you, Rod?'

And away I went, charming him, very briefly explaining IPI's service, mentioning I didn't expect him to look at our service but he was the person best placed to direct me. I found common ground, mentioning that my dad served in the Royal Australian Navy during the war, and that was it. We were best mates. We spoke for twenty minutes; he gave me a name and number to call in the ministry; and the call ended with him saying:

'Call me any time you like, Rod. And if you ever come to Sweden, let me know. I will send a car to the airport for you.'

'Thank you for your time, sir; it was a delight chatting with you.' Then, after hanging up the call, I turned to MOH. 'And thank you very much, MOH; it was a delight taking twenty off you.'

MOH paid willingly. 'It was worth it. Every dollar.'

CHAPTER 68

I CAN'T STOP

One Saturday lunchtime, not long before I gave up the grog, I was at my local pub, the Blues Point. I'd been drinking for a couple of hours, which was simply a top-up from the night before, so I was feeling no pain—those regular thoughts of having abandoned my kids were pushed well down. I figured it was a good idea to call the girls.

Brigitte, who was around eleven at the time, answered the phone.

'Brigie-Boo, how you doin' kiddo?'

'Dad, can you please not call here when you are drunk?'

And she hung up.

How dare she? I thought. Where was the respect? The gratitude for her loving father making contact, finding time to talk to his kids?

Yeah. I was sick. Deluded. Insane. And the last one to know it. It only occurred to me some months later how much courage Brigitte showed in telling me not to call.

For the time being, I kept on drinking. I kept working at IPI, making money, then spending everything on rent and booze.

Then, one fateful night, my drinking companion, Lex, suggested I should give it a rest for a while. It was a Sunday night; I'd been drinking for four days straight and, that afternoon, had watched Mike Tyson demolish his opponent. To give you an idea of the quality of company I was keeping then, I remarked to my afternoon drinking companion that I reckoned if I went into training I could beat Tyson. The fool not only agreed but suggested he manage me. How fucking low had I sunk?

The week before I was drinking with the publican, Bobby, and two blokes in their thirties, both black-belt karate exponents, when one of the barmaids came over and told Bobby that the heavily tattooed, muscular bloke at the bar was telling the girls he was going to fuck them up the arse. Apparently, he'd been released from gaol that day and was spoiling for a stink. As Bobby turned and looked him over he insolently stared back.

'Don't even finish your drink,' Bobby told him. 'Leave the premises now.'

Tough Guy walked around the bar and fronted Bobby.

'Who's going to make me?' he asked with a smirk. Before Bobby, the karate kids or the two Māori bouncers could move I put my glass on the bar, grabbed Tough Guy by his shirt front, drove my elbows into his ribs and ran him backwards, smashing his back into the solid cigarette machine. As the air left him I spun him around, knocking a heavy metal stool to the floor, him falling on top of it, me on top of him. I smashed him so hard into the stool that the back of his head hit the steel seat frame. His eyes rolled back. *He's dead*, I thought. *Good. I can't get hurt*. I stood up.

A pudgy, red-headed fucker who had obviously taken a set against me some time before started to rise from his stool, intending to get involved.

'For your life, sit down!' Bobby yelled.

The bouncers removed the groggy, would-be anal bandit from the hotel, along with his shit-scared drinking companion, and Bobby bought a round of drinks. He and the rest of the people on the bar were looking at me strangely. I can imagine what they were thinking: 'What the fuck had just happened? Was that Rod the joke-teller who just went rogue and pulverised someone half his age and half as big again?'

We were just settling back into a jocular drinking rhythm when in through the door walked Tough Guy, along with one of New South Wales's finest. One of the boys spotted them and warned me. I removed my black jacket and threw it behind the bar, leaving me in jeans and a white T-shirt. One of the karate kids took his red cap off his head and adroitly placed it on mine.

The copper and the complainant walked up to Bobby. The cop did his duty, explaining that the bloke beside him claimed to have been assaulted. While the conversation was going on I placed myself on the right-hand side of our man in blue, with the assaulted on his left. As they moved around the bar, Tough Guy looking for the thug who had tuned him up, I stayed out of his line of vision by pivoting every which way, keeping the cop between us. Bobby explained how Tough Guy's own behaviour had caused the trouble, if indeed there had been any trouble (according to Bobby he hadn't seen anything). 'Did anyone here see this bloke cop a flogging?' he asked the bar, pointedly staring at our red-headed mate. Everyone in the bar shook their heads.

The cop quickly worked out what was going on and removed the troublemaker from the premises.

Reflecting on that Sunday night, I thought about Brigitte's request for me not to call when drunk, and Lex's advice that I should give it a rest for a while. Then I did something I don't think I'd ever done before: I left an unfinished beer on the table and exited the pub.

It was Sunday 6 August 1999 at 10.30 p.m.

I ran home in a panic, convinced that someone was behind me and intended to kill me. I was shaking so much I couldn't get the key into the lock of my first-floor flat. When I did get inside, relief flooded over me, only to be replaced with a terrible sense of dread that my assassin might be lying in wait for me inside my unit. The first place I looked, and it took me five minutes to get up the nerve, was the cutlery drawer. I don't know what I expected—perhaps a deranged leprechaun to leap out with a butter knife. I progressed to the microwave, behind the TV and the freezer: all places you couldn't hide Peter Pan, let alone a grown human. I finally went to the only place big enough to hide in: the wardrobe. Again, after an interminable, terror-filled wait, I flung the door open and . . . there he was, hands raised, ready to fight, a snarl on his face. It was my reflection. I was sobbing with relief.

I picked up the phone and dialled Al's number. It was 10.45 p.m. He was fast asleep, but woke up and answered.

'Hello?'

'I can't stop,' I told him.

'Do you want to stop?'

'Yes, but I can't. I always said I would stop when I was ready. Now I'm done, but I realise I simply cannot stop.'

'Okay. What I suggest is you try not to have another drink tonight. Have a hot shower, try to get some sleep and we will deal with it tomorrow.'

The next day Al picked me up from my work in Surry Hills at 5.30 p.m. and took me to a Double Bay restaurant, and we talked. Unusually for me I actually listened. I was all out of answers, so Al's message of hope got through to me. We left the restaurant and went to the Monday 7.30 p.m. AA meeting in Edgecliff, where my steady climb back to sanity began.

CHAPTER 69

9/11

My entire attitude to life began to shift under the influence of those I met in the AA meetings. It's called Alcoholics Anonymous for a reason so, although I've seen and heard some life-changing and, at times, highly entertaining stories in meetings, I won't go into most of them. I have permission to use some names; others I've changed to maintain anonymity.

I met my sponsor, Tony Barry, as well as other AA friends: Big Wave Dave, Graham, Brewery Bill, Hendo, Actress Helen, Big Judy, John Mac (who was my sponsor after Tony) and many others. There was my mate Jimmy from Albury, who was at my first meeting in 1993. When I came back to AA in 1999 (after I'd been out for a further six years of drinking research) I attended a second meeting in Sydney. Believe it or not, Jimmy appeared—he was travelling through the city and stopped in at that very meeting! This is the coincidence we refer to in AA as a 'God Job'.

My experience working at IPI changed when I stopped drinking. Because I wasn't drinking my nights were freed up. I began working the United States far more frequently and was making strong inroads into New York stockbroking firms. I'd call the main switchboard and the girls answering would recognise me straight away.

'Hi, Rod. Are you wanting Chuck or Bill today?'

There were no more firewalls.

I made significant sales and had numerous proposals in the pipeline. I was looking at a huge payday. And I was the first one to tap the American market; the only rep who was happy to start work at 6 p.m. and finish ten hours later.

Then one night, every number I called was unresponsive. Number after number, dead air. I couldn't raise anyone by phone or email, so I packed up early and headed home.

By this time I had moved out of McMahons Point and was staying with Al at his place in Vaucluse, while Lesley was out of the city, supervising the construction of their new home. I walked in the door to see Al glued to the TV. *What is he looking at?* was my initial thought, but I said nothing. His concentration was intense.

'Do you know what's going on?' he finally said.

'Not a clue,' I replied.

'A plane has flown into the World Trade Centre. Oh, *fuck*!'

As I looked at the screen a plane entered from screen right and flew into the second World Trade Centre tower.

It was Armageddon.

Now I knew why the phones wouldn't connect. Ninety per cent of my American clients worked in those two towers. Al had worked nearby a few short years ago, and had many friends and colleagues in the towers, too.

I wasn't thinking of the commissions I was going to miss out on. My thoughts went to a particular young receptionist I had formed a beautiful friendship with. She lived at home with her mum and stepdad and dreamed of the day she would have enough money to travel to Australia. Not to see me—I was twenty-plus years her senior—but simply for the adventure of it.

I'd told her numerous stories about my time in the outback to give her an idea of what she could expect. I wept for her. Al and I both wept.

We went to a meeting the next day, having slept very little, eyes glued to the TV for updates.

I left IPI a year or so later. The writing was on the wall. RF's concept was inventive and unique but had run its course. Business began to slow down; reps were leaving in droves and RF mentioned he was going to sell his house and move up the coast.

When I heard he was planning to sell I saw an opportunity. Al had recently sold his home in Vaucluse through a well-known agent named Brad, whom he introduced me to. I posed the question: 'If I can get you a multimillion-dollar listing, what sort of commission is in it for me?'

'You'd get 25 per cent of my commission,' Brad immediately responded.

'I'll get back to you.'

Then I went to see RF.

'RF, you mentioned the other day you were planning on selling. Which agent are you going to use?'

'Oh, I've a couple in mind. Why do you ask?'

'It just occurred to me that a bloke named Brad handled the sale of my mate's home in Vaucluse. He may not suit you because he's a celebrity agent, but he got an outstanding result for my mate money-wise. And it was quick, too. Just thought I'd mention it.'

'Interesting. Thank you, RAH, I'll keep him in mind.'

Then I gave Brad a call and suggested he hand-drop a letter addressed to Richard Farrington, not 'The homeowner', into RF's letterbox in Centennial Park that day.

The following day RF called me into his office.

'In a remarkable coincidence, RAH, that chap Brad you mentioned to me yesterday left a note in my letterbox. Amazing.'

'Perhaps it's a sign from heaven, RF.'

'Well, Angie and I are meeting with him this afternoon. We shall see what he has to say. Thanks very much.'

'The pleasure is all mine.'

Naturally, RF and Angie sold through Brad, who duly paid me my commission. It was a nice little earn, and I figured RF owed me around that from bonuses that I'd missed out on by a whisker because he kept adjusting the parameters. He may have been generous with the dinners he treated us to, but he was a master of waving the carrot just a millimetre away from your nose. He was a very, very clever businessman and I feel certain that he would be quietly chuffed that I made a buck out of him in this manner. After all, he was always going to pay the house sale commission to someone. I may as well have got my chop.

I continued to spend most of my time around other sober alkies, and went to an AA meeting every day for my first five sober years. But I still had to pay the bills, so I went back to the jobs section of *The Sydney Morning Herald*. I found an ad for a media sales position at advertising company I&G. I&G placed ads in foreign-language newspapers, radio and television for mainstream Australian companies and government departments that wanted to get their message to the half of Australia's population who spoke English as their second language. Lee Hubber started the company, and he was as clever as Richard Farrington.

The work was a step up from what I did at IPI. It was cold-calling, but with the added task of thinking of ideas and projects that were worth promoting to prospective clients. Lee provided leads, but I also went looking.

One day, in a conversation with someone from one of the many Western Sydney councils I dealt with, they made a chance remark about struggling to get the message through to the local community about not putting soft plastics into the recycling bin. This led me to arrange a meeting with representatives from a dozen councils including Blacktown, Fairfield, Cumberland, Parramatta, Canterbury-Bankstown, Liverpool and others. We sold them on the idea of stumping up $5000 each for advertisements to be spread across TV, radio, and newspapers in fifteen different languages.

And we pulled it off. Lee said he'd seen nothing like it in his time in the industry. I was pretty proud of that sale.

CHAPTER 70

STOP RIGHT NOW

It was 2004 and I was approaching five years' sobriety. With Al's help I got a consolidation loan with his private bank at a very low interest rate, and I'd reduced my $120,000 debt to five figures. My girls were teenagers, and I was getting on with them really well.

I was keen to run my own business and figured I could make a go of a cafe. Through research and observation, and Al's input, we decided to buy a Michel's Patisserie franchise—a new one going into Norton Plaza, Leichhardt.

For the first month the money rolled in. We wondered—or I did, Al was far more pragmatic—just how much moolah we could make. Alas, a fortune it wasn't to be. Slowly, week by week, our income dropped. I had employed fantastic staff right from the start: Lee, my head girl, was ably assisted by Kirsten, and my daughter Laura who was saving up to travel. A little later I took on three students from the Netherlands and, after Laura left for South America, Brigitte came and worked for me for a year before she took off for Uganda. Both my daughters lived with me while they worked for the franchise.

It must have been tougher for Brigitte living and working with me than it was for her sister. At least Laura was there for the start when we still had hope. By the time Brigitte arrived, Al and I both knew we were on the skids. And it showed in me. I was working 90-hour weeks and was constantly worried about Al's investment, even though he made it crystal clear to me that he understood I was doing everything possible to make the place profitable.

In my spare time I went to AA meetings.

Nothing I did changed the income downward spiral until one day I decided to up all prices by 15 per cent. Coffee, pies, small cakes, and birthday cake special orders—which was where the real profits were—were all bumped by 15 per cent.

To my surprise, business didn't drop off—it actually increased. The number of items we were selling increased in all categories. Multiply the income by 15 per cent and, bingo, we started showing a significant profit.

Then the area representative for Michel's called by the shop and approached me over the counter. He told me my agreement clearly stated the prices I had to sell at. I told him to fuck off.

Al and I decided it was time to sell.

I dropped the prices back to the Michel's recommendation three months before we listed the cafe for sale.

It took us six months to find a buyer. When we sold and the final count-up was done, we had lost $249,000 and three and a half years of our lives. The only things we walked away with were a forensic knowledge of the franchise food business, and a stronger-than-ever friendship. As well as that, all five of our daughters—Nickie, Ginnie, Laura, Brigitte and Julia—worked in the shop and, I hope, were better for the experience.

The staff were entertained while they were there, too. One day I was on my way to see my mate Sam, who ran a coffee shop near Coles, when I noticed the centre manager, an innocuous little fella named Tim, had a scruffy individual bailed up by the shopping trolleys. There were 400 trolleys lined up, side by side in rows of twenty. Hard up against the back wall was a grubby, hollowed-out doper, eyes darting left and right. Tim was standing guard at the end of an empty trolley bay. I asked the obvious question.

'G'day, Tim. What's going on?'

'This person has been shoplifting. He was seen putting a package of sausages down the front of his tracksuit pants. I'm waiting for the police,' replied the very nervy, self-appointed guardian of Coles' profits.

'Want a hand?'

'Oh, if you would, Rod. He looks to be high on drugs and could be dangerous.'

A couple of days earlier, I'd had my varicose veins operated on and was wearing tight white compression stockings that stretched from my ankles to my groin. I'd been advised to be cautious in my movements, as any sudden exertion would probably cause the stitches to open up.

I eased Tim out of the way and took up the sentinel position, eyeballing the desperate twenty-something criminal mastermind, Leichhardt's leading sausage thief. I invited him to 'have a go, ya cunt, try to get through me'. I was carrying a mountain of pent-up anger and frustration over the failure of the business. A potentially homeless, hungry, drug-addled sausage thief seemed a reasonable target.

There were only two exits available to the desperado. The first was to run through me—a vibrating, pulsating, pumped-up ball of muscle, itching for an excuse to pulverise someone, anyone.

The second escape route was across the stacked-up trolleys; a most unlikely alternative. So, naturally, that's the one he took. From a standing jump he leapt onto the nearest trolley and, in his thong-clad feet, ran like a startled gazelle straight across them. As he sprinted across the diagonal I began a lumbering chase, aiming to head him off as he made his leap to freedom.

My aim was to maim him—not permanently, mind you. I'm not a total cunt. Just a broken limb or, if he was unlucky, a fractured skull.

He leapt, so he was just out of my reach. I increased my speed, completely oblivious to the strain on my bandaged legs. He was by now running parallel to the eastern wall, a heavy ATM ten metres ahead of him. I did the calculations and figured I could hit him with a hip and shoulder and plant the skinny prick into the ATM. *Yep*, I thought, *that should do the job. Busted shoulder or ribs at worst!* I was closing fast, but not fast enough. As he drew level with the cash machine, I was a half a metre too short. I reached out and grabbed his collar. Momentarily it slowed him, almost to a stop. He ran on the spot, his throat just inches away from retribution when, what a bastard, his collar tore away from his shirt. He blew out of his thongs and shot away from me like a marble out of a slingshot.

Fuck it. I took off after him. By this stage he was rounding the corner where Michel's was bleeding us dry, with me now ten metres behind him and losing ground fast. Then I heard a very loud voice.

'Dad, stop. Right now!' It was Brigitte. 'What the hell are you doing? What about your legs?' She had a point.

No permanent damage was done, but Tim did look at me differently from then on. The mastermind of the Great Sausage Heist avoided all penalties, bar the loss of his thongs and collar, and was never seen in the shopping centre again. I, of course, never received due recognition for my role in keeping the centre's crime level down, which I found disappointing. A simple plaque outside Coles would have done, just so the other business owners would know who to bow to as they passed our shop. I've gotten over the slight, but it did take time and some therapy.

Another day, Brigitte was on the coffee machine and I was taking orders from the line of customers when a short, fat, forty-something loudmouth stepped around the queue and demanded, in his thick South African accent, 'Two flat whites, and make it snappy.' He sat at one of our tables with his obviously embarrassed colleague, a tall, dark-skinned dude. Both of them were wearing branded business shirts. They worked for a very well-known Australian company.

I glanced up and replied, 'No table service here, mate, so you'll need to join the queue.'

He held up an empty coffee cup that hadn't been cleared from his table. 'How would you like this cup wrapped around your head?'

'Nah, I wouldn't like that at all, so why don't you take your lard arse out of my shop before I call security, sport? You and your pal won't be getting coffee from here any time soon.'

Everyone within hearing was stunned at his attitude and words. Brigitte gave me a sideways look as if to say, 'Don't do anything stupid.' I smiled at her and moved to the phone as Fatso and his embarrassed offsider moved to a table outside the shop where he sat, giving me the evil eye.

I rang his company's main number and was greeted by one of the receptionists. Before she could launch into her spiel, I said:

'Listen carefully. I want to be connected to the head of your marketing team—immediately. If I'm not, my next call is to Alan Jones, and what I have to say about your business you absolutely do not want to go to air.'

Within 30 seconds I had the head of marketing on the line.

'Mate, my name is Rod Halsted. I own Michel's Patisserie in Norton Plaza, and I've just had a short, fat South African bloke wearing a shirt with your brand all over it in my shop. He just threatened to wrap a coffee cup around my head. He is an obnoxious, self-entitled loudmouth and he's eyeballing me as we speak. If he doesn't come to the counter and apologise to me in as loud a voice as he threatened me with, my next call is to Laws or Jones, or maybe both, to explain how your company's people conduct themselves.'

'Please just give me a minute before you do anything, Mr Halsted. And I apologise on behalf of our com—'

'Mate, it's not your apology I want.' And I put the phone down. I hadn't broken eye contact with my Afrikaner pest, nor he with me. I could sense the disdain and threat bubbling from him. Then his phone rang. He pulled it from his pocket, put it to his ear and I watched all the blood drain from his face. He dropped his eyes. Then he forced his fat frame from the chair and slowly waddled over to the cake counter I was now leaning on.

'Apparently I owe you an apology,' he mumbled.

In a stentorian voice I replied, 'Sorry, what's that? I can't hear you. Speak up, man!'

He raised his voice a little. 'I said, I'm sorry for—'

'Speak up, man.'

By this stage all the staff members were giggling, customers were openly laughing and passers-by were stopping to watch the show.

'I said, I'm sorry for my poor behaviour before. I shouldn't have spoken to you the way I did.' The fucker was all but grovelling now, with equal parts embarrassment and anger.

I decided to have some more fun with him, so I explained in a loud voice how violence is never the answer to anything, that he owed his friend an apology, too, and that I accepted his apology and expected him to do better in the future. He had no choice but to stand there like an errant schoolboy and take it from me.

When I'd finished with him, I leant a little closer and, in a whisper only he could hear, I said, 'Now fuck off, and never set foot in this centre again.' And I offered him my hand, which he had no choice but to respond to. But as he reached for my hand, I turned the back of it to him and waved him away.

As he shuffled away as fast as his pudgy legs would let him, people were laughing, there was a smattering of applause and his friend, tagging along behind him, gave me a nod. I responded with a friendly wave. Another boring day at the counter averted.

I did start to wonder if perhaps I wasn't cut out for retail or dealing with the public. Well, not while so many of my customers were rude and impatient!

CHAPTER 71

WE BOTH WEPT

One day my back went on me as I was picking up a crate of cakes. I was leaving for England the next day to attend a good friend's daughter's wedding. I was on Endone for the pain, and have very little memory of my two weeks away. I do clearly remember one day, though.

After my time in London for the wedding, I caught a train to Edinburgh to meet up with Laura, who was travelling in Scotland at the time. I don't recall too much of our time together, but I do recall us travelling to Cambridge to visit a special cemetery—within which was the grave of my Uncle Rod. I'd held a lifelong desire to visit his grave and here I was, with my beautiful daughter helping her hobbling old man along.

The cemetery contains the remains of air service personnel from Australia, New Zealand and Poland. Inside there is a large stone monolith and, radiating out from it, many hundreds of small, white headstones. Carved into each is a name, rank, and dates of birth and death. It was shocking to see so many gravestones for people aged in their teens.

Eventually Laura found Rod's headstone: Flight Lieutenant Roger Hubert Halsted. He had turned 21 eight days before his death. Dead at 21; just old enough to vote. We both wept. I was so grateful to have my daughter with me on that day. Thinking about what Rod had missed out on, dying so young, not having a wife by his side into old age, not being granted children as I had been, brought out a deep sense of gratitude for all I had been blessed with.

Laura and I walked out of that hallowed place with heavy hearts but, oddly, buoyed and grateful that we had made the journey together.

CHAPTER 72

THE COCKY KILLER

I was visiting Albury when by chance I bumped into Tom Doolan, my old publican mate who had suggested I get off the grog many years before. I'd had a fight in his pub, and he suggested I drink elsewhere. When pressed he said it wasn't the fight that upset him, but what I was doing to my family. He had forgiven me for telling him to get fucked, and was happy I'd climbed onto the sobriety wagon.

Tom mentioned his family had bought a bus line in Western Australia that his son, Ben, was running. They were always in need of drivers and, if I liked, I could have a job based out of their Karratha depot. I jumped at the opportunity. Both my girls were overseas and there was nothing keeping me in the east. Plus, my memories of the west in the seventies were good ones.

I flew to Perth, then to Onslow, which was on the ocean and a short drive from Karratha. I was picked up at the airport by a guy everyone knew as Burgo.

When we arrived at Fortesque bus depot, Burgo showed me to a row of shipping containers that had been converted to accommodation. Each container had five rooms, known as dongas, which were approximately two metres wide, two and a half metres long and two metres high. They were smaller than any of the cells I'd been imprisoned in for my various DUI charges and my drug bust. I had to stand outside the door for a good couple of minutes to get my head around the fact that this was now my home, my private living space for the foreseeable future.

By this stage I was around eight years sober and had attended AA meetings at least three or four times a week, so I had come to understand the concept of acceptance. I stood there, processed the idea of living in so small a space and, repeating the AA prayer a number of times, not only accepted my new digs but decided to embrace them. I chose to see the positives.

Burgo got me started on the buses, and I became the regular driver for a crew I took to and from a mining site each day. They were a good bunch. I wasn't supposed to stop until I got them home to their camp each day, but after a quiet request from their foreman, one day I pulled into a roadside store that sold alcohol. They each jumped off and purchased a few cans, the empties of which they put in a bag, which I disposed of so their camp boss wouldn't find them.

When I eventually finished up at Fortesque some twelve months later, the boss handed me a typed letter saying what a good bloke I was. It carried twenty signatures. I've received many references over the years but none that I treasure more than this one.

In Australia, everyone ends up with a nickname. I've had too many to count over the years: in my youth I was Rocket, Bluey Bomba the Jungle Boy. I was the Red Fox at Hawthornden; then the Gouger named me the Silver Fox, because of my silver tongue and cunning nature. I've been Rockhead and Jolly. When I was driving the mining crew, I became the Cocky Killer. One day we were belting along at 100 kilometres an hour in the ancient bus I was given for the run when a flock of cockatoos flew straight across the bus's path. Three of the unfortunate birds collided with the left-hand windscreen, which not only cracked but actually popped out of its rubber seal and was perilously close to blowing in.

No problem. One of the boys finished his can and stood in the space beside the driver's seat, holding the glass in place. Problem solved. Anyway, I couldn't have called for a replacement bus. My vehicle wasn't equipped with a two-way radio. Company protocols demanded I pull the vehicle off the road, but that would mean my passengers would be hours late getting back to camp. In working conditions such as theirs, sleep is precious. So, I drove on to raucous cheers in support of the Cocky Killer. All I did was what I'd expect someone else to do in my position, but the boys loved me for it.

Because of the repetitious nature of the work, and there being nothing to do in my downtime, and because my TV gave me access to horse-racing broadcasts, I started borrowing the depot car and driving it to the local TAB, placing bets then going back to my donga to watch the results. It only took a couple of weeks of this for me to realise I was gambling the way I drank: without thinking and in large amounts. There was nothing else to spend money on in Karratha other than whores and booze, and neither held any attraction for me.

As soon as I realised what I was doing I picked up the phone and called an AA mate in Sydney. He didn't answer. So, I rang another. Same result. On my fifth call, a guy I barely knew, Geoff W, answered.

'Geoff, I don't know if you remember me. It's—'

'Rod from Sunday mornings, the Seagull Room. Yep, I know you, mate. What can I do for you?'

'Mate, I don't want to insult you, but you're the fifth person I've tried to connect with and the first to answer.'

'No insult taken, Rod. That's what we do. Keep calling until we connect. What's up?'

'Well, it's not booze, Geoff, it's gambling. I'm quickly developing an addiction to the punt. I gave it away when I stopped drinking but it's back, and it's likely the bottle will follow. I don't know if you've—'

'Rod, mate, I've been through the exact same issue. You've called the right man. The way I handled it was, I put it on the program. I clearly knew I couldn't get drunk if I didn't have the first drink, so I treated the gambling the same way. If you don't have the first bet you can't have the second, or the third, or the hundredth, if your money lasts that long. How long since you've been to a meeting?'

'Well, mate, I'm in Karratha. There's one meeting a week in this place, and I've missed the past two because I've been working.'

'Okay. Can you ask for time off when the next meeting is on? Maybe swap a shift?'

'Yeah, I can. Mate, I think you've saved my bacon. I don't want to work in this godforsaken place for a year and come home with nothing. Thank you so very much.'

'My pleasure. Make sure you look me up when you get back to Sydney.'

And the urge to gamble left me.

CHAPTER 73

GALWAY AND THE GIRLS

Once I stopped gambling it away, my money began to mount up. My two girls were both working in Galway, Ireland, at that point, so I decided to visit them. I rang Brigitte and told her I was landing in Dublin on a specific date.

'Fantastic, Dad. I'll actually be in Dublin that day, so I'll meet you at the airport.'

'What's on in Dublin?'

'Tom Waits is doing his first tour outside the States in twenty years.'

'Cool. Buy me a ticket and I'll go with you.'

'You wish, Dad. The tickets are like gold. They sold out in two days.'

I submitted my leave and booked to fly to Ireland. Six weeks later, after 33 hours from Karratha to Dublin, I was met at the airport by my beautiful younger daughter with a big hug and a huge smile.

We hopped into a cab and Brigitte gave the cabbie the address of the B&B she had booked for us.

'On your way there, mate, would you mind going via 24 Holles Street, please? I have something to pick up.'

'What are you up to now, Dad? What have you got to pick up?'

'My ticket to the concert. After I spoke to you and you said you'd be in Dublin, I decided I wasn't going to sit in a room while you went to a concert on your own. So I rang the promotor, a guy called Peter Aiken, explained my predicament and asked him for a ticket to Tom Waits. He asked me to drop by when I got to Dublin, so . . .'

The look on her face was enough, but she said it anyway. 'You never cease to astonish me with your audacity, Dad.'

'Brigitte, if you don't ask, you don't get.'

'Holles Street!' the cabbie announced.

'Would you wait for us, please, mate? We won't be long.' And into the Aiken Promotions office we went.

'G'day, you must be Colleen, I'm Rod from—'

'Australia. I remember.' She turned to call over her shoulder: 'Peter, the guy from Australia you spoke to a few weeks ago is here.'

A smiling Irishman emerged, his hand held out. 'Bloody hell, I'd completely forgotten about you, you sweet-talking colonial bastard.'

'G'day, Pete. I haven't forgotten you, old mate. This is my daughter, Brigitte: the kid I've flown around the world to see.'

He greeted her warmly, turned to his secretary and said, 'Colleen, I forgot to put a ticket aside for this bloke. Would you organise something for him to pick up at the box office tonight, please? Rod, I'm flat-out, I have to go—'

'Before you go, I said I'd pay for the ticket, and I also brought these for you. I reckon they will fit; Colleen gave me your size.' I handed him a box containing a pair of R.M. Williams boots.

'Fook me. You wouldn't credit it; I bought a pair of these last week. Colleen, don't worry about the cost of the ticket. Thanks, mate. Very much. I have to run.' And he was gone.

That night Brigitte and I walked through the Dublin drizzle to the entry gate where there was a ticket waiting for me marked 'access all areas'. We entered the huge circus tent which held, I think, around 3000 people. Brigitte headed for her seat, and I found mine. It was in a block of about 30 empty seats near the sound engineer's area. Primo seating.

Before the concert started, I wandered outside looking for water to splash on my face. I'd been up for close to 40 hours and was feeling it. There was only one other person outside: my benefactor, Peter Aiken. I stepped up to him and put my hand out, which he took.

'Mate, I just want to say a sincere thanks again. I'll be forever grateful to you for helping me share this with Brigitte.'

He held on to my hand.

'I want you to know this,' he said. 'My old man, Jim, founded this business and I've been running it now for several years. Up to this point any tickets we've given away, ever, we have paid for out of our own pockets. We have a policy of *never* giving away a free ticket. You are the first ever. I don't know how you got to me, but I do know this: you would make a sensational concert promotor—if you weren't so old!'

We both had a laugh at that. I threw water over my face then went back in and found my seat. Thirty seconds later, I was asleep. I slept through the whole show. If I'd stayed awake even for five minutes I would have found Brigitte and brought her to sit with me. Bummer. But at least she still has the 'access all areas' ticket.

Brigitte and I hired a car the next day and drove to Galway, where we visited Laura, who was working in a cafe.

Laura flew around the counter and gave me a massive hug. When she finished work all three of us went out for dinner, followed by a tour of the pubs and bars they frequented. We ended the night at a bar where the band No Banjo, friends of Brigitte's, were playing. They were outstanding—one of the best bands I've ever heard live, and that includes the Stones, Blood,

Sweat and Tears, the Eagles, Rod Stewart, Alice Cooper and numerous others.

I spent a lot of my time in Galway going to AA meetings, as well as being with my girls. One night the three of us wandered into a small pub. I paid the entry fee, which was minimal, and we took up seats close enough to the small stage that we could rest our elbows on it. Then, out strolled Australia's own Paul Kelly with his nephew Dan. We couldn't believe our luck: to be in a room of 50 people and that close to a true Aussie music legend.

Some eight years before my Irish trip, one day in Bondi, I became friends with Bazza, who tours the world and sings a bit under a different name. We enjoyed each other's company and stayed in touch over the years, so naturally I let him know I would be in Galway.

He drove over from his home to catch up over a beautiful lunch. Laura came with me. Some years later, at one of his Aussie gigs, he organised a couple of tickets to his show—and when I told him I would like to bring Laura, he gave us front-row seats.

We were seated next to a couple from an Irish dance show that was touring at the same time. At the end of the show, as he was taking his bows, he stepped to the front of the stage, bent down, and gave both the Irish girl and Laura a bunch of flowers each. It was such a beautiful gesture. It made Laura feel incredibly special and loved.

The day I was flying out of Dublin, Baz met me and we had lunch. I asked him what he'd been doing, and he said among other things that he'd attended a Buddhist conference in France for the past two weeks. He'd agreed to play one of his songs at the conference closing ceremony.

'How did it go?' I asked.

'Oh, I didn't do it.'

'Why the hell not?'

'Because the conference closes today, and I'd arranged to meet you.'

If that's not a demonstration of genuine friendship and humility, I don't know what is.

Before I left Galway, I had one last night out with my girls. While I'd been visiting I'd heard No Banjo play a number of gigs, and alongside Brigitte had many an interesting conversation and laugh with the band members.

We wandered into the wharfside bar where No Banjo was playing and found the place packed. I bought the girls drinks, and a Coke for me, and we found seats near the stage. It wasn't long before people were up and dancing, the girls and me included. I got so into it I reprised my dance routine inspired by Judy Morris in *In Search of Anna*. Before I realised it, the entire dance floor had cleared, bar myself and a girl who was clearly as demented as me. The entire bar was going off, clapping, hooting and screaming for us. The boys in the band had no intention of stopping any time soon and had managed to turn a three-minute number into twice the length of 'MacArthur Park'. At one stage I looked up to see both my girls alternately laughing hysterically and then hiding their eyes, not wanting to see their old man make a complete and utter fool of himself. I tried to leave the dance floor a couple of times only to be pushed back onto it by the raucous revellers. Finally, the band brought the number to an end, clearly understanding if I were left out there for 30 seconds longer an ambulance would be needed.

I staggered back to my two highly embarrassed but secretly delighted daughters. The entire room was giving me and my dance partner a rousing round of cheers and applause.

What a way to say goodbye to my two beauties, and to the wonderful people of Ireland. They say we should dance like no one's watching. I say fuck that. Take my advice: dance like the whole world's watching and you don't give a damn what they think.

CHAPTER 74

WHY THE FUCK NOT?

When I returned to Australia it was back to Karratha and driving the buses. My enthusiasm had waned; my Irish trip had awakened my desire for something bigger. As this thought took root, my old mate from my Variety Club days, Frank Dunphy, rang me to tell me about a television production company he had bankrolled. WTFN came into being when Frank's brother-in-law, Daryl Talbot, suggested an idea to him and asked him to finance the project. Frank's answer, 'Why the fuck not?', gave birth to the company name.

I've heard it said to choose change when in doubt. When Frank offered me a job selling space on infomercial shows such as *Mercurio's Menu* and *Coxy's Big Break* I figured that was different enough from driving buses in the barren and isolated west of Australia to qualify.

I had a few bucks saved up, so when I hit Melbourne in 2010 I decided to rent an apartment near WTFN's office in Hawthorn. The suburb was somewhat different from my previous Melbourne digs. I guess a decade of sobriety had brought a modicum of sanity to my life. Of course I rented, as always, a two-bedroom apartment, in the hope that my kids would come and stay with me now and then.

The first day I walked into the office Frank met me in the foyer and walked me upstairs to meet Daryl and his business partner, Steve. The minute I walked into the boardroom, I could tell by their body language and shared glance that Daryl and Steve were doubtful. Who was this old codger Frank had brought in to their hip company—a business employing mostly young people? I was close to 60 by then and had never worked in TV. However, I did have experience cold-calling high-level international executives, and I had worked for a media company. My referrals from Richard and Lee didn't hold back on extolling my cold-calling ability, as well as my high closing rate, so I guess Steve and Daryl thought, *What the hell? Let's give the old guy a try.*

I was introduced to Wes, who directed the sales department, and Rohan, the head of sales. Rohan was no mug, and it didn't take him long to suss out what was going on: that I was ostensibly his assistant, but that they intended to replace him with me if I turned out to be any good. And that's what happened. However, Rohan was a man of class and held no resentment towards me. In fact, we got on well. As I did with Wes, with whom I made numerous forays into the Victorian countryside, giving sales presentations.

Each of the shows WTFN produced was comprised of five segments, usually on a common theme. Each segment was valued at $12,500, or an entire show at $60,000. I was on 10 per cent commission. As with the Variety Club Special Children's Christmas Party, I couldn't see why I shouldn't sell the whole show rather than segments. It worked. In the twenty months I worked there, I sold $2 million worth of space. What I did with the commission I have no idea. I was poor when I left. I do know I didn't drink or gamble it, and that was enough.

I went close one day, though. I have no idea what made me change my route home, but at the end of a busy Friday I found myself standing in a pub, looking at the bar. I was in a trance-like state but, as I'd been advised many times in AA meetings, I put my phone in my hand rather than a drink. I rang Hendo in Sydney, who I'd also gone to when I panicked because Laura hadn't called me when she arrived in South America some three or so years before. He'd removed all fear of my daughter's future with the simple words, 'Of course everyone is entitled to their own destiny.'

'Mate, I'm standing in a pub in Melbourne and staring at the bar. I'm fucked if I know how I got here. What do I do?'

'That's cool, mate. Just turn around and walk out of the bar.'

'Okay. Mate, I've got to get past a bottle shop. Do you mind staying on the line, please?'

'No problem, mate. What have you been up to?'

And there's the AA program in a nutshell: one alkie taking care of another. One day at a time. No reward expected.

The gift for Hendo was in the giving.

The gift for me was that he answered his phone.

CHAPTER 75

THE PAST COMES KNOCKING

I don't recall exactly when I was diagnosed with hepatitis C, but it was when I was in Sydney because that's where I had my liver biopsy. That was an interesting experience in itself. I arrived at the prep rooms on Missenden Road, across from the Royal Prince Alfred Hospital and just up from Bloody Mary's and the Grose Farm Hotel—my old stomping ground in the early seventies.

I was warned by my mate Marty Pierce that the biopsy would be the most painful experience of my life. A hollow needle would be shot into my liver, and there would be no anaesthetic. I'd heard that meditation may help so, armed with the limited knowledge I had of the practice, I asked the staff to give me ten minutes alone before they came for me and to please not let anyone talk to me until the procedure had been completed.

I have no memory of what followed and felt absolutely no pain. I slowly came out of the hypnotic trance the meditation had placed me in, and opened my eyes. There, sitting on the end of my bed, was my mother. She was wearing a blue and white blouse that I loved seeing her in when I was a kid, and she had her hand on my younger self's head. Young Rod was around eight years old. And, as she lovingly gazed at her hep C-infected but sober son, she said to the young Rod, 'Look at my beautiful son.

Look what he's become.' Pride was emanating out of her, somewhat different to her anguished look when I was screaming at my wife over the phone around 20 years prior.

By the time I was working for WTFN in Melbourne, hep C had started raging through my body. My doctors decided I needed to go on interferon, the wonder cure of the day. They called me in and specified I had to bring a family member with me. I asked my youngest sister, Karen, if she would come with me. She lived in Melbourne, but we had grown apart over the years following our mother's death. To my everlasting gratitude, and her credit, she set aside old injuries and came with me.

The doctor explained the reason for her presence was because the side effects of interferon could be very nasty. The body would go through pain and trauma, but that wasn't the worst of it: the emotional effects could be devastating. It caused some patients to have suicidal thoughts and, in some cases, successfully follow through.

I agreed to the treatment regardless, and my life changed. I injected myself daily, followed the treatment plan to the letter, and found myself regularly experiencing completely irrational thoughts that would impose themselves at any time, day or night.

I informed Frank of the treatment I was undergoing and suggested he keep an eye on me in case I exhibited any unusual behaviour. It wasn't long before he gave me the nod.

'Mate, you are behaving very strangely. You are angry and the whole office is wondering what the fuck you are on. Might be time to take a holiday.'

I accepted his assessment, and went up to Daryl's office with Frank to explain what was happening. Daryl was very good about it, and he wished me well.

I was never bitter about parting with WTFN. I'd made some great friends there and had thoroughly enjoyed the work. I also left with my friendship with Frank intact. I suppose he appreciated me, too—never more so than the night we spent with my friend Hollywood at the Iguana Bar, Kings Cross, during the last days of my drinking. The Iguana was a well-known late-night hangout. Hollywood managed to irritate a white supremist Rhodesian so much that the drunken fool pulled a pistol from under his coat and put it to Hollywood's head, threatening to put a bullet through his brain.

I swiftly took him by the throat and explained that, if he fired, I'd remove the throat from his body. 'Put the weapon on the pool table. Hollywood, get the fuck out of here *now*. You too, Frank—*now*!'

He did what I asked and put the gun on the table. I looked him in the eye.

'I have two friends in here watching all this. I'm walking. If you reach for the gun before I'm out the front door, both my mates are armed. They will shoot you dead.'

And I turned and walked. Of course I didn't know anyone in the Iguana in 1999. Twenty-odd years back I'd have known half the desperadoes in there, but the Rhodesian ratbag wasn't to know that, was he?

With my health my primary concern, it was time to leave Frank and the WTFN gang and work on my sobriety.

CHAPTER 76

THE TRUTH WILL SET YOU FREE

I needed a safe place to go, so naturally I went home to Albury. Where my mates were, where I didn't have to explain myself. Where I always went when I was in trouble or needed a safe place to lie low.

I registered for the dole and started mowing lawns. The business grew rapidly; after a short time on the dole, I went to the social services office and asked to be taken off it. Oddly when I asked to be removed the person I was speaking to had no idea how to complete that request. She had to get a senior colleague. They both remarked that they couldn't remember the last time anyone had made a similar request.

I was still as mad as a hatter because of the side effects of the interferon so, irrationally, I decided to take a week off and drive to Adelaide to see my sister and her husband. On the way over I was clocked doing 139 kilometres an hour in a 100 zone in the Deniliquin area. When the matter came up for hearing in Deniliquin court, I asked my solicitor mate Brian Curphey to represent me. He said there was no point as I couldn't possibly beat the charge. I asked another solicitor, who gave me the same response. *Fuck it*, I thought. *I'll represent myself.*

I contacted my doctor, who wrote the court a letter saying I wasn't aware that one of the side effects of interferon was distraction and daydreaming. Armed with that document and a copy of my police record, which at that time ran to four and a half pages, I drove to Deniliquin with my mate Jimmy, the bloke who had warmly welcomed me to my first AA meeting all those years ago. I took Jimmy so he could drive my car home in the very likely event I'd lose my licence.

I tracked the police prosecutor down.

'Mate,' I told him, 'I don't want to spring a surprise on you, so I'm letting you know I'm defending the charge.' I handed him my doctor's letter. 'This is why. And, by the way, I've been taken off the drug recently and my concentration is fine now.'

He read the letter. 'I really appreciate you letting me know. We don't even have a copy of your driving record; it hasn't arrived.'

'That's cool, you can copy mine,' I said, handing him the police record. 'It's not pretty in the early years, but I've been off the grog for over ten years now and it's improved.'

He was dumbfounded. 'You are happy to give me a copy?'

'Yep. Best to have the truth out there.'

'And how have you stayed off the alcohol for such a long time?'

'AA, mate. It works if you work it.'

Jimmy and I went back to the courthouse and sat up the back. The magistrate seemed a reasonable bloke but was pretty severe on the drink driver who came up before me. Then it was my turn.

The case of Halsted versus the Crown was called. I stood up. The magistrate started to speak when the prosecutor jumped to his feet.

'Your honour, if I may approach?' The magistrate nodded.

The prosecutor walked to the bench and handed up my doctor's letter.

'As you can see there were extenuating circumstances, I've seen Mr Halsted's driving record and, in his early years, it wasn't good. He has spoken to me, he has been clean and sober for the past ten years, he is living an exemplary life, and I don't feel the court needs to hear this matter. I move for it to be dismissed.'

As the prosecutor sat down I thought, *Who needs a defence lawyer?*

'I can see your reasoning,' the magistrate said, 'however some sort of punishment is in order, surely?'

'Not in this case, your honour.'

This bloke wasn't just my defence attorney, he'd become my best mate.

'The punishment is $935 and five demerit points, wholly suspended upon you entering a one-year bond, Mr Halsted. Are you happy with that outcome?'

I nodded.

'I should think so,' the magistrate continued. 'Your honesty has served you well today. However, if you appear before me again within the bond period, it won't go well for you. Good luck for the future. You may go.'

The next case was called. The prosecutor got to his feet, turned and gave me a very slight nod and smile, which I returned. Then Jimmy and I left, with me behind the wheel.

I'd finally started taking my own advice. I found that the reward for honesty, at least on this occasion, was freedom.

CHAPTER 77

BYRON BAY BREAKDOWN

I was itchy for change. I'd stopped going to AA meetings after I had a drink in early January 2013. I had one beer because I got lonely and wanted a companion in my life—a woman, preferably, not a dog. After that single middy my pride and ego wouldn't let me attend meetings. Honesty had become part of my make-up, and my ego simply didn't want to stand up in front of people and say I was a day sober rather than the dozen-odd years I had chalked up before then.

I read somewhere that there were three women for every bloke in Byron Bay. It seemed like a no-brainer to move to Byron, which I did in October that year. I stopped with my old man for a day in Sydney and snuck a VB stubby from his fridge. I gulped it down instead of drinking and savouring it. The bottle was empty inside ten seconds. What to do with the empty? I couldn't put it in the box he already had a dozen empties in. Of course not; that would be normal. Guilt made me put it into my bag, taking it with me the next morning. It was insanity.

So, after having two drinks separated by ten months, I arrived in Byron Bay just after dark on a Saturday. I parked my vehicle, turned the engine off and sat there, tears streaming down my face.

I wasn't sobbing, just letting the life flow from me. I was in the middle of a nervous breakdown. I had no idea what I was doing or what I was going to do—not just the next day, but for the rest of my life. My heart was broken. I loved my daughters but had no way of showing them that. I loved my ex-wife but still blamed her for the loss of my family. And I was disgusted with what I had turned into: this weak, broken, sobbing mess of a man. I was deeply lonely and had been since the break-up of the family twenty years before.

I had an idea of what my next thought might be, and it involved a wooden box, so I circumvented it by picking up the phone and calling my sister Chris. She was always gentle with anyone in distress so when it came to family, she was the one to contact.

'Rod, what's wrong? You sound dreadful. Where are you?'

'Byron Bay. I'm lost, Chris.'

'I think you need to go to a rehab. Is there anyone you can call?'

I called a mate, Derek, whom I'd met at a Bondi AA meeting. I knew he had something to do with rehabs.

'Rocket Rod, my man. What's up?'

'Mate, I'm fucked. I think I need to go to a rehab.'

'Have you had a drink?' Only a fellow alkie would think to ask that question first up.

'Yes, mate. Two. One in January and one yesterday.'

'You don't need rehab, mate; you need a meeting. Is there one nearby tomorrow?'

'Yeah, in Mullumbimby. I'll go to that one. Thanks, mate.'

The next day I walked into the midday meeting and saw my first sponsor, Tony Barry. I sat down next to him and gave him a sideways look, which he returned with a grin. We shook hands, and listened to the chairman opening the meeting. As usual he asked if anyone was from out of town.

'Rod, alcoholic, visiting from Albury.'

'G'day, Rod,' everyone in the meeting said.

'Not to embarrass you but so we can welcome you, is there anyone here in their first 90 days?' asked the chair.

'Rod, alcoholic, day one.'

I got a sideways glance from Tony, who muttered, 'We'd better go for a coffee after this.' I nodded my agreement.

I was asked if I wanted to share, and told my story: that I stopped going to meetings because I was more interested in winning a heart than accepting life as it came at me. In other words, 'self', the ego, became primary in my life. It was exactly the same attitude I'd built over 32 years of drinking.

I'd lost sight of everything the fellowship had given me. I had my girls back in my life. I had eliminated debt and had reasonable health. (Well, better than when I was drinking—I still had hep C and type 2 diabetes.) I had grown to like myself. And I'd become used to those things, and forgotten how they had come back into my life. I'd never really connected with my Higher Power: something undefined, but in which I had the greatest faith.

When the meeting finished, we went to Tony's favourite cafe. I always enjoyed talking with him. After I told my story in the meeting he was aware of the state I was in and how I'd gotten there.

He asked me the question that cleared not just my mind but the road ahead.

'Where was God in all this?'

Now, before you start shaking your head and skipping ahead to the next bit of derring-do, take my advice: read the next words carefully. God to me, and to Tony, wasn't and isn't a religious deity. We'd both had our issues with the Catholic Church.

My issues with the church go back to my treatment by the Christian Brothers Powell and Shields—and Catholic priests such as Vincent Kiss, who raped and ruined some of my mates. So, let's not get stuck in the God thing. I use the word because it clearly identifies what I'm talking about as a Higher Power.

And in that concept, I have an unshakeable belief. I always have had. My belief is science-based: in simple terms, something non-human put the stars, planets and clouds in the sky. No human created a tree or the monkey that climbs it. Something outside this world causes the sun to rise, the oceans to ebb and rise. That thing, I have chosen to name Creator of the Universe (COTU).

Tony was essentially asking me what guidance I sought from my Higher Power.

It was a reasonable question. If I had an unshakeable belief in a power greater than anything on Earth, why would I not seek guidance from it?

That simple question shook my world back into reality.

A few days later, I was driving around with my old Albury and Drummoyne mate Doc, who now lived in Byron, when we saw a bloke cleaning his concrete driveway with a pressure washer.

'That'd be a good business to build up,' said Doc.

That's when the idea of a pressure-washing business was born. I thank COTU and Doc for that.

CHAPTER 78

LEAPS OF FAITH

Back to Albury I headed, not with my tail between my legs but an idea and $5000. As soon as I arrived, I ran the idea of a pressure-washing business past two mates: Geoff Romero, and Geoff Miller, who was also my accountant. I also went to see my mate Col Joss, for whom I'd done landscaping many years before. By this time he had a very big building and cleaning business, and I knew I'd get an honest assessment from him. 'Not a bad idea at all,' was his response.

I registered the name HiLoWash Pty Ltd with the help of Geoff Miller and my solicitor mate Brian Curphey; then I went out and bought a $1700 utility and a $600 pressure washer. That took care of half of my bank balance—all the assets I had in the world. The rest of the money I spent on radio ads on the local AM station 2AY, and on flyers, which I hand delivered.

My time at WTFN convinced me of the value of advertising, and the radio ads on 2AY, which I wrote and voiced, became central to HiLo's success. That and the start Col and his son Paul Joss gave me, with a huge yearlong contract as I started out. Many factors contributed to the business's success, not least my employees, the business ethics we lived by and the friends who stood behind me.

When I sold the business eight years after its launch, the original $5000 investment had turned into six figures in super, the outright ownership of a house, money in the bank and, most importantly, my hep C being cured.

There were three things I'd always wanted to do: a parachute jump, a bungee jump and to get up on stage and act. I'd never mustered up the nerve to follow through on any of them.

When I returned to Albury after experiencing my turning point, thanks to my actor pal and mentor Tony Barry, I heard that the Albury Wodonga Theatre Company (AWTCo) planned to put on a production of *Blackadder.* I auditioned for the part of the grotty old father, and won the role. On the weekend before the play was due to open, I went to Corowa and signed up for a solo parachute jump—none of this piggybacking for me. I did the Saturday lessons and practice, then on the Sunday I went down with my mate Trevor Orford to do the jump. Trev stayed on the ground ready to film my descent, and up I went with two experienced blokes to complete my mission.

The first guy stepped out on the right strut of the plane. I followed, and the last of our small party joined me on my left side. Here we were, trundling along at 10,000 feet, me glancing to my left then right, my companions poking their tongues out at me, me with my gob firmly shut, completely forgetting that the tongue poking was the parachutists' way of communicating. Eventually the bloke on my right gave a nod and all three of us let go of the strut and found ourselves plummeting to earth. Suddenly my two companions were way below me. *Fuck, I better pull the ripcord!* was my immediate thought as I frantically grabbed for my release handle. Then, *Fuck me, it isn't there!* hastily followed by *But why are they below me?* Finally looking up, I could see a beautiful billow of silk. When we were plummeting just after we jumped, both boys had held onto my arms. One of them must have decided to make sure the parachute opened and pulled the ripcord for me.

I'm often asked what the view was like from up there. Well, let me tell you: I don't know. For the five minutes I was in the air my eyes never left the guy on the ground controlling the big arrow, which he moved to indicate which toggle to pull. If he pointed the arrow to my right I pulled on the right toggle, and vice versa for left. I came down exactly where I was supposed to, but didn't pull both toggles down as quickly as I should have, so mucked up a perfect landing. Instead, I came down hard on my arse. The minute I was stationary, sitting on my bruised bum, lying back on the safety chute, I loudly proclaimed, 'I'm alive, thank you God, I'm alive, thank you God . . .' Trevor got it all on film.

The following weekend, after three months of rehearsals, it was time for *Blackadder* to open in the Wodonga Secondary College theatrette. Let me tell you something: waiting to go on stage was no different to standing on the strut of that plane at a vast height. It wasn't quite as terrifying, but the concentration required for both tasks was equal.

The next show was *Reservoir Dogs*, in which I played criminal boss Joe Cabot. It was a role I'd been rehearsing for back in my drug-dealing days. We opened in the same theatre, which was small, with seating for perhaps 100 patrons. In one scene, I was giving instructions to my gang, who were seated in front of a whiteboard. I was standing inches from the nearest patron in the front row, my hand resting on a wooden partition wall just above the guy's head. To emphasise a point, I slammed my open palm down on the timber. The sound in the silent theatre was like a pistol shot, and the patron levitated out of his chair and screamed. It was all I could do not to laugh. Some of the audience members weren't so self-controlled, and giggles broke out but were quickly silenced as the drama continued.

Acting was a hoot, but I couldn't be involved as often as I'd have liked as I had a business to run, which made learning lines and being available for rehearsals challenging. The following year, though, an opportunity came up that was too good to turn down: acting in a locally written production called *Heroes* as Nev, opposite John Wood of Blue Heelers fame, who filled the lead role of John.

He was a lovely, generous man to work with, as were all the cast members. But John, in particular, I got on especially well with. In one scene there were five of us in a car, supposedly motoring through the country, with my doddery character Nev asking every minute or two, 'Are we nearly there yet? I'm busting for a leak.'

When John finally pulled the car over, Nev hobbled out but couldn't make for the dunny right away as John launched into a big speech about suicide and mental health. Nev, standing back and to the side, began sucking in his cheeks, crossing his legs and generally giving the impression he was a living certainty to piss his pants. The audience began to giggle, and it became infectious. John's serious oration was given scant attention while all eyes were on Nev.

Afterwards, while we removed our make-up, John asked in a kindly manner if I wouldn't mind toning it down a notch in future so he could hold the audience's attention. I, of course, agreed. In the next performance, I turned it up a notch. Naturally. We had a laugh about that.

My final challenge in the thespian caper was an AWTCo production of *My Fair Lady* in which I played Pickering, a doddering but kindly old man. It's a role I hoped to grow into in my later years but I'm still far from, I hope, as I sit here at my desk at age 73. But I think I did the role justice, taking the forgetful side of Pickering's nature so to heart that on one memorable occasion I cut fifteen minutes from the play, completely sidelining half a dozen cast members whose lines I made redundant on that particular night.

On another occasion the musical director, Bohdan, who was in the musician's pit directing the orchestra, realised I'd forgotten my line. Looking up at me, he muttered it to me, but I couldn't hear it. He said it again, a little more loudly. Still, it fell on deaf ears. Finally, he shouted it.

As Pickering I seized upon it, crying it out loudly. The audience applauded. One thing I've learnt about the theatre is you can get away with anything as far as the audience is concerned, as long as you are convincing.

My Fair Lady played to five full houses at the Albury Entertainment Centre, an 800-seat auditorium. I sang and danced in front of 4000 people. Not bad. Of course, with their magnificent voices, Higgins, played by Tim Bishop, and Eliza Doolittle, played by Nicky Pummeroy, made me and everyone else sound better.

It was an amateur production but Joseph Thompson (the director), Bohdan, the backstage crew and the cast put on a show that would have drawn top reviews in Sydney or Melbourne. The elation I felt being involved in that production was beyond description. The fact that my father was in the audience together with Jane, my dear friends Al and Lesley, and John Wood on closing night really touched me. My old man died at age 91 but, on that night, he saw his son attempting to reach his potential and doing something he'd always dreamed of.

If you have ever had a yearning to tread the boards, take my advice: seize the day. No matter your age.

Oh, and the bungee jump? In June 2024 I travelled to Nepal for an AA conference with my fellow AA traveller, Paul. While there, on a whim, I decided to tick off the last of my three challenges. I asked the guy strapping me into the ankle harness about their safety record. 'Over fifteen years operating sixteen sites, we haven't had a single accident or death,' he replied as he finished strapping me in. I shuffled to the platform, took one look at the 101 metre drop and launched. Successfully, obviously.

I learnt an incredibly important lesson during this time. It took two months to circulate around in my skull before finally emerging as: trust the process. For me, anyway, this advice is invaluable in all areas of life. No matter the task or issue, if I've been thorough in my preparation I can move on to the next thing without wasting time going back and checking. Trust the process.

CHAPTER 79

A NEW PAIR OF GLASSES

How I've arrived at this point in my life, with good health, no money worries, no skeletons in the closet, the support of all five of my siblings and their families and more than a handful of genuine friends who will do anything for me, including pulling me up when I'm wrong, I have no idea.

I don't know how I've survived for this long, but I do know why I don't do any of the crazy things I used to do anymore. It's because I made that phone call to Al on 6 August 1999. It's because he asked me, 'Do you want to stop?' and I emphatically replied, 'Yes'. It's because he later encouraged me to go back to AA, which showed me, through others' recovery, that the way to happiness is quite simple. Be honest, deflate your ego, care for others as you'd like to be cared for. And, most importantly, accept that you are completely powerless over people, places and things.

I am even powerless over my own thoughts at times, but never over my actions—as long as my body isn't chemically altered by alcohol and drugs, and my mind isn't clouded with assumptions, secrets and resentments.

I have two beautiful daughters—one, Brigitte, who loves my company; and one, Laura, who, through bad information and ultimately me abandoning her, doesn't. I love them both equally and accept that each, like me, is entitled to her own destiny without my interference.

The most joyous thing has happened since genuine acceptance became a permanent part of my daily life. After 30 years living life as a solitary man, a beautiful, humble and intelligent woman has entered my life. What an unexpected and uplifting event to happen at 73 years young.

I look at life now through a new pair of glasses. Where I used to hate, I now sow love; where I used to doubt, I now have faith that all will be well; despair has been replaced by hope; and where I used to be needy, I am now a bloke whose nature is to give rather than take. And equally importantly I accept that knowing how to receive a gift is as important as giving.

Resentment? Take my advice . . . let it go.

CHAPTER 80

LOVE

Brigitte has brought me such joy. She is hugely successful, entirely through her own efforts in her chosen field. She's living an independent and balanced life, being genuinely humble, creative and funny, clever and kind, and above all, forgiving and giving.

Laura, who has all the talent in the world, is far too much like I was at her age. But she has a pure heart so I believe one day we will sit down, talk and listen to each other, and the truth and love will heal us.

Jane I will always love and never abandon, just as she has never abandoned me, even with the enormous pressure applied to her. I can't thank her enough for my two beautiful daughters and for standing by me when I was at my worst. She deserved much, much better.

These days, I'm taking my own advice—but I'm happy to share it, too:

- Try being honest and grateful instead of judgemental and resentful. Laugh a lot, especially at yourself, and be kind to everyone: family, friends and strangers alike. The world will be a better and happier place with you in it.

- Don't break the law. Don't sell drugs. Don't *ever* use hallucinogens, hard drugs or needles. If you must experiment, stick to straight smoko. The stuff grown using chemicals to give it extra kick will fuck you up big time. There is no doubt in my mind that field-grown marijuana has enormous medicinal value and should be legalised. Cocaine, smack, acid, meth, ketamine, ice and all the other manufactured street drugs are poison, and anyone dealing in them needs bringing down. The ones financing the illegal drug trade, the so-called legit businessmen you never hear of, should be gaoled for life. If I hadn't lived the life I have, I wouldn't be such a powerful voice against drugs and crime. Choose that life and it will almost certainly cost you more than a finger.
- Don't drive drunk.
- Don't thieve.
- Treat others the way you'd like to be treated. A happy heart is preceded by a clear conscience.
- You have to give it away to keep it. That's everything: love, money, time, attention and laughter. Especially love.
- Forgive rather than resent. Resentment and secrets kill. To that end, I contacted FiL and made my peace prior to his death.
- Know yourself.
- Be yourself.
- Love yourself.

A final note: my oldest daughter once told me, 'Dad, you should take your own advice and not give advice.' I guess you, the reader, may concur. I can only hope my mistakes will assist you on your road to a happy destiny.

ACKNOWLEDGEMENTS

Deepest gratitude to the late great Barry Humphries, who suggested, after an AA meeting at Bondi Beach one day in 2001, that I should write my memoir, to which I replied: 'One day I will, Barry, but when I do, I want to get it exactly right.'

To which he dryly replied: 'Don't get it right, get it written.'

It only took 24 years, Baz. Here it is!

Thanks to Bill Gray, Andrew Rule, Tony Wright, Bernie Leo and Barrie Cassidy for the conversations, and for taking the time to read early drafts and give encouragement. Thanks also to Victoria Owens, Chris Everingham and Megan Rigoni for their help with the photographs. A huge thank you to Chris Masters for putting my manuscript in front of Elizabeth Weiss. And, of course, also to Matt Handbury for introducing me to Robert Gorman, CEO of Allen & Unwin.

To the doctors who've kept me upright and amazingly healthy—only they and God know why I'm not in a box. Thanks to Dr Dave, Dr Mike, Dr Bill P., Dr Charles O., Dr Robyn S., Dr Peter C., Dr Jim R., Dr Rob S., Dr B.R. and the doctors at Royal Prince Alfred Hospital Liver Clinic.

Most people mentioned in this book gave permission for their correct names to be used. Some didn't, so I changed those names.

A couple of names I altered because I don't want to be shot or sued; and one person in particular, Gator, I couldn't contact, try as I did.

A special thank you to Elizabeth Weiss, Angela Handley, Brooke Lyons, Jane Fitzpatrick, Amy-May Pham-Huynh, Josh Durham and the team at Allen & Unwin for your belief in my story.

To Rob Lacey for photographing me so well and to Simon Moir of Simon Moir Classic Cars for his support.

I would not be here without my trusted and loyal family and friends. 'Thank you' will never seem enough to show the gratitude I have for every single one of you.

And finally, to Chris for proofreading, and nurturing me through the production process; you are a very tolerant sister.

It's been a blast!